TRAVEL NARRATIVE AND THE
ENDS OF MODERNITY

Over the past century, narratives of travel changed in response to modernist and postmodernist literary innovation, world wars, the demise of European empires, and the effect of new technologies and media on travel experience. Yet existing critical studies have not examined fully how the genre changes, or theorized why. This study investigates the evolution of Anglophone travel narrative from the 1920s to the present, addressing the work of canonical authors such as T. E. Lawrence, W. H. Auden, and Rebecca West; best sellers by Peter Fleming and H. V. Morton; and texts by Colin Thubron, Andrew X. Pham, Rosemary Mahoney, and others. It argues that the genre's most important transformation lies in its reinvention as a means of narrating the subjective experience of violence, cultural upheaval, and transience. It will interest scholars and students of travel writing, modernism and postmodernism, English and American literature, and the history and sociology of travel.

STACY BURTON is an associate professor of English at the University of Nevada, Reno. Her work on modernist fiction, travel narrative, and literary theory has appeared in *Modern Language Quarterly* *Modern Philology, Comparative Literature, Genre,* and elsewhere.

TRAVEL NARRATIVE AND THE ENDS OF MODERNITY

STACY BURTON

University of Nevada

CAMBRIDGE UNIVERSITY PRESS

CAMBRIDGE
UNIVERSITY PRESS

32 Avenue of the Americas, New York, NY 10013-2473, USA

Cambridge University Press is part of the University of Cambridge.

It furthers the University's mission by disseminating knowledge in the pursuit of education, learning, and research at the highest international levels of excellence.

www.cambridge.org
Information on this title: www.cambridge.org/9781107039315

First published 2014

Printed in the United States of America

A catalog record for this publication is available from the British Library.

Library of Congress Cataloging in Publication data
Burton, Stacy.
Travel narrative and the ends of modernity / Stacy Burton, University of Nevada.
pages cm.
Includes bibliographical references and index.
ISBN 978-1-107-03931-5 (hardback)
1. Travelers' writings, English – History and criticism. 2. Travelers' writings, American – History and criticism. 3. Modernism (Literature) 4. Postmodernism (Literature) 5. Travel in literature. 6. Travel writing – History. I. Title.
PR756.T72B87 2013
820.9'32–dc23 2013020641

ISBN 978-1-107-03931-5 Hardback

Contents

Illustrations

Acknowledgments

This book took more time than one might have hoped, but in the end it is better for it. I am grateful to family, friends, colleagues, and institutions for considerable support along the way. The University of Nevada, Reno, provided sabbatical leave. The Department of English provided research assistance; the College of Liberal Arts Scholarly and Creative Activities Grant Program covered permission fees for quotations and images. The department, the college, and the Office of the Vice President for Research supported presentations at academic conferences. Colleagues in the United States, the United Kingdom, and France responded: particular thanks to the International Society for the Study of Narrative, the Modernist Studies Association, and Borders and Crossings/Seuils et Traverses for their cultures of engaged discussion. The Huntington Library offered time and space for research that was funded through a Huntington/Rocky Mountain Modern Language Association fellowship. The British Library and the Library of Congress are remarkable public institutions; conducting research at each has been a pleasure.

Early on, Kathy Okerlund Nelson and Robert Nelson let me stay for weeks, and Francesca Sawaya asked good questions. Annual conversations with Pat Okker helped with the long view. Jen Hill read initial chapters rigorously and identified what was wrong: thank you. Scott Casper listened – and read the penultimate manuscript. Elizabeth Raymond and Dennis Dworkin each did much to ensure that this project moved forward. Heather Hardy supported this book at every turn.

My thanks to Ray Ryan and the two anonymous readers at Cambridge University Press for their careful engagement with my work. My thanks as well to Louis Gulino and the team at Newgen Knowledge Works for following through on details.

Words do not suffice to thank friends and family for the invaluable ordinary sustenance that makes life pleasurable and immersion in work possible. To the Burtons – Jack, Rosemary, Lisa, Steve, Sally, and company – thank you for being the most wonderful of families, year in and year out. What fine fortune it is to adventure through life together. To friends who have shared dinners, dramas, laughter, and travel over the years, many thanks: Kathy and Ron Ray, Lorie Winder Stromberg and Tom Stromberg; Dennis Dworkin and Amelia Currier, Scott Casper, Elizabeth Raymond and Jim Pagliarini, Martha Hildreth and Bruce Blackadar; Kathy Okerlund Nelson and Robert Nelson, Chris Bramwell; Francesca Sawaya; Jane Hafen; Lyn and Jack Hawkins; Judith Whitenack, Miriella Melara, and Susan Baker; Victoria Follette; Kathy and Phil Boardman, Ann Ronald and Lois Snedden, Jen Hill and Larry Cantera, Jane Detweiler and Beverly Lassiter, and Heather and Don Hardy. Here is to travel in peacetime – and to finding oneself home.

The following list of credits for permission to reproduce previously published work constitutes a continuation of the copyright page.

"Thinking," by Eric Kennington, R.A., by permission of the family of the artist. Image by permission of the Harry Ransom Center, The University of Texas at Austin.

Text from Freya Stark, *The Zodiac Arch* (New York: Harcourt, Brace & World, 1968). Reprinted by permission of John R. Murray.

Text from *Letters from Iceland*, © 1937 by W. H. Auden and Louis MacNeice, renewed. Reprinted by permission of Curtis Brown, Ltd.

Photos from *Journey to a War*, © The Estate of W. H. Auden. Reprinted by permission of Curtis Brown, Ltd.

Text and line drawing from *Seven Pillars of Wisdom*, by T. E. Lawrence, © 1926, 1935 by Doubleday, a division of Random House, Inc. Used by permission of Doubleday, a division of Random House, Inc. Any third-party use of this material, outside of this publication, is prohibited. Interested parties must apply directly to Random House, Inc., for permission.

Text and photograph from *Forbidden Journey*, by Ella Maillart, trans. Thomas McGreevy (London: Heinemann, 1937; reprinted Marlboro Press, 2003). Reprinted by permission of David Higham Associates.

Text from *Black Lamb and Grey Falcon*, by Rebecca West, © 1940, 1941; renewed © 1968, 1969 by Rebeccca West. Used by permission of Viking Penguin, a division of Penguin Group (USA), Inc.

Text from *Black Lamb and Grey Falcon*, by Rebecca West. Reprinted by permission of SLL/Sterling Lord Literistic, Inc. © The Estate of Rebecca West.

Text from *European Witness* by Stephen Spender © 1946. Reprinted by kind permission of the Estate of Stephen Spender.

Cover from *European Witness* by Stephen Spender (New York: Reynal & Hitchcock, 1946). Reprinted by permission of Houghton Mifflin Harcourt.

Panels from *Palestine*, by Joe Sacco. Reprinted by permission of Fantagraphics Books.

Excerpt from "Alley-World" from *Catfish and Mandala: A Two-Wheeled Voyage through the Landscape and Memory of Vietnam* by Andrew X. Pham. © 1999 by Andrew X. Pham. Reprinted by permission of Farrar, Straus and Giroux, LLC.

Photograph of Andrew X. Pham. Reprinted by permission of Timothy Archibald.

Text by W. G. Sebald, trans. Michael Hulse, from *The Rings of Saturn*, © 1995 by Vito von Eichborn GmbH & Co Verlag KG, Translation © 1998 by The Harvill Press. Reprinted by permission of New Directions Publishing Corp.

Text from *The Rings of Saturn* by W. G. Sebald. Published by Harvill Press. Reprinted by permission of The Random House Group Limited.

Excerpt from *The Rings of Saturn* by W. G. Sebald. © 1995 W. G. Sebald, used by permission of The Wylie Agency LLC.

Brief portions of this manuscript appeared in quite different form in the following:

"Difference and Convention: Bakhtin and the Practice of Travel Literature." *Carnivalizing Difference: Bakhtin and the Other*. Ed. Peter I. Barta, Paul Allen Miller, Charles Platter, and David Shepherd. London: Routledge Harwood, 2001. 225–245.

"Rethinking Religious Experience: Notes from Critical Theory, Feminism, and Real Life." *Dialogue* 28.4 (1995): 67–88.

CHAPTER I

Introduction: Critical Paradigms and Problems

Nothing in my life had affected me more deeply than this journey through Yugoslavia. This was in part because there is a coincidence between the natural forms and colours of the western and southern parts of Yugoslavia and the innate forms and colours of my imagination.... But my journey moved me also because it was like picking up a strand of wool that would lead me out of a labyrinth in which, to my surprise, I had found myself immured. It might be that when I followed the thread to its end I would find myself faced by locked gates, and that this labyrinth was my sole portion on this earth. But at least I now knew its twists and turns, and what corridor led into what vaulted chamber, and nothing in my life before I went to Yugoslavia had even made plain these mysteries.

Rebecca West (1941)[1]

In the early years of the Second World War, Rebecca West identified what she would call "the calamity of modern life": "we cannot know all the things which it is necessary for our survival that we should know."[2] To write of those necessary things, she turned to the travel narrative, a literary genre that would allow an admixture of personal experience and cultural observation, historical storytelling, and political call to arms. In *Black Lamb and Grey Falcon* (1941), cast as the narrative of a single "Easter journey," she works through the crisis facing Britain, Europe, and America, which she understands as a crisis of modernity. The result – more than a thousand pages of prose with thirty-two photographs, including one of the first political assassination caught on film – would be called by an early reviewer the "apotheosis" of the travel genre.[3] Though extraordinary, West's work signals much about the travel narrative's evolution to serve new cultural purposes in the twentieth century. For *Black Lamb* at once realizes the genre's potential as a means of subjective response to geopolitical crisis and articulates the newly charged ethical concern that would permeate literary travel narrative in decades to come.

Globalization, the study of imperialism, and postcolonial theory have played crucial roles in bringing travel literature and travel practices to the attention of scholars in several disciplines, including literary studies, history, sociology, anthropology, and geography. New concepts have been devised to identify and analyze cultural phenomena as pervasive as "colonial discourse" and as novel as "dark tourism"; the term "travel" has itself been troubled for its implicit reference to a privileged mobility unavailable to refugees, noncitizens, and the poor. Over the last three decades, as scholars have rethought the purposes and subjects of literary studies in light of new theories of cultural production, travel literature has come to be understood anew as what Charles Forsdick calls "a generically complex and creative form."[4] Though the account of a journey is among the oldest of prose genres, the travel narrative, like other types of literature historically deemed minor, had previously received very little scholarly attention. The field remains new and largely separate from more comprehensive literary-critical histories, however; the travel narrative and other means of writing about travel continue to be understood primarily in terms of the influential scholarship that first examined their role in European imperialism from the sixteenth to early twentieth centuries.[5] Yet, whereas some familiar tropes have remained surprisingly consistent, the travel narrative's cultural ambitions, literary strategies, and political contexts have altered significantly over the last hundred years.

Few scholars have examined travel narrative's evolution in the twentieth century, a period of profound global upheaval and transformation in which writers influenced by modernism and postmodernism reinvented the genre to serve new cultural purposes. Studies generally describe twentieth-century travel narratives in English as differing markedly from those of earlier centuries, tending more toward autobiography, literariness, and explicitly subjective observation and less toward ethnography, documentation, and claims of scientific objectivity. However, scholars have yet to examine thoroughly exactly *how* the genre of the travel narrative changed in the twentieth century, or to theorize *why* these changes occurred. No existing study considers these questions in detail. No study examines the genre's development in the context of the century's profound geopolitical changes, from world wars and the decline of European empires to globalization, or considers how these changes have played a role in the revival that travel narrative has enjoyed in the late twentieth and early twenty-first centuries. Much recent scholarship reexamines modernism in cosmopolitan and transnational contexts, including its relations with imperialism and anthropology. However, these studies deal primarily with canonical fiction and popular culture and seldom mention travel narrative: the "new modernist studies" has not taken this considerable body of primary literature seriously into account.[6] This book bridges these gaps by examining the evolution of the travel narrative as a literary genre and a strategy for thinking through modernity from the years following the First World War to the present. In so doing, it identifies distinctive, substantial changes as the genre draws from modernism and postmodernism to represent subjective response to profound, often violent cultural transformation. These changes are not limited to the 1920s or the 1980s, nor are they ephemeral. At the beginning of the twenty-first century, the travel narrative at its most serious resembles little its predecessor from the early twentieth century. This evolution occurs through a trajectory of development that demonstrates continuities that are striking and significant. Previous scholarship has failed to examine either the evolution or the continuities, for its critical frameworks, devised to investigate other questions, have precluded their recognition.

From Egeria in the fourth century to Rory Stewart in the twenty-first, European travel writing traverses the ambiguous lines between fact and fiction, claims to represent individual experience amid foreign circumstance, and makes eclectic use of other genres. At its simplest, it recounts the story of a journey using familiar conventions; at its most complex, it examines cultural and political questions that far exceed the bounds of one person's experience. Prior to the twentieth century, books based on travels and observations abroad had a distinctive role as the means by which Europeans knew about peoples and places outside their immediate experience. They recounted explorations, reported discoveries, and documented unfamiliar cultures, languages, and landscapes.[7] Travelers – often diplomats, explorers, or entrepreneurs – wrote narratives and ethnographic studies that presented themselves as truthful accounts of firsthand experience and thus important sources of knowledge. Their work often played a formative role in imperial policy. Claims deemed implausible or unverifiable could of course be dismissed as lies or discounted as literary embellishment – and often were. But in general, Europeans wrote for other Europeans in a colonial discourse that was grounded in premises that writers and their audiences shared and seldom fundamentally questioned.

Travel writing began to lose this distinctive status as European domination of the globe accelerated, more people lived abroad for imperial enterprise or traveled for leisure, new scientific disciplines were created for the study of people and places, and photographs and film were disseminated widely. These changes undermined the claims that travelers of earlier centuries could plausibly make regarding their exceptional access to knowledge otherwise unavailable to the audience at home. Tourism commodified travel, undermining the traveler's claim to authentic experience and the travel writer's claim to distinctiveness.[8] By the twentieth century, the traditional purposes of the travel narrative had been largely exhausted, and territory not already written and rewritten had become scarce. Following the First World War, victorious European nations extended their imperial reach even as independence movements accelerated in Ireland, India, and Indochina. Revolutions overthrew old empires in Russia, then China. By the end of the Second World War it was clear that the globe had entered a period of rapid geopolitical transformation in which prevailing notions of modernity, national culture, and Europe's role would be subject to new scrutiny through decolonization, migration, and new forms of cosmopolitan experience.

These changes called into question many of the premises on which travel narrative rested and the logic of the imperial discourse that it employed. Its earlier purposes – to circumscribe difference, justify empire, and confirm the logic of modernity – began to appear outmoded and intellectually dubious, as did the European traveler's presumption of expertise to discern the authentic abroad and narrate it for a Western audience. The genre had to evolve, revise its claims to seriousness, adapt to a postimperial world in which the place of the metropole was no longer secure – or fade into irrelevance. Mary Baine Campbell explains that "interest in travel writing – across a wide political spectrum – was part of the necessary reimagining of the world" that had been shattered by war, "resistance movements and wars of liberation," and eventually postcolonial immigration and globalization. "Much of the work of observing, interpreting, articulating the explosion of that world, as well as the historical development of the imperialised world that led to it," she continues, "was done through recovery and analysis of people's writings about 'foreign' and especially 'exotic' places in which they had traveled and lived."[9]

Twentieth-century travel narrative reflects the profound reimagining of the world that Campbell describes: the contexts that provoke scholars to take travel writing seriously are also the contexts that circumscribe writers' efforts to narrate their travels in a world undergoing rapid change. Of necessity, writers adapt or reject familiar themes that are ill-suited to new cultural contexts. Many aim not simply to convey information or tell a tale but, more importantly, to produce serious literature. Some write nostalgic tributes to the imperial past, depicting travel as the means for

Europeans to escape from the consequences of modernity into the security of convention. Others, sympathetic with revolutions against the inequities of the imperialized world, explicitly seek to reinvent the genre as a strategy for examining European decline and the violence of which advanced civilizations are capable. In their hands, it becomes a means for narrating firsthand the experience of what Michel Foucault calls "the history of the present" – in other words, a means for seeing the present as transient, and thus recognizing historical difference by "exposing the gaps among the various types of experiencing and knowing the world; and, through this exposition, destabilizing our own experience, so that the rupture of yet another gap may occur."[10] All demonstrate that narrating travel is a complicated act of representation that compels critical inquiry about discourse, experience, and the limits of cross-cultural understanding.

The most influential scholarship to examine the development and collapse of the imperialized world demonstrated the imaginative power that travel writing, broadly defined, had in the cultural formations of modern Europe and North America. This scholarship created a critical vocabulary and mapped out theoretical concerns that continue to matter. In *Orientalism* (1978), Edward Said powerfully called critical attention to the ways that European – chiefly British and French – writers of travel narratives, political treatises, and novels relied on discursive, ideological distinctions between "the West" and "the East" and presumed substantial authority to represent unfamiliar cultures and nations. Adapting Foucault's theories of discourse, he argued that European writers' "textual attitude" to the world constrained what they saw when traveling and largely determined how they wrote about their experiences in the Arab world.[11] Peter Hulme, in *Colonial Encounters: Europe and the Native Caribbean, 1492–1797* (1986), and Sara Mills, in *Discourses of Difference: An Analysis of Women's Travel Writing and Colonialism* (1991), also drew on Foucault – in conjunction with Marxist and gender theory – to develop conceptions of colonial discourse necessary for nuanced analyses of Europeans' texts about the peoples and places that they encountered, explored, and conquered. In *Imperial Eyes: Studies in Travel Writing and Transculturation* (1992), Mary Louise Pratt examined how "travel and exploration writing *produced* 'the rest of the world' for European readerships at particular points in Europe's expansionist trajectory" and "Europe's differentiated conceptions of itself in relation to something it became possible to call 'the rest of the world,'" specifically South America and Africa. Pratt argued that scholarly analysis of what she named "the contact zone," the space in which cross-cultural encounters occur, required "a study in genre as well as a critique of ideology."[12] Although each of these scholars examined specific strains within larger discursive traditions, their provocative analyses quickly influenced others working on a disparate array of texts and concerns. As Pratt explains in a preface to the second edition of *Imperial Eyes* (2008), the stakes were – and remain – high for scholarship that was "conceived as part of an intellectual effort to make the workings of imperialism ... available to reflection and transformation" and thus to ease its "grip on imagination and knowledge."[13]

Not all research on travel writing at the field's inception was part of this intellectual project, however. Other studies sought to demonstrate travel writing's significance in conventional literary critical terms and thus to establish it as a worthy subject for scholarly attention *as literature*. In *Travel Literature and the Evolution of the Novel* (1983), Percy Adams examined the trajectories of travel literature and the novel as European narrative traditions that developed "in parallel lines to be sure but within a historical framework of mutuality and reciprocity."[14] Entering into debates on the novel's origin, Adams argued that travel literature had played a role in the novel's development and rise to cultural prominence as significant as that of the epic and the romance; his work placed travel narrative in literary history for the first time. Paul Fussell, meanwhile, brought critical attention to twentieth-century British travel narrative with *Abroad: British Literary Traveling between the Wars* (1980). Examining dozens of travel books published by well-read, generally privileged men in "the final age of travel" and characterizing them as "a sub-species of memoir," Fussell aimed to codify the genre and identify its literary role. Such texts, he argued, are "addressed to those who do not plan to follow the traveler at all, but who require the exotic or comic anomalies, wonders, and scandals of the literary form *romance* which their own place or time cannot entirely supply."[15] Fussell's study celebrated the travel book and defended its claim to be taken seriously as literature, countering what he described as a snobbish modernist preference for the novel and the lyric poem. It was also an exercise in nostalgia for a kind of travel, sensibility, and text that he argued modernity had ruined through tourism, politics, and war. Although its broad range of reference helped establish the field within literary studies, *Abroad* rested on critical premises untouched by (if not hostile toward) literary and cultural theory that later scholars would question.[16]

In the decades since these groundbreaking studies, scholarship on travel literature has developed in various directions. Among the most influential has been work to examine the roles that travel and travel writing have played in the formation of gendered identities and literary traditions. In addition to Mills's *Discourses of Difference*, notable studies concerned with gender include Dennis Porter's *Haunted Journeys: Desire and Transgression in European Travel Writing* (1991), Karen Lawrence's *Penelope Voyages: Women and Travel in the British Literary Tradition* (1994), and Sidonie Smith's *Moving Lives: Twentieth-Century Women's Travel Writing* (2001). Porter invoked Freud and psychoanalytic theory in reading desire, guilt, and fantasy in travel writing by European men from the Enlightenment through the twentieth century, a focus chosen in part because father/son relationships figured prominently in many such texts. Lawrence observed that previous major studies "all fail to theorize a place for woman as traveling subject," for both literature and theory rested on dated tropes in which men wander and women stay home. *Penelope Voyages* reconfigured the field by exploring how "the genres, plots, and tropes of travel and adventure have been 'useful' for British women writers in supplying a set of alternative models for woman's place in society" from the seventeenth century through the twentieth.[17] Smith specifically examined narratives that demonstrate how modernity's new technologies allowed Anglophone and European women increased mobility and thus new types of identities. Whereas Lawrence and Smith, unlike Mills, dealt with writers working in a variety of genres, all shared a concern that the production and reception of travel-related writing by women had been complex in ways that criticism had yet to recognize. They sought to take into account what Lawrence described as "the different cultural freight that the woman traveler may carry."[18] Mills, eschewing any simple division between texts by men and texts by women, called for a theory capable of explaining such gendered differences while recognizing the fact that "many women write within the same discursive frameworks as men."[19]

Most studies of twentieth-century travel narrative in English have examined specific periods or specialized themes. Fussell, for example, dealt chiefly with the work of male British writers of the 1920s and 1930s. Bernard Schweizer's *Radicals on the Road: The Politics of English Travel Writing in the 1930s* (2001) and David Farley's *Modernist Travel Writing: Intellectuals Abroad* (2010) each reexamined this period, focusing on the work of four writers. Their primary themes – politics for Schweizer, modernism for Farley – countered Fussell's claims that the travel genre was damaged by politics and slighted by modernist aesthetes (interestingly, each gave West's *Black Lamb* the serious attention he denied it). The most comprehensive study of travel writing since 1960, Patrick Holland and Graham Huggan's *Tourists with Typewriters: Critical Reflections on Contemporary Travel Writing* (1998), surveyed a literary field that it defined as "predominantly Anglophone; and still primarily white, male, hetero-sexual, middle class." Taking both rhetoric and politics as their subject, Holland and Huggan explicitly sought to demonstrate that "this most hybrid and unassimilable of literary genres" still flourished despite claims that travel and travel writing had been exhausted by modernity and glo-balization.[20] Focusing on travel writing's "capacity both to fuel the expan-sionist ambitions of modern tourism and, at its best, to intervene in and challenge received ideas on cultural difference," they asked a broad range of questions about the varied ways that travel writing had "adjusted – or not – to contemporary realities, inserting itself into the late-twentieth-century discourses of postcolonialism and postmodernism, and addressing itself to new technologies and the global crises of the moment."[21]

Travel Narrative and the Ends of Modernity benefits from the work of these scholars, although its critical aims and subject matter differ. Because earlier studies analyze literature written in the decades before the Second World War separately from that written in the decades following, they do not examine the trajectories along which the travel narrative develops as a literary genre over the course of the century. Nor do they thoroughly consider the continuities between innovations of the 1920s, 1930s, and 1940s and those of the 1980s, 1990s, and 2000s. There is no counterpart in Anglophone literary studies to *Travel in Twentieth-Century French and Francophone Cultures* (2005), in which Forsdick examines the persistence of concern for cultural diversity across the twentieth century in franco-phone travel literature. This book aims to identify and analyze persistent concerns that mark the evolution of the travel narrative in English over the last century – and, in so doing, to provide such a counterpart. It focuses specifically on the genre of the travel narrative rather than travel writ-ing more broadly. "Narrative" puts into the foreground a crucial aspect of travel texts that has become more pronounced as they present them-selves not as documentary studies but as stories, as narrator's accounts of their own subjective experiences. It signals the enduring conventions of the journey and adventure tale, default paradigms with which writers con-tinue to contend in seeking narrative strategies for representing cultural exchange in globalized contact zones. For even "oppositional narratives," as Holland and Huggan point out, "cannot escape being haunted by an array of hoary tropes and clichés," and a complex oscillation between tra-dition and innovation mark the travel narrative's evolution.[22] The focus on narrative also recognizes that readers often read such texts as stories, seeking vicarious engagement with the experiences, peoples, and places they represent.

Considering twentieth-century travel texts critically *as* narratives facilitates an understanding of them in the overlapping contexts of modernism and postmodernism. This places the travel text among other narrative genres – particularly the novel and autobiography – from which it borrows freely as it becomes, in Helen Carr's words, a "more literary and autonomous genre." Scholars characterize this evolution in similar terms, although they differ on when it occurred and attribute it to different causes, from the aesthetics of modernism or postmodernism to increased awareness of cultural differences owing to globalization. Carr, for instance, describes a modernist transition in the 1920s and 1930s "from the detailed, realist text, often with an overly didactic or at any rate moral purpose, to a more impressionistic style with the interest focused as much on the travellers' responses or consciousness as their travels."[23] Hulme, in contrast, locates a "decisive shift" in the 1970s and 1980s, crediting Bruce Chatwin's *In Patagonia* (1977) for "finally … bring[ing] a modernist aesthetics to a fundamentally nineteenth-century genre" and the paucity of wilderness in the postmodern world for narrative that "increasingly emphasizes the inner journey, often merging imperceptibly into memoir." Yet the coincident strands he identifies – "the comic, the analytical, the wilderness, the spiritual, and the experimental" – all have antecedents earlier in the century.[24] Tracing both continuities and innovations as the travel narrative evolves demonstrates that the most recent innovations in the genre, often characterized as postmodern, are part of a longer history in which modernism plays a significant role.

Critical analysis of the travel narrative's development over the last century will also reveal the longer history of a crucial topic: whether and how more reflective means of representation, less constrained by imperialism, may be possible in the shrinking, globalized world of the twentieth and twenty-first centuries.[25] Although Said's analysis of the oppositional construction of "Europe" and "Orient" helped create new fields of inquiry, it did not offer sufficiently nuanced strategies for analyzing literary texts, nor did it propose an alternative model for European travel narratives. Later scholars responded by demonstrating that writing about cultural difference must be understood as involving competing perspectives and discourses. In *Critical Terrains: French and British Orientalisms* (1991), Lisa Lowe proposes "heterotopicality" to describe the complex "condition of multiple and interpenetrating positions and practices" in which discursive terrains are perpetually subject to alteration through "the continual yet uneven overlappings, intersections, and collusions" of new articulations. "The theoretical problem facing cultural criticism," she argues, is not how to fit slippage, instability, and multivalence into a conception of dominant ideology and counterideology or discourse and counterdiscourse. Rather, cultural critics might approach this question from the other direction: that is, that heterogeneities and ambivalences are givens in culture. These nonequivalences and noncorrespondences are not the objects to be reconciled or explained; they must constitute the beginning premise of any analysis.[26]

Lowe's account of cultural heterogeneity identifies not only the starting point for critical analysis but also the circumstances that twentieth-century writers of travel narratives must negotiate. In an era of increasing awareness of the fluidity of cultural distinctions, both travel and narrative appear more fraught than they once did. Iain Chambers, reflecting on the future of travel in *Travellers' Tales: Narratives of Home and Displacement* (1994), puts it directly: "In an age in which anthropology increasingly turns into autobiography, the observer, seeking to capture, to enframe, an elsewhere is now caught in the net of critical observation." Both travelers and critics, he proposes, work in changed circumstances in which new questions and new ethical obligations obtain:

> To think, to write, to be, is no longer for some of us simply to follow in the tracks of those who initially expanded and explained *our* world as they established the frontiers of Europe, of Empire, and of manhood, where the knots of gendered, sexual and ethnic identity were sometimes loosened, but more usually tightened.... It is rather to abandon such places, such centers, for the migrant's tale, the nomad's story. It is to abandon the fixed geometry of sites and roots for the unstable calculations of transit.... This means to recognize in the homesickness of much contemporary critical thought not so much the melancholy conclusion of a thwarted rationalism but an opening towards a new horizon of questions. For it is to contemplate crossing over to the 'other' side of the authorized tale, that other side of modernity, of the West, of History, and from there to consider that breach in contemporary culture which reveals an increasing number of people who are making a home in homelessness, there dwelling in diasporic identities and heterogeneous histories.[27]

At the end of modernity, whose perspectives and voices matter – to whom, how – in writing about travel and difference? Whose should, and by which criteria? What, exactly, do travel narratives represent, and for whom? What purposes does this genre serve in a rapidly changing, globalizing, postmodern, violent world?[28] These questions haunt twentieth-century travel narrative; this book examines how, and to what ends.

To understand twentieth-century travel narrative, it is necessary to examine *how* and *why* a form that had become nearly archaic not only endures but evolves into a surprisingly agile means of engaging with geopolitical issues by the beginning of the new millennium. Such an inquiry requires a complex understanding of genre, one capable of explaining "multiple discourses and discontinuous structures" as well as identifying conventions and continuities.[29] Some scholars have taken genre to be at odds with theory, which they view as a mode of conceptualizing laws and valuing essence, and better suited to history, which they view as privileging transgression and actual practice. Yet this tidy dichotomy reduces theory to a caricatured formalism and disregards history's theoretical underpinnings. Hayden White explains: "When it comes to discourse and literature ... theory is simply a mode of thought by which to grasp the (synchronic) structure of the diachronic process of which 'history' is a manifestation."[30] Genre is more productively understood, as Adena Rosmarin has argued, as a way of naming the relationship between texts, a "classifying statement" that "is powerfully persuasive not only because it leads us to perceive similarity but because it leads us to perceive that similarity in the midst of and in spite of difference" (46). As White suggests, genre is a strategy as necessary in literary study as "periodicity" is in history because it allows for a productive theorizing and historicizing of what is "always in motion, always changing, and always changing in different ways in different places on the temporal continuum" (605).[31]

Influential studies of travel writing have centered on identifying recurring tropes, explaining their power, and rereading them against the grain. Although influenced by Foucault, they have often subordinated historical specificity to the broader objective of mapping conventions that repeat over centuries across varied kinds of texts: government reports, novels, anthropological studies, travel books. As Pratt explains, this strategy foregrounds the persistence and force of imperial tropes:

> With respect to genre, I have attempted here to pay serious attention to the conventions of representation that constitute European travel writing, identifying different strands, suggesting ways of reading and focuses for rhetorical analysis.... The study of tropes often serves to unify corpuses and define genres in terms, for example, of shared repertoires of devices and conventions (and yet it is, of course, the corpuses that create the repertoires). My aim here, however, is not to define or codify. I try to use the study of tropes as much to disunify as to unify what one might call a rhetoric of travel writing. I have aimed not to circumscribe travel writing as a genre but to suggest its heterogeneity and its interactions with other kinds of expression.[32]

The tropes Pratt and others examine recur in a broad range of texts written in various circumstances, by different writers, about wildly disparate places. Their analyses emphasize the continuity and consistency with which these tropes are used and argue that they create a distinctive discourse, which David Spurr calls "the rhetoric of empire."[33] Pervasive in eighteenth- and nineteenth-century colonial texts, it persists in the twentieth century, having assumed an authoritative status that appears beyond inquiry. This imperial discourse has now been much studied.

Far less attention has been paid to travel narrative as a literary genre that changes over time, borrows and differentiates itself from other genres, and exists in relation to changing social and political relations. Only Adams's *Travel Literature and the Evolution of the Novel* has considered the genre's development in any depth. With an encyclopedic range of reference, Adams examines the development to 1800 of these related narrative genres in which protagonist and journey plot serve as a means of social commentary. Like novels, travel narratives artfully combine local detail with exoticism, realism with the stuff of romance. They mingle fact and fiction with ease: travel narratives claim to be true, yet readers often suspect that travelers lie to serve their purposes. Novels, meanwhile, often present themselves through frame stories that provide the veneer of fact to fiction. In his conclusion, Adams speculates briefly on the relation between travel narrative and novel in the twentieth century. Both genres are vulnerable to the claim of exhaustion, albeit for different reasons; much has been written on the "death" of the novel and the "end" of travel. Yet each continues to evolve, reinventing itself in changed cultural circumstances: "as the novelist finds new topics, new themes, new techniques, so does the travel writer."[34] Adams's depiction of the travel narrative as eclectic and malleable identifies genre evolution as a subject of inquiry, but does not explain how or with what consequences it occurs. A work of literary history, it sidesteps theory entirely.

To explain how and why the travel narrative changes, it is useful to remember the sustained theoretical work on genre evolution that occurred in the decades from the First World War through the Second, when thinkers such as Georg Lukács, Walter Benjamin, and Mikhail Bakhtin sought to explain the connection between modernity and aesthetic change in "a rapidly and radically modernizing world."[35] Bakhtin's major essays of the 1930s and 1940s – collected in English as *The Dialogic Imagination* – consider the nature of prose genres, their representation of language, and their evolution in response to social and political circumstance. Although he does not deal specifically with travel narrative, his understanding of "heteroglossia" and "novelistic discourse" offers strategies for examining how and why narrative genres change in conjunction with the peoples, cultures, and places they attempt to represent.[36] Bakhtin, who explicitly identifies his work as a critical response to formalist and Marxist extremes, rejects a dichotomy between theory and history: "the study of verbal art can and must overcome the divorce between an abstract 'formal' approach and an equally abstract 'ideological' approach. Form and content in discourse are one, once we understand that verbal discourse is a social phenomenon – social throughout its entire range and in each and every of its factors."[37] In his account, the most fundamental aspect of language is its social diversity: "[L]anguage is heteroglot from top to bottom; it represents the co-existence of socio-ideological contradictions between the present and the past, between differing epochs of the past, between different socio-ideological groups in the present" (291). Prose genres, specifically the novel, develop as a means of representing this heteroglossia with unprecedented fidelity. Modernity and the dominance of the novel, Bakhtin argues, compel a new understanding of genres as dynamic means of engaging with – and hence responding to – the social world.

Bakhtin's conception of genre privileges evolution and malleability over stasis and conformity, uncertainty over predictability; in his work theory and history come intertwined. He credits the novel with disrupting earlier genres' "fully formed and well-defined generic contours" and upending notions of "literature as a hierarchically organized, organic whole." The novel, he argues, is "an object of study completely different," "a creature from an alien species" that relentlessly appropriates from and parodies other genres (4). In so doing, it "novelizes" them: "In the process of becoming the dominant genre, the novel sparks the renovation of all other genres, it infects them with its spirit of process and inconclusiveness" (7). In a literary landscape dominated by the novel, discourse from "a zone of contact with the present in all its openendedness" displaces conventionalized literary forms. Other genres either change or die:

> In general, any strict adherence to a genre begins to feel like a stylization, a stylization taken to the point of parody, despite the artistic intent of the author. In an environment where the novel is the dominant genre, the conventional languages of strictly canonical genres begin to sound in new ways, which are quite different from the ways they sounded in those eras when the novel was *not* included in "high" literature. (6)

Novelization reinvigorates genres:

> They become more free and flexible, their language renews itself by incorporating extraliterary heteroglossia and the "novelistic" layers of literary language, they become dialogized, permeated with laughter, irony,

humor, elements of self-parody and finally – this is the most important thing – the novel inserts into these other genres an indeterminacy, a certain semantic openendedness, a living contact with unfinished, still-evolving contemporary reality. (7)

Bakhtin argues that the novel differs so markedly and effectively from earlier literary forms that it fundamentally transforms how genres work: "The novel ... has no canon of its own. It is, by its very nature, not canonic. It is plasticity itself. It is a genre that is ever questing, ever examining itself and subjecting its established forms to review." Other genres survive by adopting this plasticity: novelization is the means by which they escape from the "stylization of forms that have outlived themselves" and obtain "liberation from all that serves as a brake on their unique development" (39). Genres that fail to adapt, as Gary Saul Morson and Caryl Emerson explain, "come to sound hopelessly anachronistic and unsophisticated, or even like unintended self-parodies."[38] Moreover, Michael Gardiner argues, Bakhtin credits the novel with more than literary effect: he attributes a "pervasive social power" to "the counter-hegemonic or liberating potential of the novel form."[39]

Bakhtin's theory of genre and history of novelization include several lines of argument that are pertinent for analyzing twentieth-century travel narrative. First, genres evolve in response to changing social and historical circumstances. Second, in a literary context dominated by the novel, strict adherence to convention appears outmoded, mannered, and conservative. Third, genres that have become poor imitations of themselves can be revitalized by borrowing from novelistic discourse, which includes "extraliterary heteroglossia," irony, and critical self-consciousness. Fourth, novelized genres evolve in ways that not only allow for but embrace openendedness, unfinalizability, and self-scrutiny. Together, these claims help to explain *why* and *how* the travel narrative evolved over the last century. They offer ways to examine how travel narratives reflect – or fail to reflect – the century's profound intellectual and geopolitical changes. Finally, they provide a means for evaluating the travel narrative's value at the end of modernity, at what Chambers calls "the 'other' side of the authorized tale, that other side of modernity, of the West, of History."[40]

At the century's beginning, travel narrative resembles the kind of "already completed" genre that Bakhtin argues most needs innovation. Its conventions are well established: the European traveler perceives the authentic, understands it, and narrates it with a sophisticated mixture of admiration and condescension. (At his most egregious, he claims to understand his subjects better than they can understand themselves.) In the image Pratt analyzes, he is rhetorically, ideologically, often sexually, often politically "monarch of all I survey."[41] Although not solely the province of male writers, the travel narrative uses recurring tropes that predictably invoke imperial history and European notions of masculinity: adventure, discovery, freedom, domination. Locales may vary, but plots are in effect predetermined, for, as Meaghan Morris explains, "travel stories written as Voyages and Maps ... relentlessly generate models of the proper use of place and time – where to begin, where to go, what to become in between. Among the most prescriptive of genres in the canon of modern realism ..., the travel story seems strongly resistant to ... effort[s] of transformation."[42] The genre occupies a quasi-scholarly position by producing knowledge of distant peoples and places; it serves a cultural and political role by reiterating accepted discourses regarding empire and cultural difference.

Yet pressures on the genre's conventions and challenges to its authority are evident. The rapid growth of tourism in the nineteenth century had made distinctive, original angles from which to write difficult to find. Serious travelers who would write about their experiences self-consciously sought to differentiate themselves from tourists. James Buzard argues that such "anti-tourism" was not merely snobbishness but, more significantly, a modern strategy, "an important, even exemplary way of regarding one's own cultural experiences as authentic and unique, setting them against a backdrop of always assumed tourist vulgarity, repetition, and ignorance."[43] The traveler's claim to recognize the authentic and represent it authoritatively contests as well with the emergent disciplines of anthropology and archaeology, which were replacing colonial observation as the West's means for discursive management and scientific study of foreign peoples and places.[44] Revolutions and Independence movements were already signaling the eventual dissolution of Europe's empires: Europe's relation to the rest of the world was changing. The Great War killed millions, threw nations into political and economic crises, and provoked deep anxieties about cultural decline. Fussell argues that escape, not exploration, motivates many postwar travel narratives, for warm climates elsewhere promise restoration from malaise. "Some of the most assiduous travelers of the 20's and 30's," he writes, "were those whose wanderlust and all else the war had nearly extinguished."[45]

In the face of these cultural and geopolitical changes, writers must rethink the conventions and premises of a genre that is already ossifying. They do so in the context of metropolitan experience and modernist innovation. What happens, then, in travel narrative in the twentieth century? How do writers reinvent the genre to serve new purposes suited to the rapidly changing world before them? How do they break from plots, tropes, and gendered conventions so deeply established that they "resist" transformation? How do they navigate modernist nostalgia – and modernity's wars? How – or can – they reimagine national identity and cultural heterogeneity in a postimperial world? Not surprisingly, writers of travel narratives experiment in many of the ways that novelists – modernist and postmodernist – do. Their texts are more deliberately subjective, more fragmented, less earnest (or more ironic) in their presumptions, more self-conscious of their own narrativity. They incorporate other kinds of text – poetry, newspaper clippings, advertising, mass media – as well as maps, diagrams, drawings, and photographs. They attempt to jettison truth claims that presume European omniscience for personal witness that relies on contingent individual experience, seeks truth at the local level, and admits uncertainty.

Like the novel, which has "at its core … personal experience and free creative imagination," the twentieth-century travel narrative "structures itself in the zone of direct contact" with "inconclusive present-day reality."[46] It evolves, to borrow Jed Esty's phrase, by "negation, deviation, variation, and mutation."[47] Recent scholarship persuasively demonstrates that twentieth-century British narrative must be understood in its global contexts: European, metropolitan, transnational, (post)colonial.[48] In *Cosmopolitan Style* (2006), Rebecca Walkowitz argues that writers from Joseph Conrad to W. G. Sebald use "the salient features of modernist narrative" to create what she calls "critical cosmopolitanism," a mode of international engagement marked by "an aversion to heroic tones of appropriation and progress, and a suspicion of epistemological privilege."[49] Walkowitz's analysis of the mutual relation of aesthetics and politics in fiction is equally significant for understanding travel narrative. In Walkowitz's transnational, transhistorical account, writers earlier in the century develop "a specific repertoire of literary strategies" that later writers adapt and transform as all seek to "present and interpret experiences, while continuing to acknowledge the new range of experiences that shape the materials and circumstances of writing."[50] Refusing a narrow literary-historical definition, she argues for an expansive conception of modernism as a complex mode of engagement with the experience of modernity that "reflects a conflict about the content and constituency of international experience and an effort to display relationships between everyday, private activities and public, international ones." In Walkowitz's analysis, this mode begins early in the twentieth century, as made visible in the work of Conrad, "at once the most British and the most cosmopolitan of novelists," and continues to affect literary practice at the century's end, where it recurs vertiginously in Sebald's Conrad-haunted exploration of marginality and Britain in *The Rings of Saturn* (1995).[51] Twentieth-century travel narrative demonstrates a cosmopolitan articulation of experience and an ongoing adaptation of modernist strategies akin to the conceptions and practices that Walkowitz identifies in novels. At its most serious, twentieth-century travel narrative seeks to be literature that narrates modern subjects' relation to their rapidly changing, contradictory, global contexts.

To examine these aspects of twentieth-century travel narrative, as this book does, is to understand genres as evolving modes of engagement with the world and modernism as cosmopolitan in its concerns. Fussell explicitly positions his study as an elegy for a dead English genre (ironically, it appears just as a new generation of travel narratives that owe much to modernism begins to receive recognition). His outdated premises help to demonstrate what is at stake in Bakhtin's concept of novelization. Focusing on literary men of a certain class who write "displaced ... romances," Fussell privileges an apolitical aesthetic. He goes so far as to see "a premonition of the end" in the travel book "beginning to metamorphose into the war book" in the mid-1930s, a demise he attributes to "corrupters" whose work is insufficiently literary and excessively concerned with present politics.[52] In Bakhtinian terms, his analysis values "stylization" over "novelization." The very notion of genre "corruption" imagines genres to be outside history and, in so doing, refuses to recognize the significance of their metamorphosis. In the instance of the travel narrative, it effectively dismisses the genre's deep and complex relation to the particular histories of modernity and empire. Traditionally, the travel genre had refused to acknowledge its political roots. But by the 1930s, Schweizer argues, British writers had begun to pioneer

> a new tradition by employing travel writing self-consciously as a platform for voicing radical political ideas. Simultaneously, they abandoned the documentary, pseudoscientific, journalistic method that had dominated the writing of travel books in the past and instead opted for the more imaginative, introspective, essayistic, and argumentative kind of travel book that clearly aspired to be recognized as a form of literature.[53]

Schweizer's analysis of the work of George Orwell, Evelyn Waugh, Graham Greene, and Rebecca West demonstrates that these revisions to the genre occur unevenly – some innovations falter, and some elements of imperial discourse that writers seek to abandon nevertheless remain. Rob Nixon aptly characterizes the travel narrative's newfound malleability and consequent challenges when he describes the genre as a hybrid that allows V. S. Naipaul to shift between "a semi-ethnographic, distanced, analytic mode" and "an autobiographical, subjective, emotionally tangled mode."[54] Suspect though they may be, aspects of the old persist, whereas the new poses a challenge; Naipaul "negotiates the slippage between" modes "to maximize the writer's discursive authority."[55] Such oscillation is inevitable as writers reinvent travel narrative in twentieth-century cultural and geo-political contexts, for genres embody the struggle between discourse and experience, aesthetics and politics, theory and history.

The most compelling transformation in twentieth-century Anglophone travel narrative is its turn to the subjective consequences of war, vio-lence, postcolonial transformation, and Western decline.[56] This shift is not limited to the English narratives of the 1930s that Schweizer exam-ines. Instead, it is a distinctive, important development in the genre that begins in the 1920s, continues into the twenty-first century, and shapes cosmopolitan texts written in English by writers whose points of origin span the globe. These new concerns signal the genre's creative reinven-tion, its adaptation to the abrupt, often chaotic cultural and political transformation of the imperialized world. They haunt travel narratives that follow the First World War, including T. E. Lawrence's *Seven Pillars of Wisdom*, which eclectically embraces philosophical introspection, visual art, and political history. They motivate narratives of travel to the new Soviet Union and China in the 1920s and 1930s. They are central to West's *Black Lamb*, which invokes and defies all definitions of the genre, and to Stephen Spender's *European Witness*. They are signal fea-tures of travel narratives in the second half of the century, notably Colin Thubron's reflective journeys in authoritarian states in the 1980s and new nations in Central Asia after the Soviet Union's collapse. They echo as well through narratives of travel in search of authenticity – national, religious, and personal – to ameliorate the effects of modernization and war, from H. V. Morton in "the Holy Land" in the 1930s to Andrew X. Pham in Vietnam in the 1990s. Together, these texts and many oth-ers demonstrate the genre's contradictions, malleability, and seriousness; they compel a rethinking of the travel narrative's literary significance and cultural role.

The chapters that follow do not observe a strictly chronological orga-nization, for the purpose is not to claim that the travel narrative develops along a single trajectory. Instead, they argue that the travel narrative devel-ops in overlapping ways that show significant and sometimes surprising continuities from the end of the First World War to the present. Chapters 1 through 3 establish the theoretical groundwork, identify the distinctive situation of the twentieth-century traveler, and trace the influence of literary modernism and postmodernism. Chapters 4 through 6 deal with significant developments in subject matter, particularly the genre's reinvention as a means of narrating the subjective consequences of war, transformation, and decline. These developments use the innovations in narrative stance and style examined in Chapters 1 through 3 to address new concerns: the failure of nostalgia in the face of spectacular change, the violence and instability of perpetual wartime, and the recuperation of authenticity. Chapter 2 continues the theoretical work begun here by examining the particular problem of narrative authority. Chapters 3 through 6 each identify salient critical issues, noting their significance across a range of primary texts, and then analyze selected texts more thoroughly. The primary texts, written from the 1920s to the 2000s, demonstrate the recurrence and revision of modernist strategies as writers transform the travel narrative to serve new cultural purposes.

Chapter 2, "The Privilege – and Problem – of Narrative Authority" articulates the distinctive concerns of travel narrative as metropolitan experience, new technologies, and geopolitical transformation compel writers to question the genre's premises far more directly than before. By convention, the travel narrator – a modern Western subject – readily assumes the prerogative to describe foreign peoples and places with authority. In the twentieth century, however, writers often disavow any expectation to present new knowledge and instead produce narratives about individual experience and perception. Aspiring to the stature of literature, travel narrative sets aside documentary discourse for self-consciously subjective discourse. Bakhtin's theory of narration identifies what is at stake in this transition, whereas recent scholarship on flânerie reveals the critical nature of the spectatorship evident in these texts. For Bakhtin, modernity produces a world that is fundamentally social, diverse, and dynamic:

> ... all languages of heteroglossia ... are specific points of view on the world, forms for conceptualizing the world in words, specific world views, each characterized by its own objects, meanings and values. As such they all may be juxtaposed to one another, mutually supplement one another, contradict one another and be interrelated dialogically. As such they encounter one another and co-exist in the consciousness of real people.[57]

To narrate is to represent heteroglossia from within; to narrate one's own experiences dialogically is to represent one's interactions with other subjects, languages, and points of view. (To do so authoritatively, in contrast, as does documentary discourse, is to preclude their being heard.⁵⁸)

The concept of flânerie offers an understanding of spectatorship that helps to articulate the changing vantage point of the travel narrator. Beginning with Benjamin, scholars have examined modernity's transformation of mobility and perception into self-conscious, complex practices that are at once subjective and critical, aware of their own contingency yet concerned to move beyond surfaces. Some twentieth-century writers travel to distance modernity through melancholy speculation on the past. Others use the genre to grapple with modernity's consequences, narrating their travels through the upheaval caused by wars, revolutions, and globalization. Their innovations compel inquiry: How far do a spectator's privilege and knowledge actually extend? How do new technologies and geopolitical transformation alter the experience of travel and the kinds of narratives that result? How does an increased emphasis on subjective experience change a genre that had prized objective description? What are travel narrative's cultural purposes, if not to produce ethnography or instrumental knowledge?

Chapter 3, "Modernist and Postmodernist Travels" examines the ways that the travel narrative shares the aesthetic strategies and epistemological concerns of modernism and postmodernism, particularly their emphasis on contingency, discontinuity, and subjectivity. Echoing developments in the novel, travel narrative shifts to self-conscious narrators, multiple perspectives, and open-ended plots; experiments stylistically with fragments, incorporated texts, and parody; and makes idiosyncratic uses of photographs and drawings. These strategies allow writers to lay bare the historical presumptions of a genre whose claim to significance had rested on the premise that firsthand European experience constituted the basis of instrumental knowledge. In countering that premise, writers explicitly reject authority for contingency, expertise for situated observation, claims of discovery for moments of illumination.

In drawing on modernist and postmodernist techniques, the travel narrative presents the experience of travel as subjective and uncertain; its possible significance lies in the telling. In *Brazilian Adventure* (1933) and *One's Company* (1934), Peter Fleming parodies the genre's most earnest conventions, fashioning the traveler as a confident, often comic flâneur whose ease belies his lack of expertise to write about cultures and sites he scarcely knows. In *Letters from Iceland* (1937) and *Journey to a War* (1939), W. H. Auden and his collaborators devise radically new means for representing travel by juxtaposing narratives, poems, quotations, and captioned photographs. Disclaiming conventional narrative authority, Auden and Louis

MacNeice produce a multi-voiced discontinuous collage, and Auden and Christopher Isherwood depict themselves as "mere trippers ... come to China to write a book."[59] Such experimentation lays the literary ground for later texts usually credited as innovations in the genre, including Pico Iyer's self-consciously postmodern *Video Night in Kathmandu* (1988), which abandons the linear trajectory of the journey for a narrative structure that claims "to reflect not a physical but a mental itinerary."[60]

Chapter 4, "Nostalgia and the Spectacle of Modernity" considers the ways that travel narrative reclaims cultural significance by personalizing geopolitical transformation through revolution, modernization, and imperial collapse. Twentieth-century Western travelers describe a pervasive sense of mutability that takes various forms: despair about metropolitan life, yearning for an imagined simpler existence, and chagrin at finding unrest or transformation abroad. But to journey is to observe modernity's effects abroad and recognize the impossibility of retreat to a prelapsarian world untouched by revolution, social upheaval, and technology. The genre's historical ties to imperialism only intensify the familiar modernist sense of irrevocable change: although nostalgia, a quintessentially modern condition, becomes a central theme, narratives of geopolitical spectacles abroad reveal its failure as a subjective response to modernity's historical transformations. Such texts make visible the fault lines in colonial discourse. Travelers may share with ethnographers "the yearning to establish a reciprocity with the people and places they visit and about which they write," but achieving this imagined ideal nearly always falters in the face of political and textual realities.[61] Although war and tumult in foreign places offer haunting spectacles that alter Western observers' understanding of cultural difference and modernity, their own situation in the world remains largely secure, or at least unquestioned. Even in "sympathetic" narratives, as Holland and Huggan conclude, "there are gaps that the genre itself cannot help but create. Travel writing reinstalls difference even as it claims to dismantle it; the humanist desire for reconciliation ... tends to founder on the very (socioeconomic) conditions that make travel writing possible."[62]

Perhaps no text does this more dramatically than Lawrence's account of his travels in Arabia during the First World War, *Seven Pillars of Wisdom* (1926). Lawrence casts himself as both observer and costumed "man of action," at once entranced by the spectacle in which he plays a role and – like many twentieth-century travelers – chagrined at modernity's effects. His remarkably modernist narrative depicts the experiences of travel and war with unprecedented frankness: he reinvents the war story as "self-expression in ... imaginative form."[63] For other travelers, the new Soviet state and revolution-torn China provide vantage points from which to understand modernity's effects at a safe remove: travel diverts the observer from transformation at home and allows for critical reflection. In *Turkestan Solo* (1934) and *Forbidden Journey* (1937), Ella Maillart crosses Russian and Chinese Turkestan, hoping that nomadic life offers freedom from metropolitan realities. But she finds that the scene of modernity extends even to cultures she had imagined timeless. For others, travel becomes a means of deciphering the long-term consequences of modernity's violence and cultural upheavals. These concerns permeate Colin Thubron's melancholy narratives of travel through the remains of the USSR, *The Lost Heart of Asia* (1994) and *In Siberia* (1999), in which a well-read Englishman journeys alone through vast places filled with traces of older empires, meets wary survivors of the Soviet period, and reads hints of Islamist futures.

Chapter 5, "Perpetual Wartime" analyzes the development of the travel narrative as a genre for exploring deep anxieties about Western failure and metropolitan decline. In a time of global war, when violence and change are immediate and unending, travel allows no break from modernity and its consequences; the distinction between reports from the frontlines and tales from the backwoods all but collapses. Chaos elsewhere signifies the extent of a global labyrinth of national, ethnic, gender, and class conflict created by empire, urbanization, and technology. It presages – and becomes – chaos at home. Travel becomes a harbinger, narrative a way to come to terms with the shocking inhumanity of which advanced civilizations are capable and the cultural dispossession they can cause, for journeys are haunted by memories of wars past and specters of wars to come. For West, travel to Yugoslavia allows her to learn "how I shall die, and why."[64] Familiar tropes may persist, but signify differently, for few diversions are possible and respite cannot be found. The conventional traveler counts on returning safely; travelers in the labyrinth of wartime must end their narratives *in medias res*, bearing witness of what they have seen though uncertain what will follow.[65] West's work, published in the grim early years of the Second World War, is dedicated "to my friends in Yugoslavia, who are now all dead or enslaved"; it ends with a desperate meditation on the failure of civilization.

To reinvent travel narrative as a serious means of reporting modernity's violence and writing its disasters is to push the genre to startling new extremes. It is to assert that the first-person narrator is a witness whose experience can be trusted, that narrative is a meaningful strategy for understanding events so chaotic they exceed comprehension. In *Writing War in the Twentieth Century* (2000), Margot Norris argues that twentieth-century war is totalizing in new ways: the scale of civilian displacement and death, the shattering of the social order, the extremity of the violence. The nature of total war muddies conventional distinctions between the traveler who views war's prelude or aftermath and the reporter who experiences it as it happens; to write it blurs lines between travel narrative, war reporting, and the literature of witness. Travel narratives about modernity's violent ends must address its utter disruption of cultural continuity and its creation of "displaced persons," exiles, and diaspora.[66] Stephen Spender does this in *European Witness* (1946), his narrative of travel through the ruins of civilization in Germany amongst troubled civilians and displaced persons at the end of the Nazi regime. For Norris, the "changed ethical condition" of total war produces a cultural obligation to reveal and to witness, even as war becomes unrepresentable. What kinds of discourse do travel narratives use in the attempt to overcome art's inherent "incommensurability to war"?[67] Who may claim to "witness," who merely to "observe"? Who may tell whose stories, with what authority? Which stories matter to whom, and why? These questions echo through travel narratives that bear witness of the trauma of the "shattered present," the future unknown.[68] Their deep uncertainty about the legacy of modern civilization permeates texts at the century's end, including Peter Maass's *Love Thy Neighbor: A Story of War* (1996), about his journeys in war-torn Bosnia, Philip Gourevitch's narrative of travel in the time of genocide, *We Wish to Inform You That Tomorrow We Will Be Killed with Our Families: Stories from Rwanda* (1998), and Joe Sacco's graphic account of observing intifada in *Palestine* (1993–1996; 2001).

Chapter 6, "The Allure of Authenticity" examines the genre's most persistent response to the long-term consequences of global transformation and Western decline: a newly personal concern for authenticity. To search for cultures and sites deemed "authentic" is not new, nor is the use of travel narrative to document Western conclusions about the truth of distant peoples and places. In fact, the notion that travel provides a distinctive form of access to truth underlies practices as varied as Christian pilgrimage and the political fact-finding mission. In the twentieth century, however, as globalization and global war threaten identities, places, and cultural norms that had seemed secure, a new urgency inflects the search for authenticity, which evidences the crises of representation and meaning that Jean Baudrillard describes as central to postmodernity. It affects every aspect of travel, permeating phenomena as different as the ethnographer's quest to document vanishing cultures and the traveler's disdain for mass tourism's preordained itineraries. In the travel narrative, the concern for authenticity takes a distinctly inward turn, as writers journey to places of national and cultural origin, seeking evidence of belonging to ameliorate their experiences of war-time, secularization, and diaspora.[69]

Like narratives about the violent consequences of modernity, narratives of travel in search of authenticity cast the narrator as a witness whose expertise lies in firsthand experience. Centered on a personal search for surety rather than a cultural obligation to testify of events, such narratives seek to bridge the divide between the global present and views of identity and history as rooted in, and confirmed by, place. In this logic, to experience the original scene is to mitigate the effects of histori-cal chaos, modernization, and both metaphorical and literal homeless-ness. Such conceits are as flawed as they are ambitious: as Susan Stewart argues, such privileging of origins seeks an authentic past that has "never existed except as narrative."[70] Beginning with *In Search of England* (1927), H. V. Morton seeks to conserve a national life that he figures through images of rural life; his best-selling narratives "in search of" the distinct cultures of the British Isles both celebrate this notion of authenticity and demonstrate its artifice. This conflict takes center stage in *In the Steps of the Master* (1934), in which the skeptical Morton travels in the Holy Land, asking whether modern travelers can assure their Christian faith by walking where Jesus walked. Later writers also journey to places of origin, hoping to ameliorate the dislocation of emigrant life and frag-mentation of postmodernity by working out an authentic personal rela-tion to history. Andrew X. Pham undertakes such a journey in *Catfish and Mandala: A Two-Wheeled Voyage through the Landscape and Memory of Vietnam* (1999), traveling through the homeland he fled as a child refu-gee to create a narrative that will make sense of his displaced life in the United States. Rosemary Mahoney, a secular writer haunted by belief, makes a very different postmodern journey in search of authenticity in the present by traveling to global sites of pilgrimage in *The Singular Pilgrim: Travels on Sacred Ground* (2003).

The violent cultural transformations of the last century, which mark modernity's end and the emergence of an uneasily global postmodernity, pose profound ethical questions about travel practices and travel's repre-sentation in narrative. In 1945, Evelyn Waugh declared: "There is no room for tourists in a world of 'displaced persons.'" Waugh rightly understood that the stark contrast between the elective travels of a privileged narra-tor and the involuntary dislocation of "refugees and deserters" was too extreme for conventional journeying or narrative to continue unaltered.[71] He failed, however, to recognize that the genre had already been evolving for some time. Nor did he foresee its further reinvention as a strategy for understanding the consequences of the world that had just blown apart: mobility, transience, anomie, and homelessness.[72] Travel narrative now bears little resemblance to its nineteenth-century antecedent. The conclusion of this book reflects on the new cultural purposes that travel narrative serves at modernity's end and on what it may become in the future.

CHAPTER 2

The Privilege – and Problem – of Narrative Authority

[The travel book] is the most *personal* of all the literary forms except perhaps poetry: through all its vicissitudes, the author is beside you ... there he is, as he is in real life no doubt, and you feel that you know him very well. "British officers cannot go wrong in attacking at three A.M.," a statement like this, made apparently without any provocation near some little village on the Asian plateau, could only belong to the period between the Crimean and the first World War; the tough confidence of its age is in it. The same place seen today would start a very different reflection; it is the personal slant of the author that makes or mars the book of travel, and if that is taken away and mere facts are left to stand alone, the thing becomes a guide-book and falls dead.

Travel alone, therefore, is not enough. Even as a documentary it has too many competitors – the picture-books, the Sunday papers, cinerama, television – these also are documentaries and efficient for the work they do....

...The pattern becomes essential, and in the absence of a general standard, every author must provide his own. In a novel this can, and indeed should, be done unobtrusively by the selection of incidents and the building of the plot; but in travel books, or in history for that matter, the plot is there already, chaotic as a rule and shapeless, and it is the angle at which the author sees it that must bring out its meaning and create its form....

More and more then, as I see it, the travel book is becoming an interpretation....

Freya Stark (1958)[1]

The twentieth century's geopolitical transformations threaten the privileges that modern European subjects presume to be theirs: mobility, autonomy, ease of association, and the right to represent. To presume freedom of movement is to expect deference: entrée at national borders, security in the international concession, and the right to venture wherever one wishes. To presume narrative authority is to expect deference as well: liberty to keep notebooks and take photographs, access to unfettered exchange with locals, and the right to have the final word. Encounters between narrators who "like the sensation [travel] gives you of freedom from all responsibility" and officials who examine passports, refuse access to restricted areas, and search luggage for notes and film appear often in twentieth-century travel narratives.[2] The tenor of these scenes ranges from petulance to fear because the officials' actions demonstrate that travelers lack the autonomy they desire. That such is the case becomes especially clear in the context of the century's wars, cultural revolutions, and political standoffs. Disruptions of the autonomy that travelers expect call attention to the rapidly changing circumstances in which their mobility and their narratives occur. The former may be read as a figure for the latter, the presumed right to move freely wherever one wishes as a physical iteration of the privilege of omniscience.

Central to the travel narrative, though less obvious than the presumption of physical autonomy, is the presumption that being a literate European abroad grants the prerogative and even obligation to represent with authority. Like the realist novel, the nineteenth-century travel narrative rests on the premise that narrative can represent peoples and places with unsurpassed fidelity. Central among the genre's conventions is the privileged narrator whose representations rely on firsthand experience yet claim to transcend the limitations of individual perspective. A modern European subject, the conventional travel narrator confidently describes foreign peoples and places, assuming the authority to produce knowledge of ethnography and geography as well as write of personal experience. The speaker also "exhibits himself as physically more free than the reader, and thus every such book, even when it depicts its speaker trapped in Boa Vista, is an implicit celebration of freedom."[3] This stance serves to guarantee the travel narrative's truth claims: the imperial observer's mobility and command of documentary detail underwrite the text's plausibility. The traveler presents his discourse as authoritative: the first-person evidence of one who has "been there," experienced difference, and survived, one who readily assumes the expertise to represent and whose narrative – even when fantastic – brooks no questions.[4]

By the beginning of the twentieth century, the travel genre's conventions – particularly its narrator's authoritative stance – were so firmly established that they were all but obligatory. Its tropes, much repeated in travel accounts for educated audiences and echoed in the clichés of popular magazines and later films, were familiar to writers and readers alike.[5] At the same time, these conventions and tropes were increasingly ill-suited for representing the experiences of most Europeans abroad. Tourists on the exhausted itinerary of the Grand Tour or leisure cruises were not "discovering" new territory, and travelers who self-consciously sought to differentiate themselves from tourists were nonetheless aware they were neither explorers nor experts.[6] Their observations, seldom unprecedented, risked redundancy and irrelevance. In *The Desert and the Sown* (1907), Gertrude Bell described the dilemma of the earnest traveler who lacks new information to report:

> Those who venture to add a new volume to the vast literature of travel, unless they be men of learning or politicians, must be prepared with an excuse. My excuse is ready, as specious and I hope as plausible as such things should be. I desired to write not so much a book of travel as an account of the people whom I met or who accompanied me on my way, and to show what the world is like in which they live and how it appears to them....
>
> None of the country through which I went is ground virgin to the traveler, though parts of it have been visited but seldom, and described only in works that are costly and often difficult to obtain. Of such places I have given a brief account, and as many photographs as seemed to be of value.[7]

Not yet a public figure, Bell excuses her assumption of authority in her preface, then proceeds to recount her travels through the Ottoman province of Syria.[8] Her opening emphasizes subjective experience: "you must go alone" into "[t]he world of adventure and of enterprise, dark with hurrying storms, glittering in raw sunlight, an unanswered question and an unanswerable doubt hidden in the fold of every hill."[9] Yet her account mixes political detail and Orientalist description with romanticized personal observation in typically awkward ways. Although she recognizes the genre is exhausted, in practice she largely relies on convention rather than breaking new literary ground.[10]

The disjuncture between Bell's self-aware preface and her narrative illustrates the ways in which the genre had reached a breaking point. Edward Said and Mary Louise Pratt each identify two primary strategies at work in European discourse about other cultures and peoples, and their analyses explain why a specious excuse might not suffice to justify Bell's text. Although their terms differ slightly – Said uses "vision" and "narrative," Pratt "description" and "narrative" – the strategies echo those that Georg Lukács first analyzed in the 1936 essay "Narrate or Describe?"[11] Lukács argues that the nineteenth-century European novel demonstrates two "basically divergent approaches to reality": description, written "from the standpoint of an observer," and narration, "from the standpoint of a participant." This "opposition between experiencing and observing" is not merely stylistic, but rather evidence of "[d]ivergent basic positions about life and about the major problems of society" that result from capitalism.[12] Description "contemporizes" and "levels" to be comprehensive, "as part of an attempt to make literature scientific."[13] Narration, in contrast, "recounts the vicissitudes of human beings," places them in historical context, "establishes proportions," and aims to show the significance of relationships between people and things.[14] The strategies engage readers in different ways: "[w]e are merely observers" of description, whereas with narration "[w]e ourselves experience these events."[15] In Lukács's analysis, the increasing prominence of description weakens realism and compromises its ability to represent bourgeois life critically.

Said, examining European discourse about the Orient, and Pratt, examining ethnography's continuity with travel writing, make complementary arguments about discursive tactics and their limitations. Said characterizes "vision" and "narrative" as opposed strategies. The first seeks to comprehend the Orient in its entirety and depict it as static, the second to represent its historicity and malleability. "Vision" aims to subordinate individual experience to scientific representation, "narrative" to represent cultural complexity. In his analysis of the work of early twentieth-century Arabists, including Bell and T. E. Lawrence, Said finds "the defeat of narrative by vision." He writes:

> Against this static system of "synchronic essentialism" I have called vision because it presumes that the whole Orient can be seen panoptically, there is a constant pressure. The source of pressure is narrative, in that if any Oriental detail can be shown to move, or to develop, diachrony is introduced into the system. What seemed stable ... now appears unstable.... History and the narrative by which history is represented argue that vision is insufficient, that "the Orient" as an unconditional ontological category does an injustice to the potential of reality for change.
>
> Moreover, narrative is the specific form taken by written history to counter the permanence of vision.... Narrative asserts the power of men to be born, develop and die, the tendency of institutions and actualities to change, the likelihood that modernity and contemporaneity will finally overtake "classical" civilizations; above all, it asserts that the domination of reality by vision is no more than a will to power, a will to truth and interpretation.... Narrative, in short, introduces an opposing point of view, perspective, consciousness.[16]

Whereas Said focuses on the conflict between the panoptic and the perspectival, Pratt focuses on what she calls "the vexed but important relationship between personal narrative and impersonal description" in travel writing and ethnography. Travel writing, she explains, has long combined two discourses – the personal narrative and the descriptive Orientalist summa, or "particularized narrative and generalized description."[17] Easy to distinguish, they coexist in "various guises," sometimes "interwoven" from one sentence or paragraph to the next, sometimes organized into separate chapters or volumes. This persists in twentieth-century ethnography, she argues, because it "mediates a contradiction within the discipline between personal and scientific authority."[18]

The relation between these two strategies of representation reaches a critical juncture early in the twentieth century. For Said, crisis comes with the European imperative to manage the Orient's entrance into modernity in the aftermath of the First World War: Orientalism shifts "from an academic to an *instrumental* attitude." (*The Desert and the Sown*, late for the former and early for the latter, shows Bell caught in this shift.) For Pratt, crisis comes with the development of anthropology, which seeks comprehensive knowledge of other cultures by converting "the face-to-face field encounter to objectified science."[19] These changing political and intellectual circumstances make the limits of the travel narrative's presumption to speak authoritatively evident, in ways that the genre must take into account: the genre becomes critically aware of its own conventions. How far can a European narrator's privilege and knowledge truly extend, with what consequences? On what authority do they rest? What are – or might be – the purposes of travel narrative, if it no longer serves chiefly to produce knowledge? What is the role of subjective perception in a genre that traditionally prizes objective description? How do modernity, modernization, and war alter both the experiences and means of representation available to travelers?

Following the First World War, writers question the travel narrative's foundational premises, particularly the presumption of narrative authority, far more directly than ever before. They do so in these disciplinary and political contexts – and, crucially, in the literary context of modernism, with its emphasis on the subjectivity, fluidity, and contingency of points of view.[20] Modernist fiction enacts what Pericles Lewis calls "a rethinking of the relationship between the objective, omniscient narrator and individual characters with limited, subjective perspectives." The disparity between these points of view – those of an observer, on the one hand, and of participants, on the other – had been central to the realist novel and its social concerns. Modernists, however, transform "the individual protagonist into the narrator (or, to look at it another way ... the narrator into a character)."²¹ In 1924, Virginia Woolf famously argues that the novel's purpose is "to express character – not to preach doctrines, sing songs, or celebrate the glories of the British Empire."²² The following year, Aldous Huxley describes modernist narration as an apt representation of travel experience: "The God's-eye view of those novelists who really know, or pretend they know, exactly what is going on in the minds of their characters, is exchanged for the traveller's-eye view, the view of the stranger who starts with no knowledge whatever of the actors' personalities and can only infer from their gestures what is happening in their minds." Joseph Conrad's Marlow provides Huxley with an apt illustration. In *Heart of Darkness* and *Lord Jim*, Marlow recounts his experiences to European listeners in impressionistic, ambiguous narratives. His tales are about the elusiveness of meaning and the insufficiency of fact; the act of telling the story brings not clarity, but increased uncertainty. Huxley writes that Conrad "sits at a distance, he watches [his characters] acting and then wonders and wonders, through pages of Marlow's winding narratives, why on earth they acted as they did, what were their motives, what they felt and thought."²³ In Simon Gikandi's later analysis, Conrad's fiction signals a "crucial transformation in the representation of colonial space" from something to be mastered through ethnographic description to something that "proffer[s] modes of cognitive disorder that nullify the possibility of understanding itself."²⁴

Leaving the "God's-eye view" for the "traveller's view," writers challenge the travel narrative's rigid conventions and devise new ways of representing Europeans' experiences abroad. If the nineteenth-century travel narrator had generally presumed to speak with the authority of a privileged observer, the twentieth-century travel narrator would instead, as Lewis explains of modernist fiction, focus on "the perceptions and categories of a particular character" with the hope of "transforming purely subjective impressions" into meaningful, shared knowledge. "Crucial to this process," he argues, "is the notion of self-consciousness, the individuals' becoming aware of being both a subject and an object of historical processes."²⁵ Explicitly disavowing any obligation to present new data and embracing uncertainty, writers produce narratives that center on the experience and perceptions of the individual traveler. At their most serious, they cite cosmopolitan grounds: both traveler and narrative should be less provincial, more reflective, should seek to think "beyond the nation" and past first impressions.²⁶ At their most ironic, they claim authority to proclaim ignorance and invoke convention to show it false. Skeptical narrators doubt themselves; competing voices enter the text. Techniques vary: parody, reference to popular fiction and film, nonlinear form, and juxtaposition of prose, poetry, and visual images. Tim Youngs offers an incisive summary: "Much modernist travel writing is self-conscious about its own conventions. It experiments with point of view, invites critical attention to its narrator, examines the relationship between observer and observed, questions the location and use of power, parodies its progenitors, and wonders about its own function."[27] By laying bare the genre's conventions, writers subject its assumptions to scrutiny. Many explicitly foreground disparities between clichéd images and actual travel or between the texts readers expect to read and those writers actually produce.

Travel narrative's aspiration to the stature of literature is evident in this setting aside of documentary discourse (and its mode of asserting truth) for more self-consciously subjective discourses (and their competing claim to different modes of truth). For literary effect, writers combine events from different trips into a single story, omit their traveling companions, and devise composite characters. Although departures from the literal fidelity to fact that some readers of "nonfiction" might expect are occasionally noted in the text or authorial notes, generally they are not. Rebecca West's *Black Lamb*, for instance, silently combines episodes from three trips to Yugoslavia (1935, 1937, and 1938) into a narrative of a single Easter-time journey. Colin Thubron, in contrast, often prefaces his narratives with notes acknowledging his subordination of chronological fact to literary purpose. *Behind the Wall: A Journey through China* (1987), he explains, recounts a journey that "took place over a single autumn and early winter, but incorporates a few episodes from an earlier, briefer visit to China. So the book is a compression of experience, and inevitably omits many encounters made barren by people's reticence or by my poor Mandarin."[28]

Focused on their own perceptions, the narrators of some travel narratives, such as Graham Greene's *Journey without Maps* (1936), scarcely acknowledge the constant presence of traveling companions.[29] In retrospect, Greene explained the "problem of form" that he faced in seeking to avoid "the awful tedium of A to Z" in a book that could not mime the traditional European tour, lacked political urgency, and hadn't the material to be a tale in the manner of Peter Fleming. "[I]f this was an adventure it was only a subjective adventure," so his narrative would escape triviality

> only if it became more completely personal. It is a disadvantage to have an 'I' who is not a fictional figure, and the only way to deal with 'I' was to make him an abstraction. To all intents I eliminated my companion of the journey and supported the uneventful record with memories, dreams, word associations: if the book in one sense became more personal, the journey became more general.[30]

The subtitle of the *Times'* review of *Journey without Maps* concisely captures the result: "An Explorer Explores His Own Mind."[31] In Bruce Chatwin's *The Songlines* (1987), in contrast, a narrator identified as "[a] Pom by the name of Bruce" travels through Australia in constant conversation with Arkady, identified as the son of Russian immigrants.[32] Travelers whose frankness might embarrass or endanger their subjects often disguise real people, so it was not surprising that readers soon "recognised" Arkady as a man named Tolly Sawenko.[33] Chatwin, however, had invented more than a pseudonym: after he later responded that Arkady was really Salman Rushdie, Rushdie replied that the character was best characterized as Chatwin himself: "Bruce is Arkady as well as the character he calls Bruce. He is both sides of the dialogue."[34] An infamous example, *The Songlines* takes the modernist privileging of "imaginative enlargement and reduction" over fact to a new, postmodern extreme.[35] Narrative takes precedence; the traveler's subjective responses – which range from nostalgia to melancholy, euphoria to despair – become the genre's primary concern.

Yet the travel genre does not give way easily to the ambiguity and unreliability of modernist narration. Travel narratives published between the world wars are generally not as obviously experimental in style as modernist fiction, though they use many of its techniques. The similar trajectories are striking, however, and that innovation may appear later in one prose genre than another does not diminish its significance.[36] Whereas in the novel the first-person narrator comes to figure subjectivity, partiality, and unreliability, in the travel narrative the genre's long history as documentary means that the narrator always retains a tenuous claim of immediacy, witness, and truth.[37] Lewis's analysis of what is at stake for modernist novelists explains why this is so:

> The modernists differed from earlier novelists not in recognizing the fact that our perceptions of reality are always mediated by language and by consciousness – that recognition was at the root of the very form of the novel in general. Rather, the modernists were remarkable for investigating in a concerted way the possibility that the mediated nature of our consciousness might preclude our ever arriving, by rational means, at a consensus as to the nature of external reality. Modernist experiments implied that our perceptions of the outside world and of each other are so tainted by culturally specific or individually idiosyncratic values that there might be no way of arbitrating fairly between the competing claims of various individuals or groups – no eternal facts, no absolute truth, hence no absolute justice.[38]

Modernism, in short, calls into question the original premises of the travel genre, particularly its long-standing ambition to describe peoples and places so persuasively that the text is deemed veracious. The twentieth-century traveler thus writes from a precarious, uncertain position, one arguably more contradictory than the novelist's. One must ask what narrative stances were possible for travel narrators from the 1920s onward, and why, and with what consequences. The analyses of modernity advanced by Mikhail Bakhtin and Walter Benjamin provide ways into these questions. Bakhtin's account of novelistic discourse identifies both ethical and discursive consequences to narrative stance; recent adaptations of Benjamin's flânerie offer a cosmopolitan, self-conscious notion of spectatorship to counter the imperial monarch-of-all-I-survey.

Bakhtin proposes that modernity requires a new understanding of discourse, one sufficiently versatile and complex for a heterogeneous world with shifting geographical, linguistic, scientific, social, and ideological boundaries. It finds "adequate expression" through developing the novel, or novelistic discourse:[39]

> The novel is the expression of a Galilean perception of language, one that … refuses to acknowledge its own language as the sole verbal and semantic center of the ideological world. It is a perception that has been made conscious of the vast plenitude of national and, more to the point, social languages – all of which are equally capable of being "languages of truth," but, since such is the case, all of which are equally relative, reified and limited, as they are merely the languages of social groups, professions and other cross-sections of everyday life. The novel begins by presuming a verbal and semantic decentering of the ideological world, a certain linguistic homelessness of literary consciousness. (366–367)

Novelistic discourse takes as its primary concern the "competing claims of various individuals or groups" that Lewis describes. To narrate involves finding a vantage point from which to represent these disparate perceptions of the real. Bakhtin distinguishes two "stylistic lines of development" in the European novel: viewing heteroglossia from above, as a thing to be depicted in literary language, and navigating it from below, as a cacophony of discourses to be experienced dialogically. The first, he argues, seeks to manage rather than to represent: authorial voice dominates and heteroglossia remains "*outside*," as "a dialogizing background." He explicitly favors the second for "incorporat[ing] heteroglossia *into* a novel's composition, exploiting it to orchestrate its own meaning and frequently resisting altogether any unmediated and pure authorial discourse" (375). As a genre, the novel does not shift abruptly from one strategy to the other. Instead, it evolves in varied ways that build on, reify, parody, and oscillate between these lines. At his most emphatic, Bakhtin reserves the term "novel" for texts that incorporate "the fundamental heteroglossia inherent in actual language" without subordinating it to "a smooth, pure single-voiced language" (327).[40] At its richest, the novel celebrates heteroglossia's "extraliterariness" and "aspires" to represent an "abundance of embodied points of view" (411, 412).[41]

The novel's most radical innovation follows from this ambition: it creates conditions for the transformation of authorial discourse. Because novelistic discourse embraces "the spontaneity of the inconclusive present," the author "may turn up on the field of representation in any authorial pose" – may speak directly to readers, allude to events outside the narrative, polemicize, and even lie. Most importantly, "the underlying, original formal author" – not merely the narrator – "appears in a new relationship with the represented world. Both find themselves now subject to the same temporally valorized measurements, for the 'depicting' authorial language now lies on the same plan as the 'depicted' language of the hero, and may enter into dialogic relations and hybrid combinations with it (indeed, it cannot help but enter into such relations)." Bakhtin argues that this new "positioning" has "enormous … implications" for the evolution of narrative genres (27–28). Authors no longer stand outside the world they represent, but rather speak within it. "Authentic" prose discourse is hybrid and double-voiced rather than authoritative, oriented toward dialogue, not monologue: the novelistic narrator speaks "indirectly, conditionally, in a refracted way," through "the multi-languagedness surrounding and nourishing his own consciousness" (326–327).

Novelized genres thus exchange the predictability of stylized forms for the fluid uncertainty of the real. "Such, indeed," Bakhtin explains, "is the only possibility open to a genre that structures itself in a zone of direct contact with developing reality" (39). This evolution decenters the author and complicates the narrator's role. Dismantling the convention that authors or narrators have privileged access to truth from secure vantage points, it locates them within (rather than above) the social worlds they represent. As Bakhtin explains it, authors refract their intentions through the discourses of narrators and characters; narrators, whose perceptions are partial and contestable, make truth claims that may be unfounded and have voices subject to transformation.[42] Novelistic discourse is fundamentally social: it understands and represents "[o]ppositions between individuals" as "surface manifestations" of "a more fundamental speech diversity" that is inexhaustible. Its "utterly distinctive orientation" is that it "cannot forget or ignore, either through naiveté or by design, the heteroglossia that surrounds it" (326, 332). To represent one's own experiences is to represent oneself as a "speaking person" in heteroglossia. It is to show one's misperceptions and "ideological becoming" as well as one's insights and being (341).

Bakhtin's analysis is salient for understanding the evolution of travel narrative in the critical juncture following the First World War. Conventionally, the genre elides distinctions between author and narrator wherever possible: the veracity of the narrative is confirmed by the person of the author-explorer. The traveler often begins by proclaiming his credentials and authority. Richard Burton's *Personal Narrative of a Pilgrimage to al-Madinah and Meccah* (1855) illustrates this well:

> In the autumn of 1852, through the medium of my excellent friend, the late General Monteith, I offered my services to the Royal Geographic Society of London, for the purpose of removing that opprobrium to modern adventure, the huge white blot which in our maps still notes the Eastern and the Central regions of Arabia. ...
>
> ... being liberally supplied with the means of travel ... ; thoroughly tired of "progress" and "civilization"; curious to see with my eyes what others are content to "hear with ears," namely, Moslem inner life in a really Mohammedan country; and longing, if truth be told, to set foot on that mysterious spot which no vacation tourist has yet described, measured, sketched and photographed, I resolved to resume my old character of a Persian wanderer, a "Darwaysh," and to make the attempt.[43]

Burton claims two roles: that of the imperial observer who will produce certain knowledge, and that of a "character" who will feign ordinary involvement in the social world. The latter, however, is a device subordinated to the ends of the former: as the narrative proceeds it is clear that the "wanderer" never suspends his claim to imperial authority. In Bakhtinian terms, Burton's narrator plays at heteroglossia without genuinely placing his own authorial voice on the same plane as those he represents; his narrative is of the first stylistic line. Here "personal narrative" signifies the claim to objective authority through imperial experience, not the notion of subjectivity or mediated consciousness.

In the changed geopolitical and cultural contexts of the twentieth century, however, the vantage point that Burton asserts with ease becomes difficult if not impossible. Bakhtin concludes his analysis of novelistic discourse by discussing an "enormously significant" element of genre evolution. "Every age," he argues, "re-accentuates in its own way the works of its most immediate past," reading them against the grain and revivifying their images by "translating" them from one register to another (420–421). In travel narrative, the most pronounced, visible re-accentuation occurs in narrative stance. Lawrence, writing in the 1920s, could readily have justified an imperial stance similar to Burton's by invoking his popular renown as "Lawrence of Arabia." Yet he takes a very different approach in *Seven Pillars* by identifying his story as an "isolated picture throwing the main light upon myself" that is limited by reliance on "memory and my surviving notes" and partial because it omits "what the non-commissioned of us did."[44] Although he includes himself among those who had "the imaginative vision of the end," he presents that end – "Arab freedom" – as collective and natural. Lawrence qualifies his narrative authority, crediting it to style rather than imperial stature:

> My proper share was a minor one, but because of a fluent pen, a free speech, and a certain adroitness of brain, I took upon myself, as I describe it, a mock primacy. In reality I never had any office among the Arabs: was never in charge of the British mission with them. Wilson, Joyce, Newcombe, Dawnay and Davenport were all over my head. I flattered myself that I was too young, not that they had more heart or mind in the work. I did my best. . . .
>
> . . . The others have liberty some day to put on record their story, one parallel to mine but not mentioning more of me than I of them, for each of us did his job by himself and as he pleased, hardly seeing his friends.
>
> In these pages the history is not of the Arab movement, but of me in it. It is a narrative of daily life, mean happenings, little people. Here are no lessons for the world, no disclosures to shock peoples. It is filled with trivial things, partly that no one mistake for history the bones from which some day a man may make history, and partly for the pleasure it gave me to recall the fellowship of the revolt.[45]

As a narrator, Lawrence understands and declines to assume – the discursive authority that European writers customarily presume in representing foreign peoples and places. Underlying his self-description is a conception of narrative surprisingly similar to Bakhtin's:

> The prose art presumes a deliberate feeling for the historical and social concreteness of living discourse, as well as its relativity, a feeling for its participation in historical becoming and its social struggle; it deals with discourse that is still warm from that struggle and hostility, as yet unresolved and still fraught with hostile intentions and accents; prose art finds discourse in this state and subjects it to the dynamic-unity of its own style. (331)

Lawrence's frank introductory chapter describes his own uncertainty in the midst of "historical becoming" and urges readers not to invest his account with more certitude than it warrants. He characterizes himself as one participant among many rather than imperial overseer, his story as one of many possible accounts rather than history. Foreshadowing the oscillation among personal story, amateur ethnography, military report, philosophizing, and self-doubt to follow, he explicitly demonstrates a changed sense of narrative stance.[46]

In "re-accentuating" their authority, narrators like Lawrence distance their narratives from the claims to panoptic vision and comprehensive description analyzed by Said and Pratt. Bakhtin argues that such "verbal-ideological decentering" can occur only in modernity, "when a national culture loses its sealed-off and self-sufficient character, when it becomes conscious of itself as only one among *other* cultures and languages." Only in such conditions can "language reveal its essential *human* character": "[l]anguage, no longer conceived as a sacrosanct and solitary embodiment of meaning and truth, becomes merely one of many possible ways to hypothesize meaning," always in contention with others (370). Narratives demonstrate this decentering and contestability through technique – parody, double-voiced discourse, incorporated texts, competing voices – and through a focus on character (like Woolf, Bakhtin privileges character over plot). "What is realized in the novel," Bakhtin writes, "is the process of coming to know one's own language as it is perceived in someone else's language, coming to know one's own belief system in someone else's system," for plot is "subordinated to the task of coordinating and exposing languages to each other" (365).[47] The most compelling of these strategies found in twentieth-century travel narrative, as the following chapters demonstrate, evidence modernist commitment to subjectivity and cosmopolitan recognition of the geopolitical changes and cultural differences that necessitate a "reimagining of the world."[48]

The consequences of this de-centering are both ethical and aesthetic. Wlad Godzich credits Bakhtin and others with a critique of modernity that revalues social diversity against an exclusionary Enlightenment rationality: they read modernity as "the epoch that resulted from the confrontation with Otherness and then sought to avoid this Otherness at all cost by elaborating a complex strategy for its containment and eventual reduction to Sameness. Their critique inevitably seeks to restore this Otherness to its rightful, and most effective, place."[49] Bakhtin's theories concern the ethics of cognition and representation more than aesthetics and style as such. They privilege heteroglossia and dialogue in the difficult yet productive conflict with the monologic drive to control meaning, make sense, and tell a definite, compelling story. Daphna Erdinast-Vulcan argues that Bakhtin's ethical concerns are best understood in the context of recent work on the relation between subjectivity and the human propensity for narrative. Whether in narratives we write (her example is autobiography) or in how we live, subjectivity occurs on the borderline where the desire for order meets the reality of openendedness. In novelistic discourse Bakhtin finds a turn away from "authorial jurisdiction" that "anticipates the awakening of the modernist consciousness, the consciousness of an essentially secular world, where neither the fictional nor the historical subject can refer to an authorial Being – outside and above the self – for comfort and confirmation." Erdinast-Vulcan elegantly concludes that this turn signals "more than a poetic revolution: it is a paradigm shift of much wider-reaching philosophical potency":

> Even as we recognize the incurable need to aestheticize the self, to secure it within a narrative framework, and to ground it in the authorial Word, we must also be fully aware of the contingency of our narratives in an author-less existence. It is precisely in this absence of the authorial other that we become fully responsive to and responsible for the other. We are, indeed, story-telling beings who desire to be framed and narrativized into coherence, to be characters in a novel, as it were. But it is our inability to remain cocooned within those narrative frames and our recognition of the permeability and the provisional nature of our autobiographies which, in turning us out of our metaphysical home, has turned us into ethical beings.[50]

Bakhtin's critique of modernity thus helps to explain the stakes of the conflict between the security of description and the contingency of narrative that plays out in twentieth-century travel narrative. To speak authoritatively – in this instance, about peoples and places – is to preclude others from being heard: such discourse "permits no play with the context framing it, no play with its borders, no gradual and flexible transitions" (343). To narrate dialogically, from a de-centered authorial position, is to value others' voices over order, even at the price of coherence. Or, to put it another way, it is to privilege ethics over aesthetics. As Bakhtin writes of Dostoevsky and the polyphonic novel:

> the author's consciousness does not transform others' consciousnesses (that is, the consciousnesses of the characters) into objects, and does not give them secondhand and finalizing definitions. Alongside and in front of itself it senses others' equally valid consciousnesses, just as infinite and open-ended as itself. It reflects and re-creates not a world of objects, but precisely these other consciousnesses with their worlds, re-creates them in their authentic *unfinalizability* (which is, after all, their essence).[51]

At its richest, novelistic discourse attempts to balance the competing demands of representation and understanding. Such is the conundrum that travel narrative faces in reinventing itself as a literary genre centered on narration of subjective experience rather than presentation of ethnographic knowledge. Such is the ethical challenge it faces as European travelers claim that their observations abroad continue to be of significance in a globalized world, where once predominant cultures have been made conscious of being one among many.

The figure of modernity most apposite for understanding the changing, cosmopolitan vantage point of the twentieth-century travel narrator is the flâneur. "Flânerie" – defined variously as a "new state of existence," a mode of perception, and a sensibility – describes the experience of moving through heterogeneous, modern, metropolitan landscapes. It develops in the nineteenth century, "on the heels of the emergence of the city as a territory meant to be traversed," and is most immediately associated with Paris, "the most advanced and pronouncedly modern city in Europe."[52] Literary representations of flânerie abound, from nineteenth-century German travel narratives about Paris to twentieth-century English novels about independent women.[53] The flâneur appears most famously in the work of Charles Baudelaire, traversing the city's arcades, roaming its boulevards, attending to quotidian details of urban life. He (originally male) assumes with ease the privilege to roam, to speculate up close, to keep his distance, to evaluate.[54] Flânerie plays a crucial role in Benjamin's work of the 1930s on metropolitan bourgeois society. He reads it as paradigmatically modern: "The flâneur still stands on the threshold, of the metropolis as of the middle class. Neither has him in its power yet. In neither is he at home. He seeks refuge in the crowd." The flâneur is a spectator, modernity the spectacle. A collector of sensory experiences, he "goes botanizing on the asphalt."[55]

The practice of flânerie celebrates mobility and perception at a crucial historical moment, as modernity's technological innovations transform the material circumstances in which movement and observation occur. The advent of gaslight and then electric lighting allowed urban pedestrians to view once obscured sights; the proliferation of display windows and advertising filled cities with new images that explicitly linked observation with consumption.[56] In the nineteenth century, the construction of railways reshaped cities, disrupted landscapes deemed picturesque, brought speedy access to much of Europe, and allowed organized leisure travel to become an ordinary aspect of bourgeois life.[57] In the first decades of the twentieth century, railways were extended across previously inaccessible parts of Asia and Africa just as the invention of the automobile promised independence from set timetables and routes. Airplanes soon provided genuinely new vantage points from the air; eventually jets would produce a disjointed experience of places juxtaposed oddly without ground between. These new modes of experiencing the world allowed Europeans to travel extensively and see once remote cities and natural phenomena. They radically expanded the flâneur's possible field of operation: the urban pedestrian from London or Paris might now readily explore the streets of Shanghai and view the metropolis from the air. By allowing mobile subjects to observe from a safe distance or speed past, however, new technologies also promoted the superficial mode of perception that comes to be associated with tourism, which sociologist John Urry calls the "tourist gaze."

As a critical concept, flânerie usefully links specific social practices with theories of subjectivity, mobility, perception, and consumption. Building on Benjamin's work, scholars have developed the flâneur as "a general symbol of ... cultural modernity" and possible antecedent of twentieth-century "urban social identities" ranging from consumer to detective. The flâneur is "an analytic form, a narrative device, an attitude toward knowledge and its social context."[58] As Deborah Parsons explains in *Streetwalking the Metropolis: Women, the City and Modernity* (2000), "for contemporary theory he is an increasingly expansive figure who represents a variety of 'wanderings,' in terms of ambulation, nationality, gender, race, class, and sexuality. The elusivity remains, however."[59] Flânerie remains elusive precisely because it understands mobile spectatorship to be subjective and contingent – and thus to be a mode of experience capable of superficiality as well as critical delving beneath surfaces. It has the potential to be both a means of engagement with the modern metropolis and a manner of consuming it: the flâneur can be agile participant or retiring observer, sociologist or artist, Parisian or "at home in all parts of the globe."[60] At its richest, the concept celebrates modernity's transformation of mobility and perception into self-conscious, cosmopolitan practices. Its value for the analysis of travel narrative lies in its naming of the contradictions that mark the modern travel narrator's position.[61]

These contradictions are evident in scholars' use of flânerie to explain (on the one hand) and to counter (on the other) the practices of tourism. Urry understands the modern subject to be fundamentally "a subject on the move." "It is not the pedestrian *flâneur* who is emblematic of modernity," he proposes, "but rather the train-passenger, car driver and jet plane passenger."[62] Citing Benjamin's flâneur as "a forerunner of the twentieth-century tourist," he argues that flânerie is the antecedent for tourism's insatiable mode of consumption, photography, which "teaches new ways of looking at the world and new forms of authority for doing so." In his analysis, tourism homogenizes perception: although photography "*seems* to be a means of transcribing reality," it is actually a strategy of appropriation that effectively passes "itself off as a miniaturization of the real, without revealing either its constructed nature or its ideological content."[63] Tourists recognize places from having seen photographs, shoot their own images (often from designated vantage points), and rely on photographs to remember their experiences. Photography allows tourists to consume without truly observing, to capture without engaging. As John Frow explains, once photography becomes pervasive, "the shifting historical relationship between the subject and the world of sights" that produces a "nexus between travel and vision" reaches a dramatic new stage. For touristic photography confirms existing images rather than producing new knowledge: "It is a process of authentification, the establishment of a verified relay between origin and trace."[64]

For Anke Gleber, however, flânerie provides a conception of engaged critical spectatorship that counters touristic perception; in her analysis, the genealogical relation between flânerie and tourism as modes of perception matters far less than their "fundamental diversities" as "distinctive processes for the seeing and collecting of images." In *The Art of Taking a Walk: Flanerie, Literature, and Film in Weimar Culture* (1999), Gleber differentiates between flânerie and tourism as "realms of modern cultural experience."[65] Although tourism prevails among bourgeois strategies for moving through the world, it does not extinguish flânerie's potential for nuanced observation, reflection, and critique. If anything, the tourist's managed, indiscriminate gaze becomes the anathema against which the flâneur defines critical spectatorship.[66] The flâneur proceeds deliberatively, sans timetable, and may venture wherever everyday life and unusual spectacles invite, whereas the tourist heeds the guidebook and must hurry along to the next sight listed on the itinerary. The flâneur travels alone; the tourist is ever in a group. Gleber finds the most significant distinction in the flâneur's active critical faculty. Modernity and urbanization produce "a new constellation of modern images" that "create their own phenomena of perception": the flâneur reflects on "the processes of seeing" rather than merely seeing objects.[67] Tourism normalizes the extraordinary; flânerie reveals the complexity of the quotidian. Whereas tourism steers modern subjects to sights whose cultural meaning is predetermined, flânerie privileges "moments of reflection, comment, and critique." The flâneur's

> discursive reflection sets him apart from touristic consumption of prepackaged sensations and images. The flaneur distinguishes himself – or herself – from

this scenario of passive tourism as a figure who not only pursues her impulse toward drifting, but also feels compelled to retrieve these urban images in her mind, reflect on the impressions encountered, and seek to preserve them in a writing of letters or light, on either celluloid or the page.[68]

In its active engagement with visual phenomena, flânerie models a new kind of critical consciousness. For Gleber, it can be understood as "a precursor … to a theory of film" that is attuned equally to the mobile observer and "the objects and occurrences that comprise the flow of material life."[69] As such, it anticipates the kind of mobile spectatorship that travel narratives will find necessary for perceiving a world now understood to be mutable before one's eyes.

Gleber's analysis of flânerie as a distinctly modern critical consciousness helps to explain the travel narrative's increased awareness of the activity of perception and the artifice of representations. Serious travelers come to understand their movement in and observation of the world in relation to the competing modes that she identifies as flânerie and tourism, though particular subjects may of course traverse the conceptual line between (tourists may wander off the beaten track, flâneurs may gaze mindlessly in shop windows). "Over the course of the nineteenth century," Jonathan Crary argues,

> an observer increasingly had to function within disjunct and defamiliar-
> ized urban spaces, the perceptual and temporal dislocations of railroad
> travel, telegraphy, industrial production, and flows of typographic and
> visual information. Consequently, the discursive identity of the observer
> as an object of philosophical reflection and empirical study underwent an
> equally drastic renovation.[70]

This "modernization" of subjectivity and spectatorship occurs through dislocations and disruptions that make the mutability of peoples and places especially visible. It is evident in twentieth-century travel narrators' reflective analyses of visual experience, abiding interest in their own subjective responses, and explicit attention to the dramatic changes consequent to new means of transportation and representation. It is also evident in their self-consciousness as they negotiate between touristic images that precede their travels and their own firsthand observations. At the same time, through its metropolitan origins flânerie retains a reminder of the privileges of mobility and representation that even critically aware travel narrators must seek to write.[71]

Before the twentieth century, travel narratives routinely described travelers' movements in detail to comment on social mores and cultural differences, report on new means of transportation, or demonstrate a journey's rigors. In *American Notes for General Circulation* (1842), for instance,

Charles Dickens uses the confined settings of the passenger ship, railway, canal boat, and stagecoach to depict Yankee social habits. "There are no first and second class carriages as with us," he writes of the train from Boston to Lowell, "but there is a gentlemen's car and a ladies' car: the main distinction between which is that in the first, everybody smokes; and in the second, nobody does. As a black man never travels with a white one, there is also a negro car."[72] A few years later, Burton uses details of travel in Arabia to demonstrate his knowledge of local culture and his fitness for the journey:

> Shaykh Nassár ... being on his way homewards, agreed to let me have two dromedaries.... Being desirous to set out with a certain display of respectability, I accepted these terms: a man of humble pretensions would have travelled with a single animal, and a camel-man running behind him. But, besides ostentation, I wanted my attendant to be mounted, that we might make a forced march in order to ascertain how much four years' life of European effeminacy had impaired my powers of endurance. The reader may believe the assertion that there are few better tests than an eighty-four mile ride in mid-summer, on a bad wooden saddle, borne by a worse dromedary, across the Suez Desert.[73]

Dickens and Burton each recognize that their means of travel affect their perceptions. Travel by train makes rural settlements in Pennsylvania pleasurable for Dickens because they appear in picturesque fragments, at a distance, and then disappear:

> It was very pretty travelling thus, at a rapid pace along the heights of the mountain in a keen wind, to look down into a valley full of light and softness; catching glimpses, through the tree-tops, of scattered cabins; children running out the doors; dogs bursting out to bark, whom we could see without hearing; terrified pigs scampering homewards; families sitting out in their rude gardens; cows gazing upward with a stupid indifference; men in their shirtsleeves looking on at their unfinished houses, planning out tomorrow's work; and we riding onward, high above them, like a whirlwind.[74]

For Burton, riding a dromedary allows full appreciation of the desert, a "sublime" and "haggard land" with "a sky terrible in its stainless beauty." To any reader who might disagree, he retorts: "Let the traveler who suspects exaggeration leave the Suez road for an hour or two, and gallop northwards over the sands: in the drear silence, the solitude, and the fantastic desolation of the place, he will feel what the Desert may be."[75]

As Burton's challenge demonstrates, once options multiply, travel narratives reveal an increasingly keen awareness that the method of movement affects perception and experience. Twentieth-century narrators often explain that they elect the means best suited to the particular experience desired. Traveling by automobile instead of train, bicycle instead of bus, foot instead of truck becomes a key part of a narrator's self-conscious positioning. So too does traveling alone rather than in a group – or at least narrating as though one had traveled independently. Edith Wharton is one of many who celebrate the autonomy afforded by the automobile. In *A Motor-Flight through France* (1908) she characterizes this freedom visually:

> The motor-car has restored the romance of travel.
>
> Freeing us from all the compulsions and contacts of the railway, the bondage to fixed hours and the beaten track, the approach to each town through the area of ugliness and desolation created by the railway itself, it has given us back the wonder, the adventure and the novelty which enlivened the way of our posting grandparents. Above all these recovered pleasures must be ranked the delight of taking a town unawares, stealing on it by back ways and unchronicled paths, and surprising it in some intimate aspect of past time, some silhouette hidden for half a century or more by the ugly mask of railway embankments and the iron bulk of a huge station. Then the villages that we missed and yearned for from the windows of the train – the unseen villages have been given back to us!

Writing just a few years after the first Michelin guide appeared, she views motoring as a strategy for bypassing modernity's most egregious alterations to consume precisely the vista she desires.[76] As Sidonie Smith explains, for Wharton "[p]aradoxically, the modern woman becomes the woman who looks backward to the picturesque remnants of a premodern past that motoring brings into view for her."[77] Other travelers elect to travel by slow means that allow them to immerse themselves in places, interact with local inhabitants, and digress at will. In *The Places in Between* (2004), for instance, Rory Stewart walks across Afghanistan to experience rural culture and retrace ancient history as fully as possible. He must explain himself often and spends much of his journey declining rides in vehicles and shedding unwanted companions. When a regional commander announces that he will provide an honor guard for "the walking foreigner," Stewart pulls a last hanger-on aside: "I did not want to lose one group of armed men only to be given another. I told him to tell the commandant that I needed to travel alone. When we reentered, Abdul Haq sat down and talked to the young commander. 'His Excellency Rory is traveling alone for his book. He should remain alone.'"[78] Stewart's narrative, centered on his own subjective experience of Afghanistan, requires the autonomy and mobility of the flâneur.

Like the invention of new means of travel, the advent of photography alters the ways subjects perceive the world and the contexts in which they write. Photography simultaneously promises to complement narratives and threatens to supplant them. Jean-François Lyotard describes the situation succinctly: "The challenge lay essentially in that photographic and cinematographic processes can accomplish better, faster, and with a circulation a hundred thousand times larger than narrative or pictorial realism, the task which academicism had assigned to realism: to preserve various consciousnesses from doubt."[79] Europeans had produced visual knowledge of distant places for centuries, Peter Osborne explains, inventing increasingly sophisticated means of representation including linear perspective and topographical maps "to measure, survey and navigate through the widening material world they sought to know and control." They immediately found photography salient for travel because

> it was, on the one hand, a crystallisation of three hundred years of culture and science preoccupied with space and mobility and, on the other, the expression of its own time – the epoch of capitalist globalisation, the construction of a new middle-class identity and the dramatic speeding-up of transportation and communication. Photography was a representational tool refined in the service of these processes.... It introduced a mobile visual system whose realism met the demand for what was considered to be scientific objectivity, and whose ability to fascinate produced visual objects of reverie, fantasy and idealisation.[80]

Early photographers made documentary surveys of ruins in Greece and Egypt; portraits of native peoples in Africa, Asia, and the Americas; and landscape photos in Europe.

Travel narratives already often included maps, architectural plans, and ethnographic drawings; as the new technology became accessible, writers added photographs. Isabella Bird's early travel books featured illustrations, but once she became an adept photography enthusiast, she preferred her own images: her last book, *The Yangtze Valley and Beyond* (1899), includes more than 100 photographs. Bird proudly recounts her expertise – she develops her own prints while traveling, using river water – and enjoys showing prints to rural villagers to demonstrate "that I was not doing anything evil or hurtful."[81] Photographs quickly become customary, appearing in narratives as different as Bell's *The Desert*, which modestly claims to report new information and uses many of her own photographs, and Wharton's *Motor-Flight*, which covers territory so familiar that stock images suffice. Into the 1940s, travel narratives often include at least a score of photographs and a few maps, placed in the body of the text or a separate section. Fleming's *Brazilian Adventure*, for instance, includes a map, a diagram, and twenty-one photographs; Rebecca West's *Black Lamb* two maps and thirty-two photographs. Occasionally, photography assumes a major role: W. H. Auden and Christopher Isherwood's *Journey to a War* juxtaposes prose, poetry, and a "Photo Commentary" with more than sixty images. After mid-century, however, the travel narrative shifts noticeably: photos all but disappear. Thubron, who travels in China meeting ordinary citizens nearly fifty years after Auden and Isherwood, includes only a map in *Behind the Wall*. Other travel narratives, such as Pico Iyer's *Video Night*, have no photos or maps but often discuss visual media encountered en route.

By including visual images alongside prose, writers confirm that the critical "nexus between travel and vision" that Frow identifies continues to be significant. Yet remarkably, scholarship on travel narrative scarcely mentions, much less analyzes, the presence of photographs and visual images.[82] The selection of images steers readers to particular vantage points and implicitly attributes greater significance to certain sights, yet with very few exceptions the principle of selection remains obscure and relations between text and image receive casual treatment. Even original editions differ in the number and placement of photographs: Fleming's *One's Company* was published with four pages of photos in Britain, twenty in the United States. Photos often lack captions; photographers often remain uncredited. Reprints typically treat visual images as ephemera akin to cover art, excising them entirely or in part without acknowledgement. Alexandra David-Neel's *Voyage d'une Parisienne à Lhasa* (1927), for instance, originally featured a frontispiece of David-Neel disguised as a mendicant pilgrim and about twenty-five photos; the American edition published more than sixty years later has only a frontispiece of the author in European attire. The 1973 paperback of *Journey to a War* notes minor textual alterations but silently deletes the entire "Photo Commentary"; its only visual image, an unidentified Chinese political cartoon used on the cover, is the original frontispiece. The cover of the Penguin reprint of *One's Company* uses a photo of Fleming from a later book, *News from Tartary* (1936), that depicts his recurring literary persona particularly well (see Illustration 1). Both the erratic treatment of images from one edition to the next and the general disappearance of images from mid-century on further signal the travel genre's reorientation from documentation to narration. It may be read as an instance of travel narrative following modernism's lead in querying, then rejecting realist modes of representation.[83] When visual images return to the genre at the turn of the millennium,

Illustration 1. Photo of Peter Fleming, from Fleming's *News from Tartary*.

they do so innovatively, as in W. G. Sebald's postmodern *The Rings of Saturn*, which intersperses photos with text, and Joe Sacco's graphic narratives *Palestine* and *Safe Area Goražde* (2000).

What often replaces original images are scenes in which travelers contend with clichéd representations not of their own design. As the travel narrative evolves into a genre centered on subjective experience, writers must find strategies to make urbane flânerie significant to readers already fluent in the tired rhetoric – textual and visual – of empire. As David Spurr argues, the Western spectator's

> eye remains mobile and selective, constantly filtering the visible for *signs*, for those gestures and objects that, when transformed into the verbal or photographic image, can alone have meaning for a Western audience by entering a familiar web of signification. The journalist is literally on the lookout for scenes that carry an already established *interest* for a Western audience, thus investing perception itself with the mediating power of cultural difference.[84]

For the twentieth-century traveler, representing one's own subjective perception requires engagement with others who are themselves spectators. Both readers at home and strangers met in transit are insatiable consumers who already "know" foreign peoples and places through fiction, magazines, and films. This allows narrative shortcuts: Fleming can sketch what he sees in Brazil by citing scenes his audience will recognize from the popular *Wide World Magazine*. More importantly, the global proliferation of images creates fixed representations with which narrators must contend. Robyn Davidson, whose *Tracks* (1980) narrates her solo journey by camel across the Australian desert, writes of the compromise to "what had begun as a personal and private gesture" that comes when she accepts underwriting from *National Geographic*. The travel she had envisioned as an existential test of autonomy and period of immersion into local culture alters – in her perceptions and those of potential readers – with regular visits from a *Geographic* photographer and press coverage depicting her as "the camel lady."[85] Something of the authority she had presumed to be her own disappears in the transaction: she loses the privilege of self-depiction.

The complex relation between genuine exchange and image consumption becomes central in Iyer's *Video Night*, which opens with an iconic film character. "Rambo had conquered Asia," he writes. "As I crisscrossed Asia in the fall of 1985, every cinema that I visited for ten straight weeks featured a Stallone extravaganza." "[F]ifteen-foot cutouts of the avenging demon" and posters of "Suharto, Siva and Stallone" offer counter-historical visions with which Iyer's own narrative must compete. Fascinated and alarmed to see "America's pop-cultural imperialism spread through the world's most ancient civilizations," he travels to see others' experiences on "the front lines of this cultural campaign." At the end of a Stallone video on an overnight bus in Java, a fellow passenger, "a soldier just returned from putting down rebels in the jungles of East Timor, sat back with a satisfied sigh. 'That,' he pronounced aptly, 'was very fantastic.'"[86] As Iyer the postmodern traveler observes the Javanese soldier, who watches the American actor, spectatorship – and the traveler's perpetual attempt to distinguish the fantastic from the real – necessarily become the subject.

Modernity and globalization challenge the travel narrative to reinvent its strategies and its understanding of experience and observation as forms of knowledge. In narrating the perceptions of the authorial subject, is it possible to write the reflective, nuanced spectatorship that Gleber finds in flânerie? Is it possible for travel narrative to represent others dialogically, as subjects with what Bakhtin calls "embodied points of view" rather than as things? (412). Or does representation inevitably erase or consume "the heterogeneity of the subject(s) in question"?[87] Which modernist and post-modernist strategies will work for writers who challenge the travel narra-tive's conventional claims to authority? In late modernity, cognizant of the contingency of narratives and the politics of "othering," Western writers reconceive the travel narrative as a heterogeneous, dialogical cultural prac-tice. The challenge, in Iyer's words, is to invent means of narrating travel that may do justice to "the novel cultural hybrids peculiar to the tag end of the twentieth century" (10).

CHAPTER 3

Modernist and Postmodernist Travels

Though it's in keeping with the best traditions
    For Travel Books to wander from the point
    (There is no other rhyme except anoint),
They may well charge me with – I've no defences –
Obtaining money under false pretenses.

I know I've not the least chance of survival
    Beside the major travellers of the day.
I am no Lawrence who, on his arrival,
    Sat down and typed out all he had to say....

And even here the steps I flounder in
    Were worn by most distinguished boots of old.
Dasent and Morris and Lord Dufferin,
    Hooker and men of that heroic mould
    Welcome me icily into the fold;
I'm not like Peter Fleming an Etonian,
But, if I'm Judas, I'm an old Oxonian....

So this, my opening chapter has to stop
    With humbly begging everybody's pardon
From Faber first in case the book's a flop,
    Then from the critics lest they should be hard on
    The author when he leads them up the garden,
Last from the general public he must beg
Permission now and then to pull their leg.

                W. H. Auden (1937)[1]

Knowing the genre's contradictions and their own historical contingency, twentieth-century writers create new strategies for narrating travel experiences. They turn the critical eye of the flâneur on the conventions of travel and bring the concerns of modernism (and later postmodernism) to bear on the travel narrative's language, form, and purpose. They present travel as subjective, its meaning as uncertain: significance, their narratives demonstrate, lies in the telling more than in the journey itself. Self-deprecating

51

narrators disrupt the authoritative posture and imperial discourse of earlier travelers. Speculation replaces certainty; the evidence of personal experience trumps documentary data-gathering. Narratives juxtapose multiple
voices and multiple modes of representation in open-ended texts that may
refuse the established plotline whereby travel reconfirms imperial logic
and results in safe arrival home. Experimentation recasts travel narrative
as a self-consciously literary genre able to represent contingent experience
in a globalized, rapidly changing world. Implicitly, it makes the claim that
travel is better represented through heteroglossia, discontinuity, and ambiguity than through conventional tropes of exploration and adventure.

To argue that travel narrative shares in the concerns of modernism and
postmodernism is to identify aesthetic and epistemological contexts crucial for understanding both individual texts and their contributions to an
evolving genre. It is not, of course, to argue that travel narrative rejects
realism fully or extricates itself entirely from the politics and rhetoric of
empire – or even that it consistently attempts to do so. Instead, it is to recognize that, in the twentieth century, travel narrative becomes an explicitly literary genre that makes creative use of contemporary techniques to
strategic ends. As shown in Chapters 1 and 2, travel narrative as a cultural
practice is at a particularly fraught juncture following the First World
War. In a culture awash in textual and visual representations of difference,
at a time of rapid geopolitical transformation, its claim to seriousness and
continued relevance rests on the claim that first-person narrative can offer
distinctive knowledge, that critical spectatorship can and should be a productive mode of engagement with the world. To achieve this end, the genre
must not only eschew but dismantle tradition. Its innovations are bound
up with – and bound by – its situation in the history of modernity.

To understand travel narrative in relation to these predominant cultural movements is to argue for a different literary history in which modernism plays a significant role. Most scholarship on twentieth-century
travel narrative locates its primary innovations in the geopolitical context
of postwar globalization rather than in the literary-critical contexts of
modernism or postmodernism. In so doing, it discounts formal innovations that significantly reshaped the genre between the world wars and
assumes that travel narrative somehow changed between 1939 and 1960
because the world changed. Giving scant attention to aesthetics, scholars instead credit the genre's evolution chiefly to politics, although some
invoke postmodernism in discussing later metacritical texts.[2] This tendency reflects the contexts in which the scholarly field developed over
the last thirty years. In *Abroad*, Paul Fussell characterized literary travel

writing of the 1920s and 1930s as the last flourish of a romantic tradition that suffers obscurity with the ascendancy of fiction and ends with war and tourism. Concerned with appreciation more than critique, elegy more than analysis, he sought to bring attention to texts already forgotten, demonstrate travel narrative's richness, and place it in a literary history that privileged fiction and poetry. Literary modernism serves merely as a backdrop: in one of few direct references, he describes Robert Byron's *The Road to Oxiana* (1937) as sharing the collage "method" of Joyce's *Ulysses* and Eliot's *The Waste Land*.[3] David Farley's recent *Modernist Travel Writing*, which focuses on texts Fussell scarcely mentions – E. E. Cummings's *Eimi* (1933), Wyndham Lewis's *Filibusters in Barbary* (1932), and Rebecca West's *Black Lamb* – makes the first sustained argument that the "techniques or methods" of modernism play a significant role in travel narrative of the period.[4] Farley's attention to more explicitly political late modernist texts corrects for Fussell's romanticism, yet – although each recognizes travel narrative's interest in subjective experience – neither directly addresses the questions about its ethics that critical analysis of imperial rhetoric makes necessary.

Scholars who focus on travel narrative since 1960, in contrast, take the ethical obligations of first-person narration as a primary concern: Patrick Holland and Graham Huggan's *Tourists with Typewriters* and Debbie Lisle's *The Global Politics of Contemporary Travel Writing* describe a postwar period of renewal in which the travel genre seeks to demonstrates its "transgressive potential" in new ways and "resuscitat[e] itself in the face of globalization."[5] Lisle traces two narrative strategies, a "colonial vision" that mimics the privileged position of earlier travel narrators and a "cosmopolitan vision" that focuses on "the harmonizing effects of globalization." They coexist in relations that are "sometimes antagonistic, sometimes symbiotic, sometimes ambiguous": a writer might employ a "colonial vision" to interrogate its claims to authority, and a "cosmopolitan vision" might invoke heterogeneity only to manage it for the West.[6] Holland and Huggan identify their book as making "a pitch for the ethical value of travel writing, even as it demonstrates that travel narratives are unreliable in the extreme"; they conclude that the genre continues to demonstrate "possibilities for ... replenishment" because of its potential to challenge the cultural and discursive "boundaries within which travel risks being reified."[7] Lisle endorses Holland and Huggan's "ethical imperative" but concludes that the genre's self-consciousness has yet to overcome its inherent inequity: "we are, in fact, witnessing the complex rearticulation of Western authority within the most liberal and cosmopolitan gestures."[8]

Together, these tendencies – ignoring literary modernism as a possible influence and attributing ethical self-consciousness to postwar globalization – obscure important aspects of twentieth-century travel narrative and its evolution. Significantly, they fail to recognize that critical concern with the nature of spectatorship, the vantage point of the observer, the ethics of representation, and the cultural role of travel narrative become central to the genre in the 1920s in ways that persist to the present. These concerns demonstrate the travel narrative's adoption of a critical relation to modernity that – as discussed in Chapters 1 and 2 – is recognizably modernist. Rebecca Walkowitz, writing of cosmopolitan "modernism beyond the nation," argues for an expansive understanding of "modernism" that recognizes continuities and reiterations in literary strategies from the historical moment named "modernist" to that named "postmodernist." In so doing, she cites two premises: "(1) that texts may include both modernist and postmodernist elements; and (2) that a more capacious definition of literary modernism allows us to notice contradictory impulses within responses to modernity and globalization."[9] Walkowitz's reconfiguring of modernism serves the analysis of travel narrative well, for it recognizes that globalization is not exclusive to the decades at the end of the century, modernity only of concern in the early decades. Instead, from the 1920s onward, travel narrative evidences a recurring effort to reinvent itself as a genre suited to the radical transformations of the geopolitical world. Tim Youngs remarks of texts written in the 1920s and 1930s that, whereas their "formal innovations ... do heighten awareness of textual artifice and invite questions about power, they often offer little change from their nineteenth-century precursors in their judgements on other cultures";[10] Lisle says much the same about texts written in the 1980s and 1990s. The travel narrative's evolution occurs fitfully rather than in an unbroken line.

Reading together texts from this longer period makes visible the earlier origins of formal experimentation and critical self-awareness that have often been supposed to be postmodern: it is to recognize in the work of T. E. Lawrence, W. H. Auden and Christopher Isherwood, and Rebecca West aesthetic and epistemological antecedents for the work of Colin Thubron, Pico Iyer, and Andrew X. Pham. It also makes visible the genre's recursive contradictions. To be a mobile subject free to travel, observe, and write is a distinct privilege; it is also to assume narrative authority in ways that may well be fundamentally at odds with cosmopolitan ambitions to experience difference sympathetically and elusive ideals about universal understanding. Twentieth-century travelers often reveal their awareness of privilege and its consequences for the kinds of experiences they seek to have and the narratives they would write. In qualifying his stance as an English first-person narrator of an Arab revolt, Lawrence emphasizes the incommensurability between vantage points of travelers and locals, narrators and their subjects, even when shared experience is substantial and sympathies run deep. Such a sense of the incommensurable plays an important role in texts as different as Auden and Isherwood's *Journey to a War* and Iyer's *Video Night*. Auden somberly remarks the disparity between the situation of the Chinese, anxious and destitute from long civil war and terrorized by invading "foreign foe," and that of the Europeans:

> ... in an international and undamaged quarter,
> Casting our European shadows on Shanghai,
> Walking unhurt among the banks, apparently immune
>
> Below the monuments of an acquisitive society,
> With friends and books and money and the traveller's freedom,
> We are compelled to realize that our refuge is a sham.[11]

Nearly a half-century later, "the great asymmetry that governs every meeting between tourist and local" persists, and troubles Iyer:

> that we are there by choice and they largely by circumstance; that we are traveling in the spirit of pleasure, adventure and romance, while they are mired in the more urgent business of trying to survive; and that we, often courted by the government, enjoy a kind of unofficial diplomatic immunity, which gives us all the perks of authority and none of the perils of responsibility, while they must stake their hopes on every potential transaction.[12]

Writers may explicitly reject authority for contingency, expertise for situated observation, claims of discovery for moments of illumination. They may play with disavowing the privileges that they and others take to be their own: in a trope that Holland and Huggan, adapting Albert Memmi's "colonizer who refuses," call the "memsahib who refuses," the traveler disclaims the imperial ideology that determines a specific situation "while continuing to live with its actual relationships" and thus benefitting from Western status.[13] In *Brazilian Adventure*, for instance, Peter Fleming plays this role knowingly, savoring both the grime of roughing it and the material comfort awaiting him among compatriots at journey's end, the pleasure of each predicated on the guarantee of the alternative. Fleming's contemporary Beryl Smeeton performs this contradictory subject position quite earnestly in her account of going up the Yangtze on a Chinese boat in 1936. Traveling alone, she gets by with bits of Chinese and English and wears a "dressing-gown for third-class occidental ladies in the orient" of her own design. Although she elects to travel "with the Chinese," she does not surrender European privilege: her pleasure lies in the distinction of being oneself-among-the-natives. As they steam upriver, Smeeton enjoys the illusion of freedom from social constraint while retaining her status: the steamer's captain, of German descent, invites her to join him on the bridge, with its amenities and warmth, "as you are a foreign lady." The arrival of other Europeans dismays her:

> To my horror I saw some Europeans coming up the gang-plank. I had not been on my own long enough to be lonely for my own kind. On the contrary, it gave me a great lift to be the only foreigner among the Chinese, and there was a good reason for this feeling, for as soon as they saw that a foreigner was not alone they ceased to help.[14]

As Smeeton's performance demonstrates, European travel narrators cannot step entirely outside the contradictions of the positions they occupy by virtue of nationality, class, economic security, and narrative role. They may subject those positions and their imperial underpinnings to critical scrutiny. But, as Janet Wolff explains, the very vocabulary of travel impedes the effort:

> The problem with terms like 'nomad', 'maps' and 'travel' is that they are not usually located; hence (and purposely) they suggest ungrounded and unbounded movement, since the whole point is to resist fixed selves/viewers/subjects. But the consequent suggestion of free and equal mobility is itself a deception, since we do not all have the same access to the road.[15]

Holland and Huggan make a similar point a different way: "Travel writing reinstalls difference even as it claims to dismantle it; the humanist desire for reconciliation ... tends to founder on the very (socioeconomic) conditions that make travel writing possible."[16]

This chapter examines texts by Fleming, Auden and collaborators MacNeice and Isherwood, and Iyer that inventively use modernist literary strategies in ways that draw narrative privilege and the ethics of representation into critical view. Their narrative personas pointedly disavow any genuine expertise. "None of us could speak Portuguese. None of us had any relevant experience of the tropics," Fleming declares in *Brazilian Adventure*.[17] "This was our first journey to any place east of Suez. We spoke no Chinese, and possessed no special knowledge of Far Eastern affairs," Auden and Isherwood warn in the foreword to *Journey to a War*, adding, "[i]t is hardly necessary, therefore, to point out that we cannot vouch for the accuracy of many statements made in this book" (13). Iyer elaborates his lack of knowledge at length in *Video Night*:

> I make no claim to be authoritative about the places I visited. Quite the opposite, in fact. I spent no more than a few weeks in each country, I speak

not a word of any of their languages and I have never formally studied any Asian culture. Nor did I try – except in India and Japan – to consult local experts (a job best left to other experts). ...

Instead, I let myself be led by circumstance. Serendipity was my tour guide, assisted by caprice. Instead of seeking out information, I let it find me. (24)

While distancing themselves from outmoded presumptions of imperial authority, these narrators also seek to assure themselves and the readers they address directly that they are more than "trippers."[18] They aspire to be taken seriously, in literary terms and as critical observers. Each seeks to achieve substance through narrative, by finding stances within heteroglossia from which to represent subjective experience meaningfully.

The particular modernist techniques they use and the specific contexts in which they write differ; in fact, their narratives demonstrate that strategies effective in one political situation often require adaptation for another. In *Brazilian Adventure*, Fleming resolutely inverts the conventions and language of exploration to give comic high profile to a low-stakes journey, and in so doing challenges the travel narrative's pretentions. His self-assured narrator reappears in *One's Company* (1934), crossing the Soviet Union to report political news from China, a serious task for which he lacks qualification. In contrast, Auden and MacNeice, then Auden and Isherwood, discard a single narrative voice and juxtapose multiple perspectives in ways that compel readers to experience versions of heteroglossia on their own. In differing ways, with different political stakes, *Letters from Iceland* and *Journey to a War* subordinate the linear frame of the journey to an admixture of prose, poetry, and images. Writing half a century before Bruce Chatwin publishes *The Songlines*, Auden and his collaborators reinvent travel narrative as pastiche. Iyer, whose *Video Night* appears a year after *The Songlines*, opts for a different form of narrative reflexivity by turning his critical gaze on the ways that movement inflects and alters his own subjectivity. Traveling to see the globalized "not-so-far-East" and his home in America "from a different vantage point and with new eyes," he seeks not to echo previous writers who show "how one personality acts in different places" but rather "to show how different places act on one personality" (9, 26).

Brazilian Adventure **and** One's Company

In his first travel narrative, *Brazilian Adventure*, Fleming audaciously "takes his stand as a modern member of an unromantic generation."[19] He does so by assuming discursive authority with panache, invoking travel narrative conventions to show their falsity and positioning himself in counterpoint as a critical observer who can be trusted. His primary mode is parody – the practice of "imitation characterized by ironic inversion" and "repetition with critical difference" whose prominence in twentieth-century literature Linda Hutcheon demonstrates in *A Theory of Parody*. Parody – like irony – always requires a shared context: Hutcheon explains it may "be said to require a certain institutionalized sense of values – both aesthetic (generic) and social (ideological) – in order to be understood, or even to exist."[20] Adept in the "flashily impressive" jargon and "unmistakable" conventions that surround his subject, Fleming's narrator knows they're "easily guyed" because his audience knows them well from explorer narratives, adventure tales such as Richard Halliburton's *The Royal Road to Romance* (1925), and – most recently – motion pictures (130). As he declares at one point in *One's Company*, "[n]ow you could write the next bit of this narrative far better than I shall. You know the form."[21] The discourse of travel is so hackneyed, Fleming's narrator explains, that even before departing London for Brazil he and fellow expedition member Roger "found it impossible to talk of our plans without apologetically draping the pretentions of such words as Standing Camp in inverted commas"(130). Once there, they find their experiences to be "always perilously close to the pages of those books which publishers catalogue under the heading of 'Travel and Adventure'" and thus declare parody essential: "In self-defence – in instinctive pursuance of that policy of *nol admirari* which is the joint product of repression, sophistication, and all the hot air one hears – we turned to Parody" (130). Fleming assuredly disrupts traditional expectations to offer a critical vantage point. *Brazilian Adventure* is "an intensely self-conscious book," Evelyn Waugh observed in his review, because Fleming, aware "that the spirit of adventure often results in literary trash," goes "to the extreme limits of depreciation in his anxiety to avoid the pretentious."[22] Fleming seeks to write from a frankly modern point of view. To this end, he acknowledges the appeal of travel's tropes even as he undoes them: "Everyone is a romantic," he declares in *One's Company*, "though in some the romanticism is of a perverted and paradoxical kind" (44).

Brazilian Adventure begins with a confident foreword declaring that Fleming's text differs from its predecessors:

> Most expeditions have serious, scientific, non-committal books written about them. But ours was not that sort of expedition, and mine is not that sort of book. Only an alienist could have chronicled our activities either seriously or scientifically. I have, however, been as non-committal as I could.

> Differing as it does from most books about expeditions, this book differs also from most books about the interior of Brazil. It differs in being throughout strictly truthful. (5)

Though old men lament that "Modern Youth" have lost "the Spirit of Adventure," Fleming's narrator counters that "adventure in the grand old manner ... is obsolete, having been either exalted to a specialist's job or degraded to a stunt" (28). He fashions himself as a bemused critical spectator concerned to strike the right posture for recounting his experiences. A new kind of travel narrator, he is an avowed non-specialist who obtains an appointment as "special correspondent" to the *Times* (16).[23] Disinterestedness is his qualification: learning of an expedition through the Agony Column, which he reads assiduously in preference to coverage of such matters as "World Events" and "War Debts," he finds it amusing and inquires further only after the *Times* reports the expedition's intentions (13, 14). He declares he will be truthful, neither pretending nor exaggerating. Though prior accounts of "the Great Unknown" make "great play with the Terrors of the Jungle," Fleming's narrator refuses to use "the paraphernalia of tropical mumbo jumbo": "the reader must forgive me if my picture of Matto Grosso does not tally with his lurid preconceptions" (5).

The journey begins so entangled in popular clichés about adventure that veraciousness all but requires parody. The organizers propose to explore the rivers of central Brazil and discover the fate of Colonel Percy Fawcett, who disappeared in 1925 while seeking a mythical lost city. These avowed purposes, designed to gain press attention and possibly underwriting from American film magnates, provide a serious veneer for their primary goal: a profitable shooting trip.[24] The supposed expedition abandons its "never very convincing façade of scientific purpose" and surveying equipment before even leaving São Paulo (79). Despite a signed "Gentleman's Agreement," the members find themselves at odds over the sensational ambition to find Fawcett. The disputatious expedition splits up, with Fleming – whose letters to the *Times* have "guaranteed a good Fawcett 'story,' and hinted at the possibility of a very good one" – in the group that continues the quest (178, 179). In the end, the opposing contingents race each other back to the ship home, Fawcett remains a mystery, and Fleming publishes a book whose ironic inversion of convention makes it "perhaps the most popular travel book between the wars."[25]

For Fleming's narrator, honest perception requires skepticism and critical distance. By describing the Brazilian expedition as "a venture for which Rider Haggard might have written the plot and Conrad designed the scenery," he identifies even the bare facts of travel as the stuff of fiction and invites his readers to join him as critics (16). He credits "the observant reader" with more critical acuity than the expedition's organizer, in whose accounts "the actual was inextricably confused with the apocryphal" and "[f]act and fancy presented a united and imposing front" (38). He assures such readers that "[t]he advantages of being On the Spot are often overestimated":

> In the autumn of 1931 I was in Mukden a week after the Japanese had seized Manchuria; and though afterwards one behaved as though one's memories of sandbags and impassive little sentries had given one an abnormal insight into the Far Eastern crisis, one knew that in reality this was not so, and that one had been hardly any nearer coming at the truth behind the situation than if one had stayed at home and read *The Times*. Everything nowadays takes place at such long range that the man on the spot had often less chance of seeing both sides of the medal than the man at a distance.... Though it is, of course, pleasant to pick up one's misapprehensions at firsthand, and to have them coloured by one's own, and not by other people's imaginations. (83)

Fleming makes it clear that travel does not in itself guarantee insight or authority. Yet his narrator proposes to have it both ways. On the one hand, he suggests that both traveler and reader may be critical spectators whose irony and suspicion help them to discern truth. On the other, he suggests that the traveler's firsthand experience allows him to gauge the inaccuracy of literary convention: "I suppose one's first revolution – like one's first experience of anything to which one brings preconceptions coloured by literature and the drama – is always rather disappointing" (81–82). Whatever one might have supposed at home, it turns out that once you climb high enough for "a magnificent view of the Great Unknown" it all looks "familiar" (264).

In the eyes of Fleming and contemporaries such as Waugh, the new medium of film has further exaggerated outmoded conventions. The Trans-Siberian Express will call up "an intoxicating vision," Fleming's narrator observes in *One's Company*, because films and novels such as *Shanghai Express* and *Stamboul Train* have "successfully exploited its potentialities as a setting for adventure and romance" (44). One can have this "vision," however, only if one hasn't actually been on such on train and doesn't know the "nondescript smell of the upholstery" and the feeling of being in a "small, timeless, moving cell" (45). When he arrives in the "grey and dank" streets of Dover after the comic misadventure in Brazil, a poster that advertises a film as "A Jungle Epic" catches his eye:

> A Jungle Epic? Whatever those words may mean, they can hardly be applied (I reflected) to this journey which is now so near its end. The spirit of burlesque had been our titular deity. A Jungle Lampoon perhaps.

As I walked slowly through the bleak autumn streets, memory paraded for my benefit inconsequent, staccato excerpts from the comedy, like cuttings from a News Reel. (406)

Film ensures that the implausible plots and over-used language that Fleming parodies continue to thrive.[26] Though outmoded in the twentieth century, when would-be adventurers seek book contracts before they go, they persist. For the narrator, they remain pervasive, tired discourses against which the modern critical spectator must write as he "gropes for [reality] through a fog of preconceptions, misled by other people's labels" (407).

The unmistakable Fleming of *Brazilian Adventure* returns a year later in *One's Company*. The book begins with a notice:

WARNING TO THE READER

The recorded history of Chinese civilization covers a period of four thousand years. The population of China is estimated at 450 millions. China is larger than Europe.

When this book was written the author was twenty-six years old. He spent, altogether, about seven months in China. He does not speak Chinese. (13)[27]

Caution issued, Fleming proceeds to narrate his journey across Russia and into China "with the object of investigating the Communist situation" (181). He continues in the persona of the Special Correspondent (now capitalized) who frankly admits his lack of special expertise. His chief qualifications are his critical, noncommittal eye and his willingness to acknowledge his limitations. Of his visit to Moscow before boarding the Trans-Siberian Express, he notes that he is "extremely bad at sightseeing" and "wholly lacking in either an historical sense or the ability to appreciate architecture" (32, 33). As a consequence, "I saw none of the things that I should have seen. I can only tell you what Moscow looks like to the uninitiated" (33). As a critical spectator, however, Fleming's narrator has observed enough to report that the extremes of public opinion in England are "hopelessly wrong" because they are based on political opinion rather than sound evidence: "The reality falls midway between the pictures drawn by the *Morning Post* on the one hand and the Intourist travel agency on the other. Moscow is a drab, but not a desolate city" (29, 33). Later, upon arrival in Harbin, he turns his critical gaze on himself when he begins to "pass myself off on people as a Special Correspondent" without having identified what the role requires: "The great thing, I decided, was to Preserve an Open Mind. This entailed the minimum of exertion on my part and was really very easy, because I started by knowing nothing, and everything that people told me I forgot" (71).

Although *One's Company* often echoes *Brazilian Adventure*'s ironic tone, its parody is more serious. Fleming's narrator now travels alone across troubled frontiers, having taken a commission "to write a series of articles on China, each one more portentous and comprehensive than the last" (23). He still reads the Agony Column, but "merely as oracular guidance," for he already has an itinerary and professional credentials (19–20).[28] Revolution, an incidental complication in *Brazilian Adventure*, now motivates the journey. The narrator's asides on the Soviet state set the stage for his more thorough observations of violent political conflict in China, with the Japanese in Manchukuo and between Nationalists and Communists in the south. This newly serious mode appears in the narrative almost as soon as Fleming crosses the border. He writes of a young Chinese man doing "difficult and dangerous" work: "I have met, I suppose, few braver men, and no greater patriots." But he cannot say more, for "[t]o write about it would be to make [his patriotism] more futile still and perhaps – if he still survives – to endanger his life" (82). He accompanies Japanese troops on an expedition against Chinese "bandits" and photographs two men about to be executed. Though he does so "without compunction," the thought that their bodies will decay long before his photographic images materialize makes him uneasy: "It was a situation which would have put Donne's muse on her mettle" (170). In the second half of the book, Fleming's narrator reviews the political situation in a chapter titled "Hammer and Sickle" and reports an arduous journey to the anti-Communist front. He subdues parody and persona to allow earnestness. Vita Sackville-West, reviewing *One's Company*, notes that the narrative combines the familiar "light and witty touch" with "solid common sense and observation." She remarks the shift in tone from *Brazilian Adventure*: "there was something about that extravagant, high-spirited enterprise which exceeded this more sober account of the experiences of a War correspondent."[29]

Fleming's inversion of travel narrative conventions consistently links narrative authority with subjective honesty. His narrator may lack geographical or anthropological expertise, but he observes critically:

> So far I have tried to describe the Araguaya subjectively: I have tried to show what living on it was like from our point of view, from the point of view of interlopers. But this is no place (I am afraid you will be grumbling) for the subjective method: you don't go to a practically unknown part of the world to say what it was like from your point of view. Give us a few facts, a little accurate observation.
>
> I wish I could. This book is all truth and no facts. It is probably the most veracious travel book ever written; and it is certainly the least instructive.[30]

In seeing Fleming's work as being "of a debunking tendency ... depicting him as the one honest man in a profession of knaves," Fussell misses the deeper implications of such passages.[31] Fleming's self-consciousness centers more on the genre and its constraints than on himself. Though he opines freely about everything from politics to nature, he distinctly rejects the term "fact" and insists that readers understand his views are always subjective – and sometimes "half-baked."[32] In *Brazilian Adventure*, he lays an old trope to rest:

> Hitherto my imagination had not been fired by the thought that we were in a place never before visited by white men. ...
>
> I looked at those plumed expanses, aching in the heat, at the inviolable murmurous reaches of our river, and I did my very best to feel like stout Cortez. But it was no good. Common-sense strangled at birth the delights of discovery, showing them to be no more than an unusually artificial brand of snobbery.
>
> After all, common sense pointed out, the things you see would look exactly the same if you were not the first but the twenty-first white man to see them. (261)

Fleming discards the artifice of "discovery" for what will become a predominant concern of twentieth-century travel narrative: the subjective view from the front. If *One's Company* "has any value at all," he writes in the foreword, "it is the light which it throws on the processes of travel – amateur travel – in parts of the interior, which, though not remote, are seldom visited" (15). That the interior is now the site of a violent political conflict that that "no foreigner" – or at least no writer – before him has observed gives serious purpose to both journey and narrative (192).

Hutcheon observes that parody requires that readers "recognize that what they are reading *is* a parody, and to what degree and of what type."[33] Fleming's readers remark that he parodies the genre while retaining a confident, imperial stance. One reviewer, for instance, calls *Brazilian Adventure* "a refreshingly new departure" though Fleming "remains true to the old flag after all."[34] For all his debunking of the genre's pretensions, Fleming's narrator does not surrender his position of authority. Modern – unromantic, parodic, even cynical – but not truly modernist, he assuredly redefines authority as resting in the quality of one's spectatorship. His stance suits the genre parody that is his ambition while allowing him to claim that his political observations at the front should be taken seriously. It lets him pose important questions about the ethics of representation without obligating him to answer them. As Hutcheon explains, "parody's transgressions ultimately remain authorized ... by the very norm it seeks to subvert."[35] Though clearly a pointed critique of the genre, Fleming's work creates so distinctive a narrative persona that it paradoxically retains something of the aura of the adventure tale that he professes to abandon.

Letters from Iceland and *Journey to a War*

Auden's first travel book, *Letters from Iceland*, coauthored with MacNeice, constitutes an abrupt break with convention. Fleming's parodies retain traditional form: *Brazilian Adventure* and *One's Company* begin in England and end with the adventurer returning to a comfortably familiar home.[36] Auden and MacNeice, however, explicitly place *Letters from Iceland* in the genre of the "travel book" while discarding many of its usual features. *Letters from Iceland* includes a five-part "Letter to Lord Byron" using "modified Don Juan stanza[s]" in which Auden comments on British politics and culture,[37] practical information "For Tourists," excerpts from nineteenth-century texts collected as "Sheaves from Sagaland," bar graphs and pie charts, a twenty-page verse "Last Will and Testament" by both poets, "letters" to various friends at home, and a comic sequence of letters titled "Hetty to Nancy" in which a vivacious female narrator recounts a journey around a glacier, on horseback, with schoolgirls. The text is organized to juxtapose objective detail – guidebook information on currency and food; charts of habitable land and industries; graphs of exports and imports; and photographs of landscape, artwork, and workers processing herring – with subjective response presented in verse, letters, and the idiosyncratic references of the "testament."[38] Forging connections between documentary details and personal narrative is left to the reader: for instance, although the map documents "roads connecting with Reykjavik along which a car can be driven," it reveals nothing of the authors' own route (380). No single voice predominates and no single version of either author appears, for each writes from multiple vantage points; no obvious plotline runs from beginning to end. The book's most evident feature, as Marsha Bryant observes, is its "striking discontinuity," in which Auden "mixes the populism he saw in thirties documentary with the fragmentation he inherited from high modernist collage."[39] Less an attempt to create a new strategy for narrating travel than a thorough-going disruption of old norms, *Letters from Iceland* departs so completely from the genre's conventions that scholars have largely ignored it as an oddity, though similarly inventive collage techniques appear in later experimental travel texts.

Auden and MacNeice's text sets modernist subjectivity and the putatively objective ends of conventional travel writing directly against one another. Its use of modernist discontinuity and apparent randomness while declaring itself to be a "travel book" makes "the processes of perception and representation" of central concern.⁴⁰ Absent a narrative thread and explicit relations between the parts, *Letters from Iceland* leaves the significance of knowledge claims to the reader: Do bar graphs signify differently when they're linked to verse? Or documentary photographs to fictional comic letters? In a verse letter, Auden jokingly describes their project as "a little donnish experiment in objective narrative," only to counter quickly with: "Landscape's so dull/if you haven't Lawrence's wonderful wooziness" (344). The interest in the scenes before them, he explains, lies not in "the externals" of what they saw or heard, but rather in "the purely subjective feelings,/The heart-felt exhultations and the short despairs" (350). Yet the travelers' account of their exhultation and despair comes in incongruous fragments, and their feelings prove difficult to divine. By including objective information yet explicitly discounting its value, celebrating subjective response yet performing it obscurely through personal references and a ventriloquized female voice, *Letters from Iceland* prefers a diffuse heteroglossia to the authoritative voice on which the travel narrative usually depends. It calls the genre's purpose into question by demonstrating chaotically what Bryant calls "the diverse, fragmented means by which we go about making partial, tentative sense of our world."⁴¹

Contemporary reviewers found *Letters from Iceland*'s modernist innovation sufficiently engaging that they offered literary vindication: after declaring "Mr. Auden ... full of surprises," the *Times Literary Supplement* reviewer proceeds to explain and celebrate the text's methods.⁴² The *Times* review opens with a defense: "Letters from Iceland need not necessarily be about Iceland, nor even, in the accepted sense, letters, and these are in some sort neither the one nor the other." The travel book, the reviewer effectively declares, need not be about the destination but may take the subjective experience of the traveler as its primary concern. If a narrative thread runs through this "brilliantly varied book," the reviewer argues, it is that Auden, refusing a conventional "recital of collapsing tents, treacherous rocks, falling skies, and errant navigation," turns his critical eye on Europe from a distance that makes "his home truths sharper."⁴³ This interpretation borrows directly from the "W. H. Auden" found within *Letters from Iceland*, whom the reviewer cites:

> I might write [Byron] a chatty letter in light verse about anything I could think of, Europe, literature, myself. He's the right person, I think, because he was a townee, a European, and disliked Wordsworth and that kind of approach to nature, and I find that very sympathetic. This letter in itself

will have very little to do with Iceland, but will be rather a description of
the effect of travelling in distant places which is to make one reflect on
one's past and one's culture from the outside. But it will form a central
thread. (280)

In Byron's *Don Juan*, as Youngs explains, Auden finds "a model for the
literary journey as radical commentary on Europe and satire on Britain,
as well as a precedent for parodying the forms on which it draws."[44] With
the stakes not yet as high as they will soon be, Auden and MacNeice have
the leisure to experiment with modernist strategies to political as well as
literary-critical ends. "I'm going to be very up to date indeed./It's a collage
that you're going to read," Auden announces to Byron, for though "[t]he
experiment may not be a success," "I want a form that's large enough to
swim in" (182).[45]

Letters from Iceland thus identifies and poses critical issues that will have
increased urgency for Auden when he and Isherwood represent their experiences in wartime China in *Journey to a War*. In writing of an isolated,
politically insignificant nation and a people he finds free of "the least trace
of hysterical nationalism," Auden finds ample space to satirize the limits
of representation while working toward political purpose (190). He comments on serious issues throughout, telling Byron that "the John Bull of
the good old days" died at Ypres and Passchendaele and that others err in
supposing the "Führer-Prinzip" would appeal to Byron, whom he instead
imagines "in the United Front with Gide" (213, 214, 215). But these themes
do not predominate – in fact, Auden interrupts this portion of his letter to Byron because "I must write home or mother will be vexed," and
when he resumes he talks "shop" as a literary critic, positioning himself in
relation to T. S. Eliot and I. A. Richards rather than returning to "Social
Questions" (216, 249).[46] Filled with rumination, *Letters from Iceland* insists
that travel's deepest interest lies in its subjective effects – and then leaves
the meaning of those effects open to interpretation. "I hope I'm better,
wiser for the trip," Auden writes Byron late in the book, for he has seen
"the map of all my youth unroll" (326). He's come to the crucial recognition "[t]hat what we see depends on who's observing,/And what we think
on our activities," but whether this will help him "To be a better poet, better man" he cannot yet discern (335).

In the two years between the publication of *Letters from Iceland* and
Journey to a War, Auden's vantage point and global political circumstances
change profoundly. After returning home from Iceland, Auden travels
to Spain, where he spends a few months observing the Republican fight
against fascism. His last revisions to the Iceland book, written as answers

to questions from Isherwood, seem to reflect that experience. The final question – "What feelings did your visit give you about life on small islands?" – elicits:

> If you have no particular intellectual interests or ambitions and are content with the company of your family and friends ... then life on Iceland must be very pleasant.... But I had the feeling ... that for myself it was already too late. We are all too deeply involved with Europe to be able, or even to wish to escape.... [I]n the long run, the Scandinavian sanity would be too much for you, as it is for me. The truth is, we are both only really happy living among lunatics. (190)[47]

Soon commissioned to write a travel book about Asia, Auden and Isherwood decide on China, scene of British imperial interests, civil war, and invasion by Japan. Choosing their destination for political interest and titling their work *Journey to a War*, they cast themselves as earnest observers and make Spain "a self-conscious reference point."[48] The text they produce includes a long narrative in Isherwood's voice, poems by Auden – an opening sequence titled "London to Hongkong" and a closing sonnet sequence with "verse commentary" titled "In Time of War" – that invoke images from the narrative, and a "Picture Commentary" section with captioned photos, most by Auden.[49] *Journey to a War* thus boldly revises the form "large enough to swim in" of *Letters from Iceland* for the serious purpose of responding to war.

The circumstances the writers find in China heighten the stakes of spectatorship and representation in ways that push their literary strategies to their limits. Beginning with the foreword, Auden and Isherwood depict themselves as novices whose inexperience means that their narrative can only describe their own perceptions and report others' words. Ill informed about Chinese culture and fluent in no local languages, they must rely on others to explain much of what they observe. Although Auden did the leg-pulling in *Letters from Iceland*, the tables are turned in *Journey to a War*, for he and Isherwood must differentiate truth from fiction: "Some of our informants may have been unreliable, some merely polite, some deliberately pulling our leg. We can only record, for the benefit of the reader who has never been to China, some impression of what he would be likely to see, and of what kind of stories he would be likely to hear" (13). They travel from Hong Kong to Canton on a British-owned riverboat and arrive "eager to miss none of the sensational sights which had been promised us" (27). The sights are Japanese planes and warships in action, and they hope to take photographs despite posted notices warning passengers against using cameras. They first experience an air-raid while at tea in an Anglo-American missionary settlement. Isherwood finds the experience surreal:

> It was all very well for Auden to sit there so calmly.... He had been in Spain. My eyes moved over this charming room, taking in the tea-cups, the dish of scones, the book-case with Chesterton's essays and Kipling's poems, the framed photograph of an Oxford college. My brain tried to relate these images to the sounds outside; the whine of the power-diving bomber, the distant thump of the explosions. Understand, I told myself, that those noises, these objects are part of a single, integrated scene. Wake up. It's all quite real. And, at that moment, I really did wake up. At that moment, suddenly, I arrived in China. (32)

How to understand juxtaposed, disparate images and sounds as "a single, integrated scene" becomes central to Auden and Isherwood's journey, and how to present that experience for readers the project of *Journey to a War*. Though experienced in European travel, they have difficulty interpreting even firsthand experiences in China; their confusion, sometimes comical, often impedes their more serious ambitions. Being "steeped in the traditions of" the colonial romance *The Chinese Bungalow* did not, they report jokingly, prepare them for lunch with a Chinese provincial governor,[50] and the lake that Isherwood singles out on the map as possibly the furthest extent of their journey actually appears long before they come anywhere near the front (39). As British sightseers with a vague agenda, Auden and Isherwood stand out when they arrive in Hankow, the heteroglot center of "war-time China," which is full of Chinese politicians of opposed sympathies, white Russian émigrés, American and Australian correspondents, and "generals, ambassadors, journalists, foreign naval officers, soldiers of fortune, airmen, missionaries, spies" (50). When they first appear at the daily government press conference, the "inquisitively hostile eyes" of experienced reporters produce a confession: "We hastened to explain that we were not real journalists, but mere trippers, who had come to China to write a book" (53).

In so identifying themselves Auden and Isherwood pose the challenge before them. Others on the scene are surely more qualified to report the wartime chaos: the journalists who are "old hands" and "great news-men" know China intimately, and many have already "written ... so well" about the revolutionary Eighth Route Army, which entails a journey into Shaanxi province requiring more time than Auden and Isherwood "could possibly allow" (53, 61).[51] Robert Capa, whom they had met on the voyage out, has already achieved fame as a war photographer in Spain; Fleming, again a correspondent for the *Times*, is already a celebrity for his persona

as adventurer. Auden and Isherwood's literary renown at home will carry
them only so far abroad. Positioning themselves ironically from the beginning allows them to question the conventions of travel and rationales of
war without making unsustainable claims of expertise regarding the political situation. It also establishes a narrative stance that suits their attempt
to understand their own experiences in China and represent them in a
coherent manner.

To this end, they "camp" masculinity as well as literary convention, as
Maureen Moynagh demonstrates in her study of "revolutionary drag" in
Journey to a War and Bryant in her analysis of Auden's relation to documentary. Traditionally, travel narrative all but requires a performance of the
masculine expertise imbedded in its tropes. Auden and Isherwood, however, are "mere trippers" in relation to both heterosexual gender norms and
the travel genre: they aim simultaneously to continue *Letters from Iceland's*
disruption of the latter and carve out their own route beyond the former.
A "theatrical understanding of maleness" is essential to both purposes;[52]
it appears most vividly in their depictions of Capa and Fleming. They
portray Capa, a Hungarian, as a joker "more French than the French" who
concerns himself far more with aesthetics and social life than with politics (53). Though he obtains frontline photos so frank that he must "send
them uncensored to America, where they would be published as a book,"
he remains "dissatisfied" because he finds "the Chinese face unsatisfactory
for the camera, in comparison with the Spanish" and "plainly long[s] to
return" to Paris and Madrid (165).[53] Auden and Isherwood meet Fleming
and his wife Celia, an actress, at a party given by an admiral and a consul-
general in a Hankow luxury flat. He's an exaggeration of his persona, a
dashing figure who stands out even in so quintessential a colonial setting:
"Fleming, with his drawl, his tan, his sleek, perfectly brushed hair, and
lean good looks, is a subtly comic figure – the conscious, living parody of
the pukka sahib. He is altogether too good to be true – and he knows it"
(156). Performance begets parody begets irony: Fleming, who sends up the
masculine adventure type popularized by Halliburton, is in turn read by
Auden and Isherwood as the live performance of his own literary trope,
one they unexpectedly must compete with when they end up traveling
together.[54]

Auden and Isherwood's narrative ironically reiterates the power of the
genre's traditions even as it subordinates them to its own unconventional
aims. In the first several chapters of the prose Travel-Diary, they travel
from Canton to Hankow to Sian and back to Hankow. Through nationality and reputation, they have privileged access to meet local officials,

WAR ZONE

Illustration 2. "War Zone" photos, from Auden and Isherwood's *Journey to a War.*

observe Chinese soldiers and Japanese bombing runs, interview prominent expatriates including Agnes Smedley, and have tea with luminaries such as Madame Chiang Kai-shek. They travel by train, foot, and rickshaw; stay in a comfortable hotel with "pretentious, dull, and bad" food and another where military comings and goings make noise through the night; and take photos of themselves posing in the trenches (see Illustration 2) (140). One hospital tour allows them to observe gynecological surgery (and seize "the opportunity of examining" the unconscious patient's bound feet),

WAR ZONE

Enemy planes overhead

Illustration 2. (*continued*)

whereas others show them wounded soldiers (88). Although the narrative occasionally adopts the descriptive "voice of 'establishment' masculinity that characterizes British travel books," it clearly centers on Auden and Isherwood's subjective experiences and observations, with "omissions and codings" that signal a gay counter narrative.[55] One episode after another reads with as well as against the grain, juxtaposing the conventions of masculinity and travel with the real lives of literary men. In Sian, for instance, they meet Dr. Mooser, a hard-driving Swiss physician. Isherwood admires Mooser's stamina: "he rushed at life ... with his head down, stamping and roaring like a bull" (136). Mooser, he explains, "didn't quite know what to make of us.... He had no use for poetry because 'it changes the order of the words'" (137). Although his account celebrates the doctor's efficient oversight of camps for 8,000 refugees, Isherwood frames the episode with anecdotes about susceptible men, not rigor or war. He opens by describing the rickshaws of "oddly Victorian design" that he and Auden use "out of laziness, despite Dr. Mooser's warning that their upholstery often contained typhus-lice" (136). He closes with a story Mooser tells about working in Mexico a decade earlier, where he diagnosed a "queer-looking fellow with a red beard" named D. H. Lawrence (137). Though not a literary man, he knew how to interpret Lawrence's symptoms: tuberculosis.

Auden and Isherwood observe, ask questions, and report others' stories at length, yet they agree that as "casual foreigners" they lack the cultural fluency to bring back anything but "superficially depressing" impressions or to "assess" anything as nuanced as "Chinese military morale" (116). Their stay becomes a modernist series of episodes with little narrative direction, the "journey to a war" of the title perpetually deferred by miscommunication and logistical difficulty. The *Times* reviewer describes the result: they record the sights "with a deadly accuracy," in "disconnected" vignettes, with keen "thumbnail sketches of leading Chinese personalities ... and in parallel, and often in contrast, a range of British officials, missionaries, and doctors. The war is never integrated; its elements ... are exposed to view, and left at that."[56] Isherwood "presents the outline of a scene, an incident, or a character with great economy," comments another reviewer; "he does not guess at its implications, he does not integrate where the basis of integration is absent."[57] Dependent on reluctant Chinese officials for access to the northern front, they find, as Douglas Kerr explains, that "[n]either the country nor the war has a center." When they finally reach the front it disappoints, for the Japanese troops occupy their position only at night. At midday it appears "undramatic and epistemologically thin. No revelations attend it. There is no story here."[58] Frustrated by the difficulty of reaching desired destinations, they unsurprisingly are tempted to extend their break at the mountain resort "Journey's End." Like the sanatorium in Thomas Mann's *The Magic Mountain*, the resort estranges visitors from time and history: "One could arrive for the week-end and stay fifteen years" (179). A place where one could write "the book that was altogether too wonderful to finish and too sacred ever to publish," it provokes Isherwood to ask: "Why go anywhere? Why bother about the Fourth Army? It could take care of itself. What was this journey? An illusion" (179, 182).

Once Auden and Isherwood decide to travel to the south-eastern battlefront "quite independently" with their own guide, they find themselves obliged by Chinese officials to join an expedition organized for Fleming (201). At first defensive because of "a blend of anti-Etonianism and professional jealousy," they describe Fleming's attire as "almost absurdly correct," as though he had stepped from "a London tailor's window, advertising Gent's Tropical Exploration Kit" (214, 207). Their own attire, in contrast, is simply absurd: Isherwood earlier declares that he, Auden, and their servant Chiang "resemble a group of characters in one of Jules Verne's stories about lunatic English explorers" (104). Although it initially appears ludicrous for these competing performers to join forces, Auden and Isherwood recognize Fleming to be a politically savvy traveler with fortitude and "consummate skill" (208). The unexpected development allows them to prove their mettle and, simultaneously, differentiate themselves as travelers and writers.

As Auden and Isherwood tell it, traveling together produces camaraderie: abandoning their initial impressions, they become characters in a Fleming-style adventure, "[f]ollowing Peter's cue" (223). Fleming delights them by longing for his rook-rifle (mentioned in his own narratives)[59] and (in a scene out of *Brazilian Adventure*) drafting a memorandum to split up the expedition to ensure that those wishing to reach the front quickly will not be hindered. Isherwood describes their climb up a steep mountain track: "Laughing and perspiring we scrambled uphill; the Fleming Legend accompanying us like a distorted shadow. Auden and I recited passages from an imaginary travel-book called 'With Fleming to the Front'" (214).[60] Echoing Fleming and Roger, they amuse themselves through parody. At day's end they fall asleep exhausted while Fleming types into the night. Later, they travel the last stretch to the front at Meiki through a downpour. Isherwood rides ahead with the Chinese members of the group, singing drunkenly and talking to his horse in German. Auden and Fleming walk, arguing about Soviet Russia and arriving "in the highest of spirits and muddy from head to foot" (221). Now congenial compatriots (often in league against Chinese officialdom), they spend their last evening together drinking cognac and arguing over "the meaning of the word Civilization" and the question, "Had China anything to learn from the West?" (231). They part company with regret, having "all three enjoyed our expedition together." Auden sums up the experience: "Well, we've been on a journey with Fleming in China, and now we're real travelers for ever and ever. We need never go farther than Brighton again" (232). His declaration underscores their departure from tradition. Having kept up with Fleming, and distinguished between the persona and the man, they incorporate him into their own story, self-consciously casting the experience as a set piece. In effect, they subordinate the Fleming Legend to their own project.[61] Kerr reads this as a failure: "Isherwood cannot emulate the confident authority of Fleming's Asia discourse, but nor can he escape its genre. So his travel book implodes, turning its own inadequacies into comedy."[62] Far from imploding, however, Auden and Isherwood's narrative moves forward on its own terms, signaling their preference for modernist ways of writing travel.

Journey to a War's use of juxtaposition constitutes its most thorough de-centering of convention, most visible modernism, and deepest endorsement of subjective spectatorship. By placing Isherwood's voice in counterpoint with Auden's – or "Isherwood's" with "Auden's" – and the writers' voices in counterpoint with those of people they meet, using poetry to frame prose, and following up word with image, *Journey to a War* provides a representation of heteroglossia that offers no single point of entry or univocal line of analysis. Extending their critique of travel conventions to the relation between narrative and images, they call attention to the ambiguous role of photographs by giving them an unusual prominence. The "Picture Commentary," a discrete section of more than sixty photos that follows the prose text and precedes "In Time of War," uses placement and captions to provoke yet leaves interpretation to the reader. The photos of individuals identify nearly all by type: Reporters, Coolies, White Russian Restaurant Proprietor, Ambassador, Shanghai Business Man. (Only a few, including Fleming and Mooser, have proper names.) The section begins with the powerful and prominent – a photo of General and Madame Chiang Kai-Shek labeled "The Chiangs" – and ends with "Unknown Soldier." Captions linking adjacent photos often assert political or ethical significance – casualties labeled "The Innocent" and "The Guilty" – yet leave their terms ambiguous (see Illustration 3). Some pair individuals of similar physical build and differing ideology: "Chou En-lai (communist)" shares a page with "Du Yueh-seng (capitalist)." "Even in this most particular and naturalistic of media," Kerr observes, "Auden seems to be drawn toward generalization, allegory, and myth. The images are not unmoving, but they are subject to an eerie depersonalization."[63] "Children in Uniform," a set of two photos captioned "With legs" and "Without," obscurely shows none of the foregrounded figures below the hip.

At times, Bryant argues, Auden and Isherwood's renditions of an experience in photos, prose, and poetry are at odds with one another, forming "an unsteady triptych."[64] One representation throws another into question, or a juxtaposition of image and text invites yet refuses interpretation. The Travel-Diary suggests that they were never in grave danger, yet the Picture Commentary's photos of the writers in the trenches give differing impressions: Auden poses nonchalantly with a Chinese soldier, while Isherwood and another soldier appear vulnerable to attack, looking off in the distance at what the caption calls "Enemy planes overhead." Auden's inclusion of stills from the Nationalist film *Fight to the Last* along with apparently genuine on-the-scene shots of soldiers and refugees calls into question any implicit claim that photos provide documentary support for the text.[65] His use of the title of Andre Malraux' 1933 novel *La Condition humaine* to identify photos placed opposite the film stills compounds the

WAR ZONE

The Innocent

The Guilty

Illustration 3. "The Innocent" and "The Guilty," from Auden and Isherwood's *Journey to a War.*

ambiguity, for Malraux' novel had not been made into a film. Together these incommensurate juxtapositions produce a "schizophrenic figuration of 'frontline' experience," "blurring" the nature of the stance from which Auden and Isherwood observe the scene of war.[66]

This blurring of their positions as observing subjects is evidenced most starkly in the disjuncture between Auden's poems, which frame the volume, and Isherwood's prose. *Journey to a War*'s contemporary reviewers found this formal bricolage to be its most difficult feature. A few celebrated its modernist fragmentation for its verisimilitude of the contingency and discontinuity of wartime experience. Others, however, saw the text's refusal to integrate its multiple vantage points as an aesthetic failing best resolved by asserting that one text was central, the other peripheral. Bad metaphors abound: the *Times Literary Supplement* reviewer describes the book as a "sandwich" (with photographs as "condiments"), Waugh as a pantomime costume with "hind and front legs of a monster."[67] Scholars have tended to examine the text's prose, poetry, and photos in dialogue with one another – particularly the relation between poetry and prose – without imposing a rigid narrative line.[68] John Fuller, for instance, argues that the "occasionally grandiose" moments in the poetry are "calculated to counterbalance the self-deprecatory comedy" of the Travel-Diary.[69]

The poems that open the book introduce serious themes that surface sporadically in the prose, then reappear with force in the poems at the book's close. The dedication to E. M. Forster juxtaposes Auden and Isherwood's role as observers of war's "Madness" with the modernist concern for "inner life" that is central to Forster's novels (11). The opening sequence, "London to Hongkong," considers the practices of travel and empire and opens the text with "an expression of ambivalence about the nature of journeys, or at least about the journey as utopian impulse, and the journey as escape."[70] To the question "does the traveler find … [p]roofs that somewhere there exists, really, the Good Place?" the poet replies,

> No, he discovers nothing: he does not want to arrive.
> The journey is false: the false journey really an illness
> …
> But at moments …
> … the trance is broken: he remembers
> The hours, the places where he was well; he believes in joy. (17)

The last poem in the sequence sets the stage for the journey by describing the "modern city" of Hong Kong; the first page of the following Travel-Diary reports their departure for Canton by river boat. Although the prose and photo sections center on social observation and political detail, the closing sonnet sequence, "In Time of War," and the "Commentary" that follows return pointedly to the opening themes. The sonnets place the Sino-Japanese war as an episode in the troubled evolution of civilization from innocence to grim necessity, a sign of the horror that threatens East and West alike in late modernity: "And maps can really point to places/ Where life is evil now:/Nanking; Dachau" (274). *Journey to a War* ends with the speaker hearing two intermingled sounds: "the distant mutter of guerrilla fighting" and "the voice of Man"; he gives the final word to the latter, who hopes to "outgrow my madness" and imagines a future in which "the forces of the will" "construct at last a human justice" (300, 301).

Journey to a War's greatest significance for the evolution of the travel genre lies in its modernist insistence that although complex events may occur as an "integrated scene," no single voice, mode of representation, or subjective observer can represent them fully alone. Late in the narrative, Isherwood underscores the logic of giving heteroglossia precedence when he considers memory's susceptibility. Traveling by steamer, he observes that a port hole, like a picture frame, severs image from context and aestheticizes once-prosaic details. "Memory in the years to come," he adds, "would prefer this simple theatrical picture to all the subtle and chaotic impressions of the past months. This, I thought – despite all we have seen, heard, experienced – is how I shall finally remember China" (234). Where Fleming retains narrative privilege in order to parody it, Auden and Isherwood deliberately cede it to one another and to other voices, keeping chaotic impressions alive by refusing to privilege one simple picture. The Travel-Diary emphasizes this by ending with an exchange between touring writers and expatriate activist on knowing where to begin. Like the "Commentary," it ends with another's voice. After describing the gulf between Chinese and Europeans in Shanghai, ideologically "too grossly wide for any bridge," and the ludicrous extremes of British solipsism, Isherwood writes:

> And the well-meaning tourist, the liberal and humanitarian intellectual, can only wring his hands over all this and exclaim: "Oh dear, things are so awful here – so complicated. One doesn't know where to start."
>
> "I know where *I* should start," says Mr. [Rewi] Alley, with a ferocious snort. "They were starting quite nicely in 1927." (253)

Moynagh argues that Auden and Isherwood's "predominantly ironic gaze" serves a serious modernist purpose: they are "critiquing the pretentions and limitations of Western intellectuals like themselves, while insisting, at least obliquely, on the value of bearing witness." Among the most compelling realities to which they attest, in Bryant's words, is the difficulty of understanding and making ethical sense of "decentered experience devoid of the man-making feats that structure linear plots."[71] Through its deliberately disjointed form, *Journey to a War* underscores what Auden and Isherwood learn as mobile spectators: though men might imagine war to be sensational and diagram it as "lucid and tidy," they can attest that actual experience is nothing like that: "War is bombing an already disused arsenal, missing it, and killing a few old women.... War is untidy, inefficient, obscure, and largely a matter of chance" (202).

Video Night in Kathmandu

By the 1980s, modernist subjectivity and experimentation no longer startle as they once did. The literary techniques that modernist novelists had devised in investigating "the possibility that the mediated nature of our consciousness might preclude our ever arriving ... at a consensus as to the nature of external reality" have become quite familiar.[72] Postmodernist fiction echoes and amplifies these techniques, at times to metacritical extremes that question the very existence of the real. Like the novel, the travel narrative continues to makes inventive use of modernist techniques, but – at the same time – it continues to bear a commitment to representing – and valuing – firsthand experience in real geopolitical contexts.[73] Travel texts written later in the century vary profoundly, from those relatively conventional in style to experimental texts that push the concept of narrative so far that initial reception centers on how to read them and what their genre(s) might be. Of such works in English, Chatwin's *The Songlines* has been most prominent; in French, Michel Butor's *Mobile, étude pour une représentation des États-Unis* (1962), dedicated "A la mémoire de Jackson Pollock," and Roland Barthes's *L'Empire des signes* (1970).[74] As discussed in Chapters 1 and 2, increased critical concern for the ethics of representation figures prominently in both postwar literary production and scholarship on imperial discourse and travel writing. Pico Iyer's *Video Night in Kathmandu: And Other Reports from the Not-So-Far-East* presents itself as a narrative written in and about a world that has changed profoundly: "Scarcely forty years ago, most of the world's secret places were known only to adventurers, soldiers, missionaries and a few enterprising traders; in recent years, however, the secrets were open, and so too was the world – anyone with a credit card could become a lay colonialist" (6). Where Auden and Isherwood examine the ethics of representation through irony and experiment, and deal with the cultural battles of globalization only indirectly, Iyer makes these matters his primary themes. Despite his ambition to bridge differences between the West and the "Not-So-Far-East," however, *Video Night* falters because the romance of his own subjectivity ends up trumping the narrator's critical spectatorship.

Iyer's narrator presents himself as a cosmopolitan subject with a keen eye. "[A] British subject, an American resident and an Indian citizen," he is "accustomed to cross-cultural anomalies and the mixed feelings of exile. Nowhere was home, and everywhere" (24). Despite several years of writing guidebooks in Europe and analyzing "World Affairs" for *Time* magazine, he remains a romantic who savors being in "alien parts" where "we speak more simply … move more freely, unencumbered by the histories that we carry around at home, and look more excitedly, with eyes of wonder" (23). Well-read in the genre (he quotes Fussell's criticism as well as writers from Rudyard Kipling to Paul Theroux), he explicitly places his text in counterpoint to convention. To readers seeking a "vivid day-to-day account of a journey through Asia," he recommends Peter Fleming and John Krich (25–26). For travel experiences he deems timeless, such as spending nights in a Mogul palace, viewing a "rare and sumptuous cremation," or climbing "live volcanoes in the dead of the Javanese night," he advises descriptions "by travelers more observant than myself" (10). Although Iyer's narrator retains the traditional theme of discovery, he approaches it by dwelling selectively on two themes: "the brand-new kinds of exotica thrown up by our synthetic age" of "willy-nilly collisions and collusions between East and West" and his own subjective placement in that world (10). Hoping that "home is, finally, not the physical place, but the role and self we choose to occupy," he travels "to discover what resided in me and where I resided more fully" (9).

Iyer's narrative of his journey of self discovery adopts an explicitly postmodern trajectory that fractures both geography and temporality. From beginning to end and within each chapter, he declares, the text reflects "not the chronological sequence of my movements so much as the twists and turns of my thoughts as I tried to make sense of the places I saw" (25). Drawing from "seven months crisscrossing the continent [of Asia] on four separate trips" taken "over the course of two years" (5), his first-person narrative is organized as a series of national vignettes tied together by the themes of self-discovery and cross-consumption between East and West. *Video Night* leaps from Bali to Tibet, the Philippines to Burma; it omits Korea entirely, excludes most of Indonesia, and says nothing of the politically unreachable destinations of Vietnam, Cambodia, and Laos. It jumps from 1985 to 1984 to 1986, seldom specifying dates or even seasons. Within chapters, time passes, for Iyer often returns, weeks or months later, to see whether he or a place has changed. Between chapters, time seems to reverse: "It was my first night in Asia" appears at the beginning of the sixth of twelve chapters (151). Both the fifth and eighth chapters begin in Hong Kong, yet Iyer's narrator describes the disorienting cacophony of arrival in the latter as though this visit were his first: "Suddenly, like almost everyone else on almost every trip through Asia I found myself at Hong Kong's Kai Tak Airport" (221). Such discontinuities leave the narrative without a continuous plotline and depict self-discovery as iterative, not developmental. In each nation, Iyer cycles from innocent arrival to disillusioned romantic, only to do it again in the next. The geopolitical contexts that matter are of his own choosing, for though Iyer cites both imperialism and capitalism his sense of history is, as Paul Smethurst explains, "spectral rather than causal," for he knowingly "stand[s] outside" historical facticity in preference for anomalies that fit his themes.[75] Iyer's traveling discards beginning, middle, and end for a condition of perpetual mobility.

In counterpoint to its iterative account of subjectivity, *Video Night* proposes a thematic "mental itinerary" designed to provide a "progressively more complex" understanding of contemporary Asia's relation with Western capitalism (25, 27). The plotline thus comes from perception, not travel or geography. Iyer groups chapters by his sense of each nation's relation with the West, beginning with "fairly simple and straightforward discussions of the most basic kinds of meeting … along the tourist trail" (Bali, Tibet, Nepal, China); proceeding to "some of the forms of Empire still to be found in the East" (the Philippines, Burma, Hong Kong); and ending by exploring how "some of the East's deepest cultures" adapt "Western influences, and make them distinctively their own" (India, Thailand, Japan; 27). From the opening description of audiences watching Rambo to the closing chapter, "The Empire Strikes Back," Iyer's narrator pays particular attention to cross-cultural adaptations of language and image. The text has "little description of physical or architectural beauty" but much of popular culture, from T-shirt slogans and restaurant menus in Kathmandu to nightclub performances in the Philippines and baseball in Japan.[76] Each chapter reiterates the claim that understanding contemporary Asia requires observing its relations with Western cultural products. "Revelations both mid-boggling and earth-shattering did not in fact lie around every corner" in Kathmandu, the narrator declares, but "the best enchilada of my life" did (86, 87). He watches movies – and movie audiences – in nearly every chapter.[77] Despite frequent references to the British Raj and the American military presence in the Philippines, he concerns himself with cultural, not political, domination. As Holland and Huggan argue, Iyer views the new "hybrid cultural forms" of "the East" as arising "not so much out of an imperialist imposition as out of a process of symbolic exchange involving the reindigenization of imported forms."[78]

To observe this symbolic exchange, Iyer's narrator refuses organized tours in order to wander independently as a flâneur who may talk with whomever he chooses. Trinh T. Minh-ha outlines the view that privileged travel in the era of tourism becomes "a socio-historical process of dispossession" that produces "a real identity crisis." To achieve meaningful experience, the traveler then seeks "to *imitate* the Other, to hide and disguise himself in an attempt to inscribe himself in a counter-exoticism that will allow him to be a nontourist."[79] Iyer's imitation comes through exchanges that he writes as personal friendships, despite the inequalities inherent in the circumstances in which the exchange occurs. He grounds his cultural and political analyses in such experiences: "Whenever I got carried away by the thrill-a-minute frenzy of the political scene," his narrator writes of the Philippines, "the friends I made in Manila brought me back to the simple realities of a system that had reduced its men to rags and driven its women to brothels" (180). His conversations with bar girls, security guards, and expatriates all center on their senses of identity, perceptions of the West, and desires. Many scenes deal with the acquisition and reuse of Western culture: studying English, copying fashions, mimicking Madonna. Including others' voices to the degree that Iyer's narrator does might be read as a way of recognizing heteroglossia: many people he meets get to tell their own stories. Yet he most attends to – and most savors – exchanges with characters whose naïve idealism he admires: Maung-Maung, an earnest trishaw driver in Mandalay who works assiduously to serve his tourist clients, and Sarah, a religious waitress in Manila who longs to study nursing.

Video Night thus recapitulates old notions about the romance of travel and the West's discursive relation to the East at the same time as it questions them. Like Fleming's narratives, it inverts genre expectations – in this instance, temporal and physical itineraries – without disturbing their underlying logic (Iyer may have read Fussell, but apparently not Said). For all its attention to hybridity and synthesis, in the end *Video Night* reiterates the West's discursive authority over the East. As Malini Johar Schueller argues, "[d]espite the migrant, homeless, global identity that Iyer overtly charts as his qualification, presumably for a decentered perspective, the 'I' of the text presumes a Westernness and whiteness that is geopolitically located.... [A] privileged cosmopolitanism that can position itself as unmarked."[80] This is most acutely evident when Iyer, who grounds his

claim to cross-cultural authority in personal experience, uses that authority to pass judgment on others' identities. In the Philippines, for instance,
he pronounces mixed-race children of Filipinos and U.S. soldiers playing
along the streets "not exactly All-American" solely on the basis of their
physical appearance – a categorical claim of precisely the sort he professes
to refuse (167). He laments Filipino vocalists' mastery of Joan Baez, the
Beatles, Bruce Springsteen, and Julio Iglesias. Although he recognizes that
their technical brilliance makes such vocalists stars across Asia, he finds
it regrettable because the feeling seems "borrowed" rather than genuine:
"as a form of self-expression, this eerie kind of ventriloquism made me
sad" (174).

The conversations that Iyer's narrator seeks with locals often disappoint
him because their instrumentality prevents the unbounded exchange that
he desires. Too often, he writes, "each of us was a symbol to each other,
both to be cherished and to be put to use.... The happiest aspect of traveling in the developing world is that it allows cross-cultural exchanges in
which each party can give something to the other. Yet the fact that both
parties have something to gain from the giving is surely the saddest thing."
(276). The identity markers that he deems genuine seem to exceed economic realities: Sarah's persistent hopefulness, Maung-Maung's self-reflec-
tive writing, and his own longing to find a place that feels like home. But
neither Sarah nor Maung-Maung has the luxury of setting economic concern aside: each writes of constant financial struggle. Sarah, a correspondent so faithful that she sends him birthday greetings though she cannot
afford her own medicine, writes "plaintive and affectionate letters"; the
last, "heartrending" letter he cites hopes for tuition assistance and perhaps
even marriage to her "best friend" (367). "Friendship" clearly signifies very
differently for Sarah, struggling to survive in Manila, and "Dear Pico,"
whose privilege allows him to quote her and move on.

The old paradigm of East versus West remains surprisingly secure
throughout *Video Night*, despite the "Not-So-Far" of the subtitle: Iyer
characterizes the West as "a masculine culture, dedicated to assertion,
virility and power, while Southeast Asia seemed feminine in its texture, all
softness, delicacy and grace" (215).[81] In the end, he revises his thesis, but
not its primary terms: "I began to suspect that my original formulation
should, if anything, be reversed: the East was increasingly moving in on
the West," for the "Orient ... was taking over the future, a realm that had
long seemed an exclusively Western dominion" (358, 361). As Holland and
Huggan observe: "For all its vivid celebration of paradox and hybridity
in the encounter of East and West, *Video Night* communicates a strong

sense of what Iain Chambers has called the 'Eurocentric domestication of space.'"[82] That domestication becomes most visible in Iyer's conclusions about his own cosmopolitan subjectivity. Despite his apparent comfort with a performative sense of self – "in one country I found myself an American journalist, in another a former British schoolboy, in yet another a homecoming Indian relative and in a fourth a plain tourist" – the once restless Iyer seeks an idyllic life removed from cultural complexity (26). "It was only when I returned home that I felt homesick," he writes, "not just for the gentleness and grace that I had found in many parts of Asia, but also, and more deeply, for the gentler self it had found in me. It was not corruption that stayed with me from my travels, but purity" (363). While finishing the book, he decides "to put my visions of Japan to the test" through the distinctly Western dream of living "a life of Thoreauvian quiet" abroad.[83] In that desire, he shows himself vulnerable to a variant of the fashion he describes glibly in *Video Night*: "Japan was fast becoming the Paris of the '80s, the place where the young went to be young" (361).[84]

More than a decade later, Japan his primary residence, Iyer revisits themes of globalization and displacement in *The Global Soul: Jet Lag, Shopping Malls, and the Search for Home* (2000).[85] Writing of *Video Night* and *Global Soul*, Lisle argues that "cosmopolitans like Iyer define, decide and ultimately erase cultural difference on their own particular terms while claiming to base these judgements on universal criteria."[86] In this regard, Iyer, whose attention to his own subjectivity often occludes critical observation, proves less skeptical about narrative authority than Fleming's formally self-conscious narrator and less concerned with the ethical consequences of representation than Auden and Isherwood. The final line of *Video Night* demonstrates this by equating Iyer's own elective quest for "home" with the uncertain existence of Ead, a Bangkok bar girl with a "broken heart" and a taste for Western goods who has returned to her rural village of necessity (308). He imagines her there "alone with her thoughts" and ambitions: "And I realized, when I did, that I had never left Asia at all; while she, like all the others, could never quite go back" (373, 374). Despite his deep immersion in a postcolonial heteroglossia in which, in Kwame Anthony Appiah's words, "we are all already contaminated by each other" in complex, inequitable ways, in Iyer's narratives his affinity for order, purity, and having the last word prevails.[87]

Travel narrative from the 1920s to the present participates in the literary innovations best-known in other narrative genres, particularly fiction. It owes much to modernism, which allows writers to open up an exhausted narrative form and reinvent it as a means of representing critical, subjective spectatorship of a world undergoing radical change. Largely abandoning the vantage point from the summit, with its claim to mastery over all that lies below them, travel narrators turn instead to the critical insights available on the ground and in the street. Such innovations make it possible for the travel genre to take on difficult, politically complex themes by offering a firsthand view from the frontlines, in narratives of the subjective experience of chaotic historical transformations. The following chapters explore these developments in detail.

CHAPTER 4

Nostalgia and the Spectacle of Modernity

> One could not help wondering about the Tibetans away to the south.... They shut themselves up in their mystical Buddhism and only allow the twentieth century to penetrate drop by drop, so as to be assimilated gradually. On the other hand, Siberia in the north, under the lash of the second Five Years Plan, is being mechanized. What, exposed between the two influences, and still Moslem, is Central Asia going to do? Will it revolt against the priests or against the agents of Russian manufactured goods through whom its own artisan class is disappearing? Serving alternately as a Chinese frontier against the hordes of the Occident and as a buffer for Russia against the growing imperialism of Japan, is it possible for it to become independent and remain true to itself?
>
> Ella Maillart (1937)[1]

In the twentieth century, travel narrative reasserts its cultural significance by personalizing contemporary geopolitical spectacle. In 1907, Gertrude Bell described the dilemma of the traveler who had no new information to report, only personal experience. Within a decade, however, the First World War and the Russian Revolution signaled the onset of an era of profound geopolitical upheaval that would continue through the Second World War, independence movements, the creation of regimes, and the collapse of empires. There was suddenly much to understand as Europe's internal relations and its relations with the larger world changed rapidly and chaotically. The travel narrative finds new purpose as a means of observing modernity's effects abroad and explaining them to home audiences uncertain whether such changes are to be celebrated or mourned. Modernization, cultural transformation, and the violence consequent to geopolitical events become significant concerns in the genre that persist to the present. In narratives about travels with the Arab revolt, through the new Soviet state, across the frontlines of the Chinese civil war, inside regions officially closed or nations newly open, and into twenty-first-century wars "on terror," writers from

Europe and North America narrate the consequences of modernity and globalization through the firsthand observations of a critical spectator.

These upheavals signaled the spectacular entrance into modernity of nations, regions, and peoples that Europeans had long imagined as existing in some earlier stage of – or outside – history. To understand the genre's concern with contemporary spectacle as an important part of its evolution thus involves rethinking the nostalgia for imagined worlds that recurs in travel narrative. Why do modern travelers often narrate their experiences in terms of nostalgia for a world prior to modernization, global diaspora, and global war?[2] If not explicitly anti-modern, twentieth-century travel narrative is nonetheless often preoccupied with imagined worlds *before*: before whichever war is, for a particular place, The War; before urbanization or modern technology; before the end of empires, or beginning; before so many narratives had been written. Many writers narrate quests for pastoral forms of life that they suppose will be unmarked by the malaise of the metropolitan center. Barry Curtis and Claire Pajaczkowska astutely describe the logic of such nostalgia, which blurs historical understanding with subjective desire:

> Travellers and tourists seek places of "unspoilt" beauty.... The unravaged haunts of beauty offer an experience of time before the vitiating effects of modernity and all the losses of innocence that it entails. The journey and its destination are often described as a passage through symbolic time.... The historic past in all its sedimented inevitability is sought in relation to a personal, pre-emptive moment – the Arcadian prelude to industrialization, the innocent hedonism of the primitive, precolonial world, and the unity of self which preceded adulthood and modern self-consciousness.[3]

Thus Swiss writer Ella Maillart, whose disenchantment with the metropolitan West spurs her to travel in Asia, explains herself in *Turkestan Solo* (1934): "Wherever I go, it is always the secret of ... simple, straightforward races that I seek, peoples whom a fair sky is sufficient to content. Only by returning to their way of living, can we ever hope to find a way out of the bog in which we vainly stumble."[4] Such sentiments persist: more than half a century later, American Mary Morris, "weary of life in New York," travels "in search of a place where the land and the people and the time in which they lived were somehow connected – where life would begin to make sense to me again."[5] This sense that travel promises a privileged access to a prelapsarian world is especially evident in the surprising number of writers who seek to recapitulate famous journeys known from earlier travel books, as though the imprimatur of a more pristine time will guarantee the quality of the experience.

Scholars have rightly made much of these preoccupations. Patrick Holland and Graham Huggan, for instance, discuss the tendency for travel writers to seek "solace for a troubled present in nostalgic cultural myths" by invoking what Ali Behdad calls "belatedness" and what Renato Rosaldo terms "imperialist nostalgia."[6] Scholars sympathetic with the genre's conventions, such as Paul Fussell, as well as those critical of its ethics, such as Edward Said and Debbie Lisle, often give its nostalgia center stage.[7] Yet as Maillart and Morris demonstrate – and Curtis and Pajaczkowska make explicit – nostalgia occurs in, and must be understood in, the cultural and political contexts of modernity. For as Svetlana Boym explains, nostalgia, "like progress, is dependent on the modern conception of unrepeatable and irreversible time." Once thought to be a distinctly "European disease," it comes in many variants, from the original mourning for a distant homeland to a deep longing for lost times and places, from idealizing what once was to wistfully imagining what might have been.[8] Nostalgia signals the complexity of the present. A powerful strategy for constructing history, it privileges some stories and effaces others, mixing cultural and political imperatives as it fixes the past in narratives salient for the present.[9] Nostalgia is a means of grappling with modernity's consequences, a subjective response to the spectacle of change, a prerogative of cultures that consider themselves advanced, a practice intrinsic to modern life: to "have" nostalgia is to "be" modern.

John Frow argues that modernity typically defines itself by constructing a mythical relation between "modernity" and "tradition," with the former standing for the present, the latter for a sacralized, nostalgic version of the past. Modernity's "structural oppositions" are "potentially endless but formally homologous":

> [a]uthentic and inauthentic experience; community and society; organic and mechanical solidarity; status and contract; use value and exchange value.... The relations between traveler and tourist, between the exotic and familiar, between immediacy and the forms of human association belong to this structure, and they continue to operate as powerful experiential categories.[10]

In this discursive structure, nostalgia is inherently reactionary; it exists counter to modernity. Yet as a cultural practice, twentieth-century nostalgia proves to be "an irreducibly plural phenomenon" that "takes on very different forms and dimensions."[11] In fact, recent scholarship argues that nostalgia can be a constructive, even radical mode of engagement with modernity that is oriented toward improving the future rather than idealizing the past. In their work on "generations of nostalgia" among refugees from Nazism, Marianne Hirsch and Leo Spitzer describe these divergent views: on the one hand, nostalgia as "indiscriminate idealization" that can be not only escapist but dangerous; on the other, nostalgia as "a resistant relationship to the present, a 'critical utopianism' that imagines a better future."[12] Travel narratives demonstrate nostalgia's irreducible complexity, for they both invoke and question modernity's "structural oppositions" at every turn, particularly when they take cultural and political change as central themes. To read travelers' nostalgia without reading its production through modernity thus elides its significance in twentieth-century travel narrative. It is to privilege the romantically anachronistic over the politically engaged, with Fussell, or to take unreflective escapist tales to be representative of a genre, with Lisle. To do so is to deny the significance of the travel genre's many experimental texts and serious meditations on the consequences of cultural chaos and war.

Modernity – as the context in which critical observation occurs and as a spectacle to be seen – becomes a fundamental preoccupation of travel writers in the twentieth century. Edward Said famously argues that the recurrent trope of eighteenth- and nineteenth-century travel narrative is timelessness, with the world beyond Europe excluded from history.[13] In the twentieth century, however, even narratives framed as quests for a pastoral freedom from urban malaise acknowledge that modernity cannot be evaded and that its pervasive effects require interpretation. Nostalgia often signals the scale of spectacular change that travelers can neither negate nor manage. Maillart's desire for simple rural life, for instance, comes entwined with serious interest in the effects of Soviet collectivization, which brings "schools, hospitals, newspapers, wireless, tractors, and the cinema" to Central Asia, where "Mohammedans are rising in revolt."[14] Significantly, many travel narratives explicitly take modernity's transformations as their primary concerns: writers travel to observe wars, cultural revolutions, and globalization firsthand. (Auden and Isherwood are neither the first nor the last to "journey to a war"; Iyer's interest in the reach of mass culture is not unique.) In Colin Thubron's analysis, such mutability "haunts" twentieth-century travel narrative, which acknowledges the irreversibility of change with a mixture of nostalgia about the almost-past and curiosity about the future-in-the-making. The traveler

> knows that his moment is fleeting. He encounters a culture at an instant of transition (since everything is in transition) and knows that if he returns next year things will be different. So he catches the moment on the wing, and stops it in Time. In Norman Lewis's *Golden Earth* [1952], for instance,

we see a Burma, just post-war, which has since vanished for ever.... A feeling of mutability haunts many travelogues. The traveler moves in the past tense (probably), not the present of the guidebook or the academic study – recording not what necessarily is, but what for an instant was.[15]

In a century of unceasing, chaotic change, the travel narrative takes the vexed temporality of modernity as its subject, seeking to witness the present as it becomes past and to read signs of possible futures.

This chapter and the next examine the travel narrative's critical engagement with modernity, first as a spectacle the Western traveler experiences abroad and then as a labyrinth of perpetual war that neither traveling observer nor observed can escape. War and the collapse of empires accelerate the transformation of cultures and landscapes that travelers already experience as overdetermined "textual *zones*" built of "several different kinds of knowledge: historical, political, anthropological, cultural, mythical, and experiential."[16] The geopolitical changes that challenge Europeans' assumed right to represent simultaneously throw their prior knowledge into question, compelling them to consider modernity's consequences anew. If, as Paul Smethurst notes, imperialist travel writing uses "mobility in the service of empire," twentieth-century travel narratives about cultural and political upheaval might be understood to use mobility in the service of mutability, as a means of making sense of change *in medias res*.[17] From the 1920s onward, the travel genre finds new serious purpose: to narrate large-scale transformations through the mobile critical spectator, who goes to the frontlines to experience firsthand "what for an instant was" and speculate what may become. Travel becomes a means of understanding modernity's global reach through observing its irruptions and metamorphoses abroad. Narrative makes visible the ethical consequences of revolution and capitalism far from the Western metropolis: in the cities of the Soviet Union, the deserts of Arabia, the villages of Central Asia.

Travel narratives about the new Union of Soviet Socialist Republics written in the late 1920s and early 1930s demonstrate the genre's new critical purpose particularly well. The Soviet social experiment and the state's ambitious plans for modernization fascinated and alarmed Western observers. Inventing itself at Europe's edge, in a place long thought both spiritual and dangerous, the Soviet Union offered mutability and spectacle on a monumental scale. Histories, novels, and travel accounts had long depicted Russia as a site of extremes, capable of civilization (and thus of being European) yet at heart barbaric (or at best incomprehensible). At the time of the revolution, Western images of Russia combined tropes of mysteriousness and difference known from Astolphe de Custine's influential travel account *La Russie en 1839* with newer iterations drawn from the novels of Dostoevksy and Tolstoy.[18] Intellectuals and popular writers, leftists and conservatives alike sought to go to the Soviet Union to observe history intensified, view the future in the making, and write what they saw. Some, such as Theodore Dreiser, went as guests of the state; others, like Walter Benjamin, traveled on their own initiative. Gradually, as the new state stabilized and received formal recognition from Western nations, travel became easier and an obligatory itinerary emerged: Lenin's tomb, Soviet schools, the state apparatus, collective farms, dam construction on the Dnieper River, and an autonomous republic or two.[19] Travelers' politics and motives varied from idealistic sympathy with the revolution's ambitions to opportunism to deep anxiety about the emergence of a new kind of political state. Some hoped to find the new Jerusalem, others to see the Russia they had imagined from literature before it disappeared.[20] Travel books proliferated wildly: by 1933, Peter Fleming could joke that he had stayed in Moscow for "four days, or nearly twice the length of time considered necessary by those intending to write a book on Modern Russia."[21]

In this historical moment, writers from across the political spectrum share the conviction that the transformation of Russia matters not just for its own citizens but for themselves: to see the spectacle there unmediated, they argue, is necessary for understanding the future of the West. Serious travelers who value "the inheritance of European humanism" must concern themselves with Russia, Robert Byron declares in *First Russia, Then Tibet* (1933), for "[t]he forces at work are older than the Revolution, and will long survive it.... Hence the shock of their emergence and the universal curiosity as to their future part in history."[22] Such curiosity cannot be sated by the new media of newsreels and film alone, journalist Ada Chesterton explains in *My Russian Venture* (1931), because they present only selected, distanced fragments of the real: "though impressed, we are keenly conscious of how much remains unshown. In the throes of earth-shaking experiment, with humanity itself uprooted, Russia excites a persistent interest which the most inveterate propaganda for or against the Soviet cannot still." To comprehend the "world-historical experiment" fully, the wary Western traveler must observe firsthand, unconstrained by the Soviet state. "I desired only to see and hear and judge for myself," Chesterton writes, "without guidance and quite unsupervised."[23] Walter Benjamin, who explores Moscow in 1927 "in the manner of a Baudelairean *flâneur*," finds vignettes through which to explain complex social realities in everyday life on the street: "the complete interpenetration of technological and primitive modes of life, this world-historical experiment in the new

Russia, is illustrated in miniature by a streetcar ride."[24] A Marxist sympathetic with Soviet ambitions, Benjamin often uses such quotidian detail to contrast social conditions in Moscow with those in modern Europe. An "astonishing" mix of "naïve desire for improvement" and "boundless curiosity and playfulness" drives the immediate transformation: "Each thought, each day, each life lies here as on a laboratory table. And as if it were a metal from which an unknown substance is by every means to be extracted, it must endure experimentation to the point of exhaustion. No organism, no organization, can escape this process."[25] However, Byron, a traveler known for his appreciation of Byzantine art, takes a different stance. Far more skeptical about the experiment, he views it as a moment in the long evolution of civilizations: his hope is to see Russia "not as reactionaries and enthusiasts both see her, in ethical relation to the present, but in cultural relation to the future." The truly extraordinary phenomenon, he argues, is not Bolshevism itself, but historical change:

> Russia can give much to the traveler who wishes to enlarge his experience and knows how to do so by seeing things not as he wishes them to be, but as they are: Past, present, and future exhibit a continuous interaction, rapid and conscious as a film, whose novelty and scale are equaled in no other part of the contemporary world. I found little time for dislikes. I could only observe and be thankful that such a spectacle had not been denied me.[26]

Though their politics differ, the earnest journalist, the Marxist flâneur, and the aesthetic traveler each view Russia's radical transformation as a spectacular event, one that compels them to devise critical stances from which to comprehend and narrate.

Byron's use of "spectacle" to describe the "continuous interaction" of past, present, and future in the Soviet Union reveals the complex ways that tumultuous geopolitical transformations fascinate Western travelers. Spectacle has been much studied as a modern form of presentation orchestrated to specific ends, seen in public displays as varied as Britain's Great Exhibition of 1851, "world's fairs," Nazi rallies, and popular history as presented in wax museums and films.[27] Thomas Richards, for instance, analyzes Victorian exhibitions and imperial imagery to demonstrate how spectacle serves nineteenth-century capitalism as "a theater through which it might reproduce its fundamental imperatives in a striking and memorable way" and thus effectively create "a truly national commodity culture."[28] Said specifically characterizes the relation between nineteenth-century European writers and the space of the Orient as spectacular in nature. In the narratives of Richard Burton, Gustave Flaubert, and others, he argues, "the Orient is *for* the European observer": such texts present the Orient as "spectacle, or *tableau vivant*" staged before the observer in encyclopedic display.[29] The "*spectacular* form," in his analysis, manages the "*epistemological* difficulty" of cultural difference through clichéd, disciplined formulations of "the exotic and strange"; the understanding it produces is achieved at the price of barring "the Westerner's full participation." Such a relation privileges assertions of "comprehensive vision" over narration of diffuse, historically specific experience.[30] "Spectacle" thus effectively characterizes both a mode of presentation and the mode of perception that it creates, each comprehensive in ambition.[31]

To identify an event or experience as spectacular is to name the epistemological challenge that it poses to comprehension and narration. Jonathan Crary argues that spectacle's most crucial consequence lies not in the mode of perception it produces, but in the "fundamental reorganization of the subject" that follows.[32] Crary identifies a critical genealogy centered on the historical conjuncture of the "technological perfection" achieved by synchronizing image and sound in film and television and the rapid ascent of fascism and Stalinism, which make strategic use of these new media to "incarnat[e] models of the spectacle." "The full coincidence of sound with image, of voice with figure," Crary writes, "not only was a crucial new way of organizing space, time, and narrative, but it instituted a more commanding authority over the observer, enforcing a new kind of attention."[33] In his analysis, these newly intensified forms of spectacle have the capacity to obliterate individual perception – a concern first articulated by Benjamin, whose *Arcades Project* of the late 1920s and 1930s considers the consequences of urbanization, mass media, and modes of observation, including flânerie. The reconfiguration and proliferation of spectacle produces a "sweeping remaking of the observer" that threatens sustained attention and comprehension, "a crisis in perception itself." Spectacle's greatest danger, in Crary's account, lies in the possibility that it can produce a present that obliterates historical knowledge. But siding with Benjamin's critique over Guy Debord's nostalgic pessimism, he speculates that spectacle's effects may be disrupted strategically "through counter-memory and counter-itineraries."[34]

By calling attention to spectacle's reciprocal reorganizing of human observers, space, time, and narrative, Crary identifies what is at stake when writers create vantage points from which to write the calamitous history-in-the-making of the twentieth century. The spectacular forms of representation that Said finds in earlier travel accounts have considerable purchase because they promise the security of comprehensive vision from a safe remove. To do so, they figure the world as lying before the observer, static and knowable. But in an era of "world-historical" change, panoramic vision from a position of safety no longer suffices, for it no longer persuades: to understand mutability, one must see for oneself and narrate while both observer and event are in motion. "Being a spectator of calamities taking place in another country," as Susan Sontag explains, "is a quintessential modern experience" potentially fraught with epistemological and ethical consequence.[35] How to be a spectator – responsively and ethically – concerns many twentieth-century writers who take historical tumult and violence as their subjects. In travel narratives about geopolitical transformation, their focus alternates between Europeans as anxious observers and complex phenomena that they cannot fully comprehend, immediate experience and its consequential relation with past and future. For these travelers, the apposite analogue for "seeing things … as they are," in Byron's words, can no longer be the static *tableau vivant* but rather the new medium of film, capable of showing history as "continuous interaction." Film's narrative capacity trumps the frozen moment of the photograph (interestingly, this occurs at the same time as anthropology comes to value mobile observation in the field over the fixed vantage point of home).[36]

This chapter examines texts by T. E. Lawrence, Ella Maillart, and Colin Thubron that aim to narrate the experience of geopolitical transformation on the ground rather than from a static vantage point secured by European expertise. Each finds the cultural consequences of modernity's rapid, uncertain changes compelling in ways that unsettle the observer, push familiar assumptions to the limit, and require novel narrative means. Lawrence finds representing his wartime travels in alliance with Arabs doubly challenging. Anguished by British abandonment of the revolt after spending three years "in the naked desert, under the indifferent heaven," he seeks to write frankly about the chaos of war and his own irreversible transformation, for his experience has "quitted me of my English self, and let me look at the West and its conventions with new eyes" (29, 31). At the same time, his reflective, often melancholy narrator must compete with the spectacular image of Lawrence as costumed historical actor already widely known from newsreels. Maillart and Thubron each travel to experience the cultural and economic consequences of revolutionary transformations in Asia. For Maillart, who seeks an alternative to metropolitan modernity in the far reaches of the Soviet Union and China, the chaotic realities of modernization and 1930s politics intrude on pastoral dreams. By traveling independently among the peoples of Central Asia, however, she hopes to obtain a fuller comprehension of present and future than that promulgated as the official line. Thubron, haunted by mutability, writes of peoples in flux in the decade after the Soviet collapse, rewriting past and future through competing nostalgic narratives, some for an imagined Islamic "time before frontiers," others for the security of authoritarian rule.[37] Reinventing themselves in a globalized world, many long for the immediate pleasures of Western capitalism that Thubron himself travels to understand in the larger context of modernity.

Seven Pillars of Wisdom: A Triumph

Seven Pillars of Wisdom, a remarkable "vast labyrinth of a book," comprises nearly 700 pages of text and – in the original edition – more than 125 paintings, drawings, maps, and photographs, many in color.[38] Lawrence's first-person narrative of his wartime experiences in Arabia juxtaposes scenes of political maneuvering with ethnographic descriptions, moments of camaraderie with pages of earnest introspection. He recounts traveling in costume yet knowing it unwise to assume "the privileges of both societies," learning to lead men when he prefers books, and feeling himself to be an "empty soul" and "godless fraud" (254, 502, 548). The book's "sophisticated, eclectic" visual art, overseen by Eric Kennington, complements its prose: formal portraits of Arabs and Englishmen, Vorticist-inspired illustrations, evocative drawings "reflecting states of mind," and photographs of Jidda and Damascus.[39] Decorative capital letters open every chapter and each page beginning with a new paragraph, with occasional odd turns of phrase devised to ensure that sentences begin with specific letters and paragraph and page endings coincide. Yet *Seven Pillars'* textual and visual modernism belies this ordered surface. The opening leaf, an elaborate Kennington woodcut titled "The Eternal Itch," depicts the world as a "Boschian landscape of human torment and folly" filled with faceless beings and disparate images: warfare, primitive rites, a gramophone, sport, and violent death.[40] In watercolors and drawings with titles such as "Strata," "Thinking," and "Nightmare," Kennington symbolically imagines Lawrence's conflicted state of mind; in comic line drawings, he satirizes his rhetorical posture. In Dennis Porter's words, *Seven Pillars* presents itself, text and image, as "a complexly determined product of the early twentieth century, characterized by heterogeneity and fragmentation."[41]

Despite *Seven Pillars'* complexity, the cultural contexts in which it first appeared have constrained its reception ever since. Well before Lawrence's narrative reached even private audiences, Lawrence the man and his wartime actions had been made into public spectacle by American journalist Lowell Thomas. Thomas's illustrated lecture "With Allenby in Palestine" filled packed halls in London in 1919 and installments of his celebratory *With Lawrence in Arabia* appeared in *The Strand Magazine* in 1920. *The Strand* advertised Thomas's account as "The Greatest Romance of Real Life ever told"; he portrayed Lawrence as "a modern Arabian knight."[42] Distinguishing Lawrence from the spectacular "Lawrence" became such a preoccupation that when *Seven Pillars* finally appeared in 1926, with a military abridgement, *Revolt in the Desert*, forthcoming, the *Times* published an "account of the history and the nature of the singular original ... to correct legends long current and to preclude others still unborn."[43] Graham Dawson observes that *Seven Pillars* can be read as Lawrence's effort "to elicit recognition of himself as a man more complex than Thomas's adventure hero," and indeed the text's comic drawings of Lawrence in Arab dress, which exaggerate his short physical stature, effectively debunk Thomas's larger-than-life imagery.[44] Reviews opened with obligatory references to the writer's notoriety. Herbert Read hopes futilely that "topical interest in Colonel Lawrence's book will have subsided" by the time his review appears in 1928, but even in 1935, when the public edition appeared shortly after Lawrence's accidental death, his narrative still competed with his reputation.[45] The *Times Literary Supplement* review, "Lawrence of Arabia," evokes "the thick-spun legends that enveloped in veils of mystery one of the most remarkable men of the century."[46] E. M. Forster opens his review by pointedly discounting the myth: "The little fellow who is labeled for posterity as Lawrence of Arabia hated the title." Forster concedes that critics can only hope to "protect him from the sharks" and "governesses," for "legend will probably flourish" even as text and man are "analyzed, estimated, claimed."[47] Forster was prescient: Lawrence as historical figure has continued to overshadow *Seven Pillars* as text, with literary and cultural studies concerning themselves primarily with his veracity, psyche, and sexuality.[48]

On a cursory reading, *Seven Pillars* resembles late nineteenth-century travel narrative, with such documentary features as ethnographic and historical overviews, journey maps, synopses and itineraries, and fact-laden appendices. Lawrence explicitly invokes British predecessors: Charles Doughty, who had "first understood" the significance of Wadi Hamdh, "the greatest valley in Arabia"; and "Palgrave, the Blunts, and Gertrude Bell amongst the storied travellers" who have crossed the Great Nefudh, whose company he would enter were "business" not at hand (158, 250).[49] He credits Bell with introducing him to Faiz el Ghusein, who becomes secretary to Emir Feisal, and borrows her title, "the desert and the sown," to describe "[t]he difference between Hejaz and Syria" (76, 328). He is candid about his geopolitical ambitions:

> All men dream: but not equally. Those who dream by night in the dusty recesses of their minds wake in the day to find that it was vanity: but the dreamers of the day are dangerous men, for they may act their dream with open eyes, to make it possible. This I did. I meant to make a new nation, to restore a lost influence, to give twenty millions of Semites the foundations on which to build an inspired dream-palace of their national thoughts. (24–25)

The subtitle, "A Triumph," suggests an unambiguous journey undertaken by a "man of action," with "a theme ready and epic to a direct eye and hand" (549). This is the analysis Said advances, reading Lawrence as instrumental agent and taking *Seven Pillars* as evidence for his own larger argument about imperial hegemony. Although he observes that Lawrence's work demonstrates "the conflict between narrative history and vision," he quickly concludes that the conflict ends with narrative defeated.[50]

From the beginning of *Seven Pillars*, however, Lawrence signals that his experiences – and, necessarily, his narrative – differ from those of his predecessors. He positions the narrator so frankly in the introductory chapter that he withheld it from the subscription edition (it was restored to the text several years after his death).[51] In wartime, Lawrence explains, as Britain's "essential insincerity" toward the Arabs fractured their shared dream and compromised his own position, he found himself "continually and bitterly ashamed" by his role and began in his official reports "to conceal the true stories of things, and to persuade the few Arabs who knew to an equal reticence" (25, 26). Now, Lawrence determines to write "a narrative of daily life, mean happenings, little people": not an official history of the spectacle made famous by Thomas, but a narrative of his own subjective observations (24). "In this book," he explains, "I mean to be my own judge of what to say" (26). In the text that follows, the narrator's depictions of peoples and places and stories of military action come intermingled with anxious introspection and startling directness that are utterly modernist. He opens the first chapter by reflecting on the madness "inherent in our circumstances" as men driven by "a purpose so ravenous that it devoured all our strength" (29). He envisions their journey as a secular inversion of pilgrimage:

> My thoughts as we went were how this was the pilgrim road, down which, for uncounted generations, the people of the north had come to visit the

> Holy City, bearing with them gifts of faith for the shrine; and it seemed that the Arab revolt might be in a sense a return pilgrimage, to take back to the north, to Syria, an ideal for an ideal, a belief in liberty for their past belief in a revelation. (78)

A modern man who has preferred "the theory and philosophy of warfare especially from the metaphysical side" to soldiering, he seeks "the equation between my book-reading and my movements" now that circumstance places him in the field (188).

Late in *Seven Pillars*, Lawrence's narrator explains that by casting a man who had longed "for the power of self-expression in some imaginative form" as "a man of action" in the Arab Revolt, historical "accident, with perverted humor," has offered him an epic theme. But he must refuse, for "[t]he epic mode was alien to me, as to my generation" (549). Instead, he devises a narrative suited to the contradictions and uncertainties of his experience. Once a dreamer, then a skeptic among believers, the narrator finds that their success leaves him melancholy rather than triumphant. On the eve of the entry into Damascus he reflects:

> After supping I tried in the blankness to think forward: but my mind was a blank, my dreams puffed out like candles by the strong wind of success. In front was our too-tangible goal: but behind lay the effort of two years, its misery forgotten or glorified. Names rang through my head.... Yet the men had changed. Death had taken the gentle ones; and the new stridency, of those who were left, hurt me. (638)

His narrative ends anticlimactically, in the chaotic aftermath of a supposed victory he finds hollow. While they discuss "ceremonial antics a world of work awaited, inside and outside": creating a "façade" of order in war-torn Damascus, restoring public services and the rule of law, burying the decaying corpses of the dead (648, 651). He finds himself lonely at the mu'adhdhin's call to prayer on the "first night of perfect freedom," "the event sorrowful and the phrase meaningless"; when the work is done, Lawrence, "ragged nerves ... jangling" asks "leave to go away" (652, 658, 660).

Though *Seven Pillars* is contemporary with *Ulysses*, alludes to *The Waste Land* and *Portrait of the Artist as a Young Man,* and self-consciously privileges subjective perception over the God's eye view, few analyses have explicitly considered it to be modernist.[52] The critical tendency has been to read the narrative's heterogeneity and fragmentation as evidence of the author's psychological state rather than as purposive elements. In such readings, these characteristics are flaws to be rectified or problems to be explained. Read, for instance, dismisses *Seven Pillars* as unheroic, visually "incongruous," and "difficult to bring into any definite focus. So much of it is vivid, but the author's mind behind it all is dark, and obscured by divided aims." He unabashedly prefers an epic hero like Doughty, "a great patriarch among men … inquiring but full of certainty," to "Colonel Lawrence … a soldier spoilt by introspection and self-analysis; a man with a load on his mind."[53] Reading *Seven Pillars* chiefly in terms of Lawrence's psyche remains the dominant strategy even decades later, fueled further by biographical disclosure in the 1970s. Even Clare Brandabur and Nasser al-Hassan Athamneh, who celebrate *Seven Pillars*' "imaginative" admixture of confession, autobiography, and romance seventy years after Read dismisses it, still understand Lawrence's literary work as evidence of "deep division of the self" and "self-loathing" over his Orientalist role. "Clearly," they conclude, "the opposition between 'vision' and 'narration' in *Seven Pillars* stems from an unresolved conflict in the author himself, a struggle which caused Lawrence terrible suffering and apparently led to his early death."[54] Such claims privilege biographical assumption over modernist complexity at every turn.

Reading *Seven Pillars* as a modernist narrative of chaotic geopolitical transformation, however, reveals its contradictions to be literary innovations that demonstrate the complexity of Lawrence's experience. No longer bound by the imperial discourse of official reports, Lawrence produces a text of "vast interior" and "contrary effects" in which his first-person narrator frankly recounts experiences that "quite upset his theories" about Arabs, warfare, Britain, and himself.[55] Forster praises him for struggling to create a form faithful to his experience's ambiguity and discontinuity:

> Here is a young man, describing himself as he was when still younger. He has discovered that he can lead an Arab army, fight, bluff, and spy, be hard and disciplinary, and this is exhilarating; but the course of his inner life runs contrary. That course is turbid, slow, weighted by remorse for victory, and by disgust against the body.

To answer "What is this long book about?" with "It describes the revolt in Arabia against the Turks as it appeared to an Englishman who took part in it," Forster explains, is to elide what matters most: "That is what the book is about, and *Moby Dick* was about catching a whale. For round this tent-pole of a military chronicle T. E. has hung an unexampled fabric of portraits, descriptions, philosophies, emotions, adventures, dreams."[56] The result – "something unique to our literature" – suits Lawrence's generation, which inhabits a world Forster characterizes as "this terrible modern mix-up."[57] The oscillations and dissonance of Lawrence's narrative represent the incoherence of his experience: he is an imperial actor deeply skeptical of empire, an intellectual who longs for liberation from his thoughts, a Briton dressed as a Bedouin who "never renounces his difference."[58] During a forced march from Azrak to Akaba, the narrator reflects:

> I seemed at last approaching the insensibility which had always been beyond my reach: but a delectable land: for one born so slug-tissued that nothing this side fainting would let his spirit free. Now I found myself dividing into parts. There was one which went on riding wisely, sparing or helping every pace of the wearied camel. Another hovering above and to the right bent down curiously, and asked what the flesh was doing.... [A] third garrulous one talked and wondered, critical of the body's self-inflected labour, and contemptuous of the reason for effort. (451)

Seven Pillars "may take the form of a journey that begins with a departure and ends with a return," Porter observes, "but such symbolic closure fails to reduce the contradictory energies that traverse it," produced through the "double overdetermination" of author and text.[59]

In this analysis, *Seven Pillars*' discursive shifts and unconventional visual art demonstrate a modernist understanding of the difficulty of ethical representation. For Lawrence, writing the spectacle of history-in-the-making is an act of stewardship that requires fidelity to Arab viewpoints as well as British, to thought and feeling as well as action. Time allows hindsight but does not simplify the responsibility: he writes and rewrites, asking military and literary figures to read his preliminary manuscript and – like other modernists – creating stories of origin that become part of the narrative itself.[60] Both engaged participant and critical observer, he seeks to narrate the messy truth of his experience as he perceives it, not tell a "romantic tale" (562). Such a project requires something beyond the prewar travel conventions ready at hand, though Lawrence does not abandon them wholesale. He depicts many distinct characters with nuance and empathy, from leaders such as Feisal and Auda abu Tayi to the Ageyli servant boys Farraj and Daud (though these depictions owe something to fiction, they are individualized actors rather than types).[61] Of Farraj's response to Daud's death, for instance, he writes, "I was not astonished to see Farraj look dark and hard of face, leaden-eyed and old, when he came to tell me that his fellow was dead; and from that day till his service ended he made no more laughter for us.... The others offered themselves to comfort him, but instead he wandered restlessly, grey and silent, very much alone" (508). Yet he makes predictable use of ossified conceptions of race and national character when he describes the Ageyl as "unthinking" and

Illustration 4. "A Literary Method" (Kennington), from Lawrence's *Seven Pillars of Wisdom*.

explains the political dynamic as one between Arab leaders with "completeness of instinct," and British officers with "centrifugal minds" (509, 214).[62] Lawrence sends Kennington to Arabia so that his color portraits will benefit from live sittings and firsthand experience. Yet *Seven Pillars* also caricatures nuanced portraiture by depicting "literary method" as entomology: Lawrence stands before a specimen frame, pinning each character in place (535) (see Illustration 4). Kennington's cartoon foregrounds the challenge of finding a vantage point by simultaneously showing Lawrence as "Lawrence," the character in Arab dress, skewered with his fellows in both armies, and as the Author, towering over them. In depicting authorship as visual arrangement, it echoes the narrator's descriptions of his "picture-making memory" and his role as the armies prepare for action: "My business was to see every one with news, and let him talk himself out to me, afterwards arranging and combining the truth of these points into a complete picture in my mind" (413, 600).

In *Culture and Imperialism*, Said argues that "the extremes of self-consciousness, discontinuity, self-referentiality, and corrosive irony, whose formal patterns we have come to recognize as the hallmarks of modernist culture," evidence the shocked response of European culture at the juncture when it can no longer escape the consequences of empire. Grouping Lawrence with Conrad, Forster, Joyce, and other modernists, he suggests that modernism's signature literary innovation is "a new encyclopedic form" of which *Seven Pillars* – like *Ulysses* – may be an instance. With "a circularity of structure, inclusive and open at the same time," and a "strange juxtaposition of comic and tragic, high and low, commonplace and exotic," this new form ironically attempts to contain difference by substituting aesthetic unity for "the once-possible synthesis of the world empires."[63] Said may well be right about both modernism and Lawrence's ambition – Forster observed that he "yearned to create a single work of art out of [his inner] life and out of his military experiences."[64] *Seven Pillars'* unprecedented juxtaposition of lengthy narrative with multiple forms of visual art proclaims its encyclopedic nature: Lawrence will represent his subjects fully, from every vantage point available. At the same time, the text's surface elements assert its aesthetic unity: the use of synopses at the beginning of each book, the visual features that echo the order of medieval texts, the singular subtitle, "A Triumph."

Whether encyclopedic modernist texts achieve the unity they proclaim, however, is questionable: as discussed in Chapter 2, critical accounts of modernist narration center on its compelling demonstration that "a consensus as to the nature of external reality" is impossible, for fragmentation undoes any assertion of unity.[65] Lawrence's narrator, looking back, concurs: he explains the anguish and disorientation that come from incessantly working to see the world complexly, "through the veils at once of two customs, two educations, two environments" (32). Even as *Seven Pillars* draws on the travel genre's conventions, it gives increasing precedence to subjective perception over the course of the narrative, disrupting his account of the campaign with long musings on "strangeness and pain," "free-will," "futility," and "myself" (31, 511, 552, 563). It oscillates between pragmatic, documentary language and a self-consciously literary "foregrounding of verbal signifiers," between evocative portraits of the external features of men and speculative drawings of their inner lives.[66] The text's visual depictions insist on Lawrence's multiplicity: he is an Oriental expert filled with disdain for "ordinary generals," an impassive public visage concealing chaos in "Strata," a dark cloud overshadowing the journey in "Thinking," a defenseless bare figure fleeing a monster in "Nightmare"

(320). Together, *Seven Pillars'* text and visual art constitute "a mélange of discontinuous, sometimes conflicting narratives."[67] Ambitiously encyclopedic rather than deliberately disjointed as the later *Journey to a War, Seven Pillars* deftly uses dissonance to represents the modernist spectator's subjective experience of history-in-the-making. Modernity's chaos prevails: for all his "riding a thousand miles each month upon camels: with added nervous hours in crazy aeroplanes, or rushing across country in powerful cars," Lawrence cannot control the spectacle before him (502). Any closure he might claim is uncertain, any triumph transient.

Turkestan Solo and *Forbidden Journey*

A member of the Swiss national hockey and ski teams, Maillart competed in sailing at the 1924 Paris Olympics, then dabbled in documentary filmmaking. Sharing the disillusionment and restlessness common among modernist intellectuals, she went to the Soviet Union in 1930, "ostensibly to do research for a book on Russian silent films."[68] Instead, Maillart ended up writing a book about her travels: *Parmi la jeunesse russe: de Moscou au Caucase* (1932). Its modest success allowed her to launch a career as a traveler who supported herself through writing.[69] An artless, often naïve account, it covers no original territory but helps to explain the recurrent themes of Maillart's most successful work, *Des Monts Célestes aux Sables Rouges/ Turkestan Solo: One Woman's Expedition from the Tien Shan to the Kizel Kum* (1934) and *Oasis interdites/ Forbidden Journey: From Peking to Kashmir* (1937).[70] Not literary by inclination or education, Maillart comes to present herself, as George Orwell would observe, as "the kind of person who never wants the journey to end, who is genuinely more interested in marching through empty steppes and past ruined temples than in getting home to write a book about it; but at the same time, of course, sufficiently civilized to retain a sense of strangeness in the wilderness."[71] Her narratives about travels in Central Asia demonstrate well the role nostalgia plays role in travelers' engagement with modernity and spectacular transformation.

In hindsight, Maillart described her first journey into the Soviet Union as a quest for an antidote to a political climate in which "[g]rowing uneasiness and lack of security seemed to confirm what Spengler had called the 'Decline of the West.'" Russia alone "seemed to have escaped from the general trend. Though opinions differed about its value, something new seemed to be taking place in the east. Why not go there?"[72] *Parmi la jeunesse russe* opens with a familiar theme: "il faudrait aller à Moscou;

les russes y vivent des heures inoubliables." On the train to Moscow she reflects:

> Je roule vers un pays dont je n'imagine rien. Trop de données opposes se sont rencontrées en moi et s'y sont annulées, y faisant le vide.... c'est ... une abstraction vers laquelle je vais: vers la plus téméraire experience des temps modernes.
>
> Je veux particulièrement connaître les aspirations nouvelles des jeunes, ceux de vingt ans, ceux qui ne connurent pas l'ancien monde, ceux pour qui le nouvel état semble être bâti.[73]

Once there, however, Maillart's narrator finds herself less intrigued by the lives of urban youth in Moscow than by the collision between modernization and rural life in the Caucasus, where collectivization aims to transform illiterate peasants into modern workers. Unlike Western observers such as American Margaret Bourke-White who celebrate Soviet industrialization, Maillart views these changes with caution. Bourke-White's photographs depict "the land of embryo industry": an "agricultural people who were striving to become industrialists" in a nation "trying to do an astonishing thing."[74] Maillart, however, finds that travel in mountain villages tempers her initial hope that industry will solve Russia's problems. She reconsiders her optimism after seeing the uneasy coexistence of superstition and secularism that rapid transformation produces. Her narrator observes a "curieux mélange de deux époques" in the discordant rites that commemorate the death of a young communist: his family constructs a mannequin of their lost son, complete with his revolver and books.[75] Eventually, Maillart speculates whether modernization is truly beneficial; perhaps, she concludes, the antidote for European decline is not an experimental utopia but rather a return to what she perceives as the simple purposiveness of rural life.

This modernist nostalgia becomes Maillart's signature concern in *Turkestan Solo* and *Forbidden Journey*. Disheartened by Europe's uncertainty and eager to escape urban materialism, in *Turkestan Solo* she "hasten[s] to take stock of what remains of the ancient life before modernity overtakes it" and to observe a way of life that might elude politics (171). Venturing deep into Russian Turkestan, she climbs Tien Shan and then travels to the ancient cities of Tashkent, Samarkand, and Khiva.[76] In *Forbidden Journey*, she travels west from Peking to Sian, across the desert into Sinkiang, and crosses the Hindu Kush into Kashmir. Each narrative juxtaposes Maillart's subjective reflections with cogent descriptions of the people she meets and places she experiences. Her narrator

wishes passionately to experience authentic ways of being untouched by
"the vitiating effects of modernity."[77] She romanticizes "the ways of the
nomads, ways that are as old as the world" and "crav[es] to understand
the thousands of diverse lives that make up humanity."[78] Her motives
more existential than ethnographic, she seeks a meaningful way to live.
"The nomad's life enthralls me," Maillart writes, for "[e]verything must
be relearnt again, before life can be truly gauged. What life is worth is
a conception we have all lost, more or less. But in contact with primitive, simple peoples, mountain-dwellers, nomads, and sailors, it is impossible to ignore the elemental laws. Life finds its equilibrium again."[79] The
"elemental laws" that she imagines urban Europeans to have lost value
physicality over social life, immediate experience over politics. Rooted in
stasis and continuity, they locate meaning in cyclical patterns rather than
the irreversible temporality of modernity. Having seen the consequences
of collectivization and dealt with Soviet and Chinese bureaucracies, she
envisions a life outside of geopolitical realities, free of restraint.

Yet the "equilibrium" that Maillart desires rests on contradiction:
she seeks to escape modernity but come to terms with it, to learn traditional ways of living while exercising utterly modern freedom herself.
In *Forbidden Journey*, she writes of long weeks traveling by horse with a
camel caravan:

> I loved the primitive way of living which gave one back that hunger that
> transforms every morsel one puts under one's tooth into solid satisfaction;
> the healthy weariness that made sleep an incomparable voluptuousness;
> and the desire to get on that found realization in every step one took.
>
> … I wanted to forget that we had, inevitably, to return home. I even lost
> the desire to return home. I should have liked the journey to continue for
> the rest of my life. There was nothing to attract me back to the west. I
> knew I should feel isolated amongst my contemporaries, for their ways had
> ceased to be my ways. (88–89)

Maillart understands her nostalgia to be a longing to forget the modernity of which she is constantly aware. Even as she savors the possibility of
discovery and cites tales from ancient history, the practical circumstances
of travel amidst cultural chaos require her to attend constantly to the present. As a European woman traveling alone in a Central Asia, the Maillart
of *Turkestan Solo* must respond frequently to queries about her marital
status. Although taken with the notion of "primitive" ways, she recognizes that the privileges modern women take to be theirs cause suspicion
by violating local custom. Knowing that her difference may increase the
risk of rape, she prudently carries neosalvarsan and a syringe in case she

contracts syphilis through "Mongolian trials and tribulations" (316–317). Some of Maillart's sharpest observations have to do with the consequences of the USSR's abrupt modernization for women. As she declares to a Soviet bureaucrat, she wants to go to Uzbekistan for its fabled past and, more urgently, to observe "the Mohammedan women in their harems before they have all been liquidated. And to get some idea what the liberation they owe to the Soviet Government has meant to them" (21–22). There she meets peasant women who now attend school, interviews factory workers, and befriends Maroussia, a dancer turned lorry-driver who hopes to become a mechanic. Liberation has been tumultuous: many Uzbek husbands object to women's independence, and Maroussia must fend off coworkers' sexual advances. When Maillart asks the director of an embroidery collective of 400 women about "the family dramas that they say take place in connection with unveiling," the "precise and intelligent" Muslim woman replies, "it's always the same story: 'I won't have you go out like that,' says the man. We've established a small court for dealing with these family differences. It's the husbands who have to be made to see reason.... But education will open their eyes in time" (223, 224). A keen observer of the local effects of geopolitics, Maillart intersperses passages of introspection with detailed accounts of the cultural consequences of conflict between a near-medieval "force of habit" and "the will to do that the Soviets have brought with them" (242).

Turkestan Solo and *Forbidden Journey* cast the European traveler's usual assumptions about mobility, ease of association, and narrative authority in sharp relief, for Maillart's insistence on crossing borders, visiting dissidents, taking photographs, and writing notes challenges the order of controlled societies and makes visible the instability of places riven by spectacular change. In *Turkestan Solo* she slips away from others in her party near the frontier between Kazakstan and Kirghizistan to visit a Trotskyist exile:

> My intention must be kept secret from my companions ... for they might not like it. They do not know I have no political convictions whatever, and that curiosity is merely my motive. Also they might be afraid of possible accusations of having taken a politically unsound person with them....
>
> ... If he is under observation I shall be caught, and my journey will end abruptly, then and there....
>
> But I am determined to risk it. The risk spurs me on. (42)

She takes chances by taking hundreds of photographs with her Leica camera, at times in violation of custom or government restriction, and by writing notes about her experiences. At one point, a Soviet officer

I REFILL MY LEICA

Illustration 5. Photo of Ella Maillart refilling her Leica, from Maillart's *Forbidden Journey.*

confiscates her camera. Later, detained by local authorities for not reg-
istering, she realizes that her possessions pose risks: "it will be easy for
them to find some photograph I should not have taken.... And all the
notes I left lying about! Have I at least destroyed the records of my visits
to the exiles?" (287).[80] Photography allows Maillart to document peoples
and places, yet it accentuates her difference when curious onlookers watch
her use the Leica or return her gaze through a dropped lens. Two photographs in *Forbidden Journey* dramatize this momentary reversal of spectator and spectacle. In one, she shows Mongolian men photographs from
Owen Lattimore's *Desert Road to Turkestan*, hoping the novelty will sate
their "insatiable curiosity" about her person and possessions; in another,
a crowd looks on as she refills the Leica, seated out of doors on rubble,
dressed in a plaid skirt (81) (see Illustration 5).[81]

   Turkestan Solo and *Forbidden Journey* narrate Maillart's travels as a critical spectator who, in Charles Forsdick's analysis, "favors a *flânerie* that
constantly defers the journey's end."[82] Although she prefers to travel independently, at a reflective pace, realities governing the movement of foreigners circumscribe her options. Each narrative opens with a problem:
what mixture of strategy and subterfuge will the journey require? The first
chapter of *Turkestan Solo*, "Lets and Hindrances," recounts a game of dog-
gedness and chance: Maillart petitions the Society of Proletarian Tourists

and calls on the People's Commissar for Justice and the Commissariat for Foreign Affairs, all in search of a way to travel to the Tien Shan. At last a random opportunity to join a mountaineering expedition allows her to obtain a visa to leave Moscow for Turkestan. Later, she frames the foreword to *Forbidden Journey* with a scene of her earlier disappointment on the USSR's eastern frontier:

> from the heights of the Celestial Mountains I could descry, on a plain far away and further still to the east, the yellow dust of the Takla Makan desert. It was China, the fabulous country of which, since my childhood, I had dreamed.... But I had found it impossible to secure the visa necessary to enter Chinese Turkestan ... isolated from the rest of the world owing to political troubles. If I went on I should be arrested at the first Chinese village. Sadly I retraced my steps, turning my back on the limitless unknown that beckoned. (xiii)[83]

Forbidden Journey begins with Maillart in Peking in 1935, undeterred by the list of Europeans recently expelled from Chinese Turkestan, an area now "more 'taboo' than ever" where the central government has no authority and "kidnappings and assassinations ... are always possibilities" (3, 4). These impediments only spur her on:

> The desire to undertake the journey to Turkestan took a firmer and firmer hold on me, and I began to perceive the means by which it might be realized.
>
> I must, above all, avoid the known routes. Following them, one was bound to be sent back. The thing was to chance entering Sinkiang at some point where there were not as yet any orders relating to foreigners; then, as quickly as possible, make for Kashgar on the north of the Pamirs, and there to put oneself under the protection of the British consul, so as to avoid being taken for a spy, as every foreigner was, and arrested. (5)

Peter Fleming, acquainted with Maillart from a chance meeting in London and collaboration as correspondents in Manchuria, is in Peking with similar ambitions. Recognizing they must take an unexpected route across the desert, the travelers strategically devise a plan built "in a ramshackle way on circumstance by opportunism and a little imagination"; reluctantly, they surrender the autonomy that each prefers in order to join forces.[84]

The old Etonian who appears in *Forbidden Journey*, Maillart's most nuanced and literary narrative, resembles the persona Fleming creates in his account of their journey, *News from Tartary* (1936), more than the celebrity who later appears in Auden and Isherwood's *Journey to a War*.[85] Maillart appreciates "Peter's brilliant intelligence, his faculty of being able to eat anything and sleep anywhere, and ... still more his horror of any distortion of facts and the native objectivity with which he recounted them" (8–9). He proves to be "the best of comrades," for she can "be absolutely frank" with him and admires his aplomb (147). They survive the physically arduous, politically difficult journey through "egotisms that worked together, each helping the other": Fleming, adept at cajolery, more than once "reverse[s] a situation which seemed more than dubious for us," Maillart handles their medical and veterinary crises with skill; he speaks some Chinese, she some Russian (148, 236). Although each chafes occasionally at the other's manner, they joke comfortably, like seasoned comrades. The alliance lasts without crisis through the seven months it takes to travel the 3,500 miles from Peking to Kashgar to India, crossing deserts and mountains by train, horse and donkey with camel train, and motor vehicle. They part company in Delhi when Fleming flies home on Imperial Airways, Maillart on Air France: her book ends with a photograph of the travelers smiling broadly at the airfield, Maillart in plaid skirt with her Leica, Fleming in pressed khakis with his pipe.

Fleming's presence in *Forbidden Journey* serves as a constant reminder of modernity's inescapability. His ease as an imperial subject contrasts starkly with Maillart's alienation: "we did not see things from the same angle" (88). Fleming's imagination is oriented toward England: he longs for the *Times*, reads Macaulay, and is "not a little moved at the sight" of a homemade Union Jack (186). His obligations back home drive them: he "wished to travel as quickly as possible.... Whereas I wanted to dawdle in my usual fashion, as if I had the whole of eternity before me" (9).[86] Maillart, for whom Europe "seem[s] so far away that it might as well be dead," longs to explore side valleys and savor local customs, but while she "dream[s] of discovering ... unknown ways of living," Fleming desires to kill "some rare bird for the Zoo" (98, 78). His haste exasperates her, and she "ma[kes] no bones about telling Peter what I thought of people who travelled too fast and took no time to learn anything about anything" (240). His presence compels her to acknowledge the placement in modernity that she cannot elude:

> Though I liked the companionship and it had considerably ameliorated the anxiety of our wait at Lanchow, it nevertheless deprived me of the greatest thrill the sense of discovery had given me on previous journeys. I had lost the intense joy, the intoxication, of blazing my own trail and the proud sense of being able to get through alone, to which I had become accustomed. Above all, a piece of Europe inevitably accompanied us through the mere fact of our association. That isolated us. I was no longer thousands of miles from my own world. I was not submerged by, or integrated into,

Asia. Travelling in company, one does not learn the language so quickly. The natives do not make their own of you. You penetrate less deeply into the life about you. (46)

The political turmoil that Maillart finds across "the Asiatic chessboard" conclusively precludes the romantic submersion in "a huge unmodernized stretch of territory" she once imagined (221, xvi). Having hoped to step outside history, she finds herself obligated to make sense of its consequences: "[A]t the heart of Asia, where I expected to find myself amongst poor men but free," she regrets, "I found economic slavery and national antagonism as strong as in any part whatsoever of the present-day world" (137). Here Maillart's perceptions differ most from Fleming's. *News from Tartary* aims both to tell a good travel story (Fleming never entirely discards his earlier persona) and to report, objectively, "the evidence of reliable people" regarding civil unrest in China and the intentions of the Soviet Union in Asia. It ends on a light note, as the disheveled travelers arrive in a hotel lobby in Srinagar where "Anglo-India, starched and glossy [in evening dress], stared at us with horror and disgust."[87] *Forbidden Journey*, in contrast, laments from the beginning that "[m]odern war, the necessity ... of militarizing a country if it was to maintain its independence ... was the West's gift to the Far East.... Progress indeed!" (18). Whereas Fleming provides political analysis, Maillart asks anxious questions: "What is going to happen? Did the Soviets ... fear England might get the upper hand in a Moslem republic in Turkestan? ... Heaven knows" (221).[88] Her narrative ends in sober recognition of geopolitical realities: with "[s]hadows of war ... hovering over Europe," the travelers must hurry home by air (298). This allows her to contrast the immersion of overland journeying with the spectacular, hurried view from above: having been "in the habit of moving at the same rate as people did a thousand years ago," she now finds herself "every day flying over new countries inhabited by different races. Centuries of history! Cradles of religions! They seemed to be huddled into a little space" (299). As the lights of Paris appear on the horizon, she suddenly understands, "with all the strength of my senses and intelligence, that Paris, France, Europe, the White Race, were nothing.... The something that counted in and against all particularisms was the magnificent scheme of things that we call the world" (299–300). Ever troubled by Europe's parochialism, Maillart uses the view afforded by the airplane to make a last gesture toward the equilibrium she has sought. Iterating her own sense of the interrelation of individual experience and geopolitical change, she views the modern world on the brink of global war with what Rebecca Walkowitz will later call critical cosmopolitanism.

The Lost Heart of Asia and *In Siberia*

The late-century traveler's "dilemma," Colin Thubron would explain in 1984, is that the "sense of the extraordinary is inevitably dimmed" once "[k]nowledge is on the end of a telephone, and the aeroplane has overseen everything." Yet in the decades between Lawrence's travels and Thubron's, violence had irreversibly transformed both the "flawed and disillusioned world" of Europe and the distant places that mobile observers would traverse: "[W]ithin thirty years after 1914 some seventy million people had been violently slain – and these not in Outer Mongolia but in the very heart of Western civilization. . . . The old dream of utopia has become the nightmare of the dystopia, the nuclear holocaust."[89] Unlike Lawrence and Maillart, who observe modernity's effects while still hoping that arcadian freedom may be possible outside Europe, Thubron travels through decidedly modern societies fissured by decades of violence and upheaval. Beginning in the late 1960s, he travels across Asia from the Levant to the farthest corners of Siberia, seizing the moments when war pauses or state control relaxes enough for a writer given to "[t]he frisson of solitary travel – travel in a boyish euphoria of self-sufficiency."[90] In the 1970s, he walks across Cyprus, where Greeks and Turks live in "nervous cohabitation"; in the 1980s, he travels alone by car in the pre-*glasnost* Soviet Union and by train, foot, and bicycle in pre-Tiananmen China; in the 1990s, he journeys through the remains of the Soviet empire; and in the new century, he retraces the ancient Silk Road through Iran and war-torn Afghanistan.[91]

The half-century following the Second World War offers myriad spectacles of cultural transformation as new nations emerge from old empires across Asia and Africa and state consolidation in the Soviet Union and China produces controlled societies whose scope, violence, and eventual collapse fascinate and frighten the West. In *The Lost Heart of Asia* (1994) and *In Siberia* (1999) Thubron narrates his travels in fledgling nations just emerging from the Soviet Union and in the isolated, vast eastern province of the newly open Russia. There he seeks to understand modernity writ large through the quotidian details of the transient present: the uneasy mix of old and new cultural loyalties in conditions of mutability, the modes of affiliation that work after politics and technology have separated people from places of origin. Thubron first traces out these themes a decade earlier in *Among the Russians* (1983) and *Behind the Wall: A Journey through China* (1987). Like Lawrence and Maillart, he seeks to immerse himself fully: he learns Russian; he learns Mandarin. Unlike Lawrence, whose narrative must handle his public role as well as his solitary reflection, and Maillart, who must write history-in-the-making in a world headed for war as well as her own story, Thubron enjoys the literary freedom to focus wholly on the subjective perceptions of the traveler and the strangers he meets. Though conscious of the scale of the changes he observes, he refuses spectacular representation in order to comprehend the consequences of cultural upheaval in individual lives. Discounting the grand view from above, his narratives recount his interactions with ordinary people who are living restless late modern lives amidst geopolitical uncertainty, hope, disillusionment, and fitful globalization. Though they follow geographical itineraries and chart the routes traveled, Thubron's narratives give precedence to the critical observer, suiting experience to narrative purpose by collapsing temporal fidelity and proceeding episodically. Breaks within chapters signal the end of one anecdote and the beginning of another more clearly than they do a night's rest or a week's travel onward. Salient historical and geographical details appear as the narrative requires, never as separate disquisitions. For the narrative through-line is the traveler's subjective coming-to-understand, his struggle to bridge the epistemological chasm between what he knows and what he hears, between his experiences of history and modernity and those of people he meets.

Thubron's travel narratives bear a distinctive signature: assured voice, comfortable erudition, and literary, even lyrical style.[92] Peter Hulme, writing of *In Siberia*, describes it well: "Although not without self-deprecating humour, Thubron's narrative persona radiates an unfussy authority: he knows the history, he speaks the language, he gets around without difficulty – but he flaunts nothing. His spare literary style, combined with modest hints of shyness and sensitivity, exude integrity."[93] The narrator's secure position permits him to acknowledge ambivalence and wander purposively without purpose. He begins *Among the Russians* by reflecting on his situation as a postwar British subject who travels alone to understand "this country I feared":

> I belonged to a generation too young to romanticize about Soviet Communism. Yet nothing in the intervening years had dispelled my childhood estrangement and ignorance. My mind was filled with confused pictures: paradox, cliché....
>
> ... And I was deeply prejudiced. Nobody from the West enters the Soviet Union without prejudice....
>
> But I think I wanted to know and embrace this enemy I had inherited. I felt myself, at least a little, to be on his side. Communism at once attracted and repelled me. Nothing could be more alluring to the puritan idealist

whose tatters (I suppose) hung about me as I took the road to Minsk; nothing more disquieting to the solitary. All my motives, when I thought about them, filled up with ambiguity.

As the genre's quintessential figure – a solitary observer – Thubron must explain his existence repeatedly to people he meets in collective societies: "Solitariness here is rare, odd. It was not catered for. I found myself apologizing for it."[94] Asked "are you a group?" and "are you alone?" almost daily, he finds himself the object of curiosity, his independence the sign of his difference. Thubron turns these queries, which reverse the roles of seer and seen, into an unanswered refrain that follows his persona on later journeys. In China, a Yangtze steamship radio operator intensifies the questioning: "'Why are you alone? . . . Aren't you with your work unit?' . . . 'Why aren't you married?'" "I had not the English, let alone the Mandarin, to answer this," he muses.[95] A decade later, a cynical assessor he meets in a Siberian village near the Mongolian border startles Thubron as he falls asleep by "ask[ing] out of the blue: 'And you? What are you doing here?'" This time, the narrator echoes the query and silently replies:

> What was I doing? My eyes opened on the night. I was trying to find a core to Siberia, where there seemed none; or at least for a moment to witness its passage through the wreckage of Communism – to glimpse that old, unappeasable desire to believe, as it fractured into confused channels, flowed under other names. Because I could not imagine a Russia without faith.
>
> But I said to him: 'I came to look at the grave-mounds of Pazyryk.' They had yielded the world's most intimate nomad artefacts. 'They're only ten miles from here. You know of them?'[96]

Such queries no longer truly surprise, for they are variations on the questions he seeks more obliquely to answer about the people among whom he travels. Thubron uses the moment to scrutinize his tendency to seek a still point of order beneath modernity's chaos.

The travel narrator who seeks to experience the moment of mutability in which past fractures into future must fight impulses to privilege the obvious over the evanescent, the stuff of legend over the ordinary. He must acknowledge what he observes though it refutes what he desires. Thubron – better versed in geography and history than many among whom he travels – repeatedly juxtaposes easy Western misreadings that would produce romantic spectacle with the uncertain confusion of life on the ground. Seeing families in Canton as they eagerly welcome expatriate relatives who bring consumer goods from Hong Kong, he reflects, "I watched them in selfish gloom. Unconsciously, I suppose, I was demanding that they conform to my puritan concept of Communism, or to some pastoral simplicity. But they robustly refused. They had no intention of feeding my romanticism with their suffering. They wanted those televisions."[97] Beginning *The Lost Heart of Asia* in an airplane high above Turkmenistan, Thubron reflects on the nostalgic center that gives the narrative its title: "It was a childish concept, I suppose – that the world had a heart – but it had proved oddly durable" (1). He uses the spectacular vantage point to imagine possible futures:

> The old order – all of Soviet Central Asia – was cracking apart, and its five republics, artificially created by Stalin, had declared their sovereignty a few months earlier. Uzbekistan, Tajikistan, Kazakhstan, Turkmenistan, Kirghizstan – suddenly the Soviet tide had ebbed from these shadowy Moslem nations and had left them naked in their independence. What would they become? Would they hurl themselves into the Islamic furnace, I wondered, or reconvene in a Communist mass? I could conceive their future only in the light of powers which I already knew: Islam, Moscow, Turkey, the West. (3)

Such speculations anticipate that grand narratives can subsume contemporary disarray: that the Soviet era will prove a violent irruption in a continuous Islamic history, or that globalization will remake the entire world as a simulacrum of the West. Yet once he is on the ground he quickly finds that real-life complexities insistently refuse the pre-made narratives he has at hand.

Thubron presents himself as an observer who oscillates between being haunted and compelled by the mutability before him. His narratives trace both the decadent ease of nostalgia and its fundamental error.[98] In *The Lost Heart*, he traverses the Oxus, "the immemorial divide between the Persian and Turkic worlds," by train. In the "precious minute" of crossing the river, he allows himself to "fanc[y] that it scarcely belonged to the present at all" – and then returns to the actual scene before him, in which "the span of a new lorry bridge" superannuates "antiquated ferries" (53–54). The train north from Samarkand takes him through the Gates of Tamerlane, where he looks past the "rashes of modern graffiti" to see ancient "sanguinary inscriptions" and envision Uzbek khans in battle (198). Tashkent has "the sweep and grandeur of a true capital," but he finds few "remnants of the czarist city" and "scarcely a trace of native costume" (198, 199). Its future is up for grabs: "The hotel guests were mostly on business. An Israeli foreign office agent was scouting to open an embassy.... Two Chinese delegations were trying to nose out trade.... An American Mormon had started a food-processing plant ... and the KGB, who had once harassed him, were now pestering him to sell them things" (202). Thubron opens *In Siberia* by evoking a spectral "bleak beauty, and an indelible fear," a place where "[e]ven now the white spaces induce fantasies and apprehension" that draw him inexorably (1). He speculates: perhaps Siberia will become "a pole of purity and authentic 'Russianness'" now that Moscow "succumbs to the contagion of the West," perhaps it will "fracture" (3). As the journey begins, "[f]or the last time, the future looks shapely and whole," for it "lives in the simplicity of maps" (3). Travel undoes this simplicity. Months later in a bleak village north of the Arctic Circle, he spends evenings conversing with Nikolai, a Russian doctor working among the Entsy people, who hopes him to be a kindred soul (Colin/Kolya/Nikolai).

> 'So what are you doing here?'
>
> 'I'm looking at Siberia.'
>
> 'And what do you see?' He gestured out of the window. 'Anything?' Into my silence he pursued: 'What did you expect, Nikolai?'
>
> 'Nikolai, it's too long ago to remember!' But I had been looking for patterns, of course. I wanted their security. I wanted some unity or shape to human diversity. But instead this land had become diffused and unexpected as I travelled it. Wherever I stopped appeared untypical, as if the essential Siberia could exist only in my absence, and I could not answer Nikolai at all.
>
> 'I didn't expect anywhere as bad as here.'
>
> 'This is extreme.' (137)

Prodded by an educated man to explain, Thubron must acknowledge (if only to himself) the disparity between his longings and the messy realities of a fractured society.

Such conversations play a crucial role in *The Lost Heart* and *In Siberia*. As Julia Gergits and James Schramer explain, "on all of his travels, Thubron seeks out friends of friends, strikes up conversations with strangers, and finds himself invited to weddings, parties, and dinners."[99] These scenes put his subjective speculations in narrative context: they personalize the complex histories before him and populate the vast spaces he traverses.[100] The everyday narratives of the people he meets surprise him by revealing nuanced differences he had not anticipated. In *The Lost Heart*, sharing a hotel room in Turkestan with a Kazakh metal worker who "can't understand what the Uzbeks say" shows Thubron "the traveller's illusion that everyone is assimilated but himself" (315). When devout young men gathered from several republics to study at the medreseh in Bukhara startle him by calling "this conservative backwater" "a godless place," he realizes that "all the time they considered themselves strangers here, just as I was" (76). Such "[e]veryday encounters, gathered impressions, and an equal receptivity to archaeologists and homeless drunks enable but also anchor his speculations."[101] More importantly, by challenging his assumptions they force him to rethink the value of what he knows. Thubron travels in Central Asia at "the ideal moment," William Dalrymple observes, for in the wake of Soviet collapse and Islamic fundamentalism he finds "a people who were openly asking fundamental questions about themselves."[102] Comfortable in his own persona as solitary Englishman, he learns that questions about identity are more complex – and more unanswerable – than he has supposed. The artist Zelim and his wife Gelia, a teacher, whom he visits in Bukhara, have "no real homeland" to which they could return should the new republic dissolve into ethnic conflict, for she is Tartar, he half-Chechen. "'[P]eople are bewildered now,'" she explains:

> A boy came to me yesterday and said, "My father is Ukrainian, my mother Tartar, so what am I? I suppose I'm just Russian." And I couldn't answer him.... As for these Moslems, they don't feel any identity really. They may call themselves Uzbeks or Tajiks, but it doesn't mean that much to them. They were Soviet before, and that was that. We all had this idea that we were one people, that we would melt into one another.... And now we're left with nothing. (87)

Thubron knows the history of Stalin's strategies for managing Moslem citizens in Central Asia, but has no answers for the future. When Gelia speculates that Zelim's mother, who reads Soviet memoirs, may care for her across ethnic lines because she loves her son, the traveler can only reply "weakly: 'I hope so'" (88). For the irreversible temporality of modernity – marked by exile, forced resettlement, and ethnic opportunism – has severed the kinds of connections between peoples, and peoples and places, that some imagine might still obtain.

Though Thubron the traveler eschews many of the comforts that would distance him from fortuitous exchanges with strangers, Thubron the narrator cannot fully elide the differences of class, knowledge, and mobility that allow him to be a mobile spectator of others' experiences. Dalrymple's description of Thubron eerily echoes Kennington's cartoon of Lawrence: his narrative makes his encounters into "a series of lives pinned dispassionately to paper like the butterflies of a Victorian collector."[103] This spectacular relation between the observer and his subjects remains visible because his presence invites not only personal queries but also insistent speculation about the exotic West. Thubron may be the first foreigner many have met, but globalized media have already introduced fun-house images of the world beyond the old Soviet empire. A Turkic woman he meets in *The Lost Heart* asks him about the West "with the wan amazement of someone enquiring after another faith's paradise," for "[s]he had seen American drama on television, and the West now appeared to her as delectable as it had once – under Moscow's censor-ship – seemed sordid" (190). The medreseh students ask about Salman Rushdie and the West "with mixed repudiation and awe. There was a haunting Westerner in every one of them" (76). Young Turkic merchants question him incessantly at a tea-house, for to them the West "shim-mered in an El Dorado beyond their reach, but their black eyes settled on me as its exemplar" (257–258). Later, in *In Siberia*, a Ukrainian informer and his Burgat friend, whom Thubron meets near Lake Baikal, gaze at him "with a passion to pin down, penetrate" and ask endlessly about public figures (Margaret Thatcher, Princess Diana), hunting, salaries, and Sherlock Holmes (153). Thubron uses his visit to Siberia's Institute for Physics in Akademgorodok to comment comically on the passion to get inside another's difference and his own discomfort when made a subject of speculation. At the institute, an enthusiastic scientist named Sasha asks to examine him in a hypomagnetic chamber that "opens up psycho-physical recesses not normally explored." Told that sensitive "cos-mophiles" may experience the sensation of being transported out of the body, he gamely subjects himself. Feeling nothing, he jokes about false science. To Sasha he diplomatically pleads weariness and insensitivity; to the reader, whom he trusts shares his skepticism, he wryly concludes, "I'm not cosmophobic ... I'm just English" (70, 72).

In Siberia's most compelling moments comes when Thubron's ethical sense collides with the obligation to understand. Siberia's recent history is unbearably violent; scenes of death litter its vast north. The narrative begins in Yekaterinburg, where Bolshevists murdered the last czar and his family, and closes in Kolyma, where many thousands died in Stalinist work camps. In Vorkuta, Thubron meets a life-long member of the Communist Party who spent twelve years in the camps and, at eighty-seven years old, lives out her days working at an organization dedicated to Stalin's victims and watching a Mexican soap opera. His insistent questions make him "feel like a voyeur, ashamed," but he presses on as she rocks on the sofa nervously, touching his hand as though he requires comforting. He asks:

> 'What was it like, the work?' I think: perhaps, day to day, it was not quite as people have written it, perhaps only the worst was recalled, the uncommon.
>
> ...
>
> And were the guards cruel, I ask, or only callous?

'They just did what they were told,' she says. 'After all, if we escaped, they would end up like us.'

I don't like this easy understanding. I want her to be angry. 'Did they think you guilty?' (44–45)

"[I]t is easy to misjudge those times," he realizes, "to forget how isolated people became … until ascertainable truth became a dangerous rarity" – and then he presses her again:

'And you,' I pursue, 'did you ever imagine yourself guilty?' …

'No, absolutely not. Nor did the others with me. But I should have been released in 1948, and it didn't happen. …'

I lose her down a great labyrinth. I can't disentangle her shadows.

…

But something is plaguing me. I can't bear her acquiescence. I say cruelly: 'But what was the purpose in the end? To so much suffering …'

She looks back at me, and suddenly her eyes begin to water. She glances away again.

For the first time she seems unable to answer. She repeats: 'Purpose?'

… The word seems to torment her. Her eyes are brimming, so that I feel ashamed of what I have asked. Her hand alights on mine. (46, 47–48)

Months later, near the Chinese border, he meets a retired schoolteacher nearly ninety years old who spends her days writing a four-volume local history yet "cannot bring herself to indict Stalin" (212). Siberia's extremes form an indecipherable palimpsest: "I have not inhabited these horrors as she has. It is those who have inhabited them who may measure, mitigate, even excuse them. Twenty million dead, to Agrippina Doroskova, is far more forgivable than sixty million. To me both figures bulge towards the unimaginable" (213). In these exchanges with elderly survivors, Thubron marks both the insufficiency of narrative and the limit of his capacity to comprehend experience so utterly different from his own.

It is fitting, then, that Thubron ends his narrative without resolution, juxtaposing his revulsion as a Western witness of the Soviet past with the measured responses of a generation that has had to move on from that history to live insistently in the present. Fedor, a Russian Jew, takes him surreptitiously through the soon-to-be-destroyed remains of a tran-sit camp near Magadan that Fedor's friend, having "lost his memory," had survived. As the first – and last – outsider to see the camp, Thubron wants "time to write down things, to remember," but must make do with "dashed-off notes" that evoke "violent snapshots" (273). Fedor's obses-sion with the camps has made him "touched … with melancholy," but not impractical: he hurries Thubron along "furtively" and brings waders and lighted helmets so they can explore the icy punishment block where prisoners scratched their names on walls (272, 273). Later Yuri, a geologist, drives Thubron through snowy mountains on a "half-visible track" to Butugychag, a labor camp where 25,000 political and criminal prisoners mined radioactive uranium. Hiking through snowfall, they enter the compound, Yuri "indifferent," the narrator's "heart-beat quickening, as if we were entering a cathedral or a morgue" (275). In that setting Thubron finds himself haunted by Stalin's spectacular intention to create an empire that would "last through all imaginable time. The past had been reorganized for ever, the future preordained." He longs for his guide to share his horror and "call this place an atrocious mystery"; he wants confirmation that it will never happen again. But Yuri, whose grandfather, a postman, spent five years in the camps for joking about Stalin, hesitates. "We're not the same as you in the West," he replies, "We're late with our history here." Perhaps, he concludes, "we spiral a little … a little upwards" (277). Unlike Thubron, who travels to experience mutability, understand history, and glimpse the future, Yuri lives in the present and has a quotidian measure of freedom. He allows only that he wishes his grandfather were still alive, for "people can joke about anything now. We've still got that" (278).

In twentieth-century travel narratives about geopolitical transformation, the critical observer seeking to comprehend the consequences of modernity refuses spectacular representation for the vantage point on the ground, where one can see the "continuous interaction" of past, present and future firsthand. Such narratives acknowledge nostalgia's persistence as a response to modernity while demonstrating its failure as a means of understanding its irreversible temporality. Instead, drawing on modernism's commitment to subjective perception, writers adapt travel narrative to new purpose, as a means of cosmopolitan engagement with world-historical change. In so doing, they invest the genre with a newly critical concern for the ethical consequences of representation.

CHAPTER 5

Perpetual Wartime

[I]t was in Cologne that I realized what total destruction meant.

My first impression on passing through was of there being not a single house left. There are plenty of walls but these walls are a thin mask in front of the damp, hollow, stinking emptiness of gutted interiors. Whole streets with nothing but the walls left standing are worse than streets flattened. They are more sinister and oppressive.

… One passes through street after street of houses whose windows look hollowed and blacked – like the open mouth of a charred corpse; behind these windows there is nothing except floors, furniture, bits of rag, books, all dropped to the bottom of the building to form there a sodden mass.

…

The great city looks like a corpse and stinks like one also, with all the garbage which has not been cleared away, all the bodies still buried under heaps of stones and iron.

Stephen Spender (1946)¹

In "the bloodiest century in the human history of the world," violent conflict, exacerbated by modernity's technological innovations and global reach, becomes travel's perpetual context: world wars, civil wars, wars for independence, genocides.² Whereas some twentieth-century Western writers travel to observe the consequences of spectacular transformation in distant places, others travel to witness the origins and effects of war closer to home. Ruin left by wars past, anxiety over future conflagrations, and contemporary chaos permeate the travel narrative. The metropolitan center signifies differently: once a secure launching point, it now often appears as the site of corruption and alienation depicted in *Heart of Darkness* and *The Waste Land*. Modernity's consequences shadow the entire journey: travel provides an ephemeral interlude but seldom resolves the narrator's subjective concerns or uncertainty about the future. The modernist counterpart to the explorer who returns to the imperial capital to report his successful expedition is the metropolitan observer who travels to understand the irreversible modernity that enmeshes both narrator and subjects, forever altering the terms of their engagement. Circumnavigating the globe and seeing much of the British Empire, Aldous Huxley wrote in 1926, made him "richer by much experience and poorer by many exploded convictions, many perished certainties."[3] He was not alone in his disenchantment; as Helen Carr observes: "One of the most pervasive moods in travel writing of the inter-war years is a certain world-weariness, springing from disillusionment with European civilization and dismay at its impact on the rest of the world."[4] The period of global change and crisis leading up to the Second World War signals to many what Oswald Spengler called "the decline of the West"; the unspeakable genocide and recurring wars that follow exceed their worst premonitions. Travel becomes a means of narrating the violence of which late modern civilizations prove capable, of attesting to their inhumanity (from bloody revolution to genocide in the name of the nation) as total war shatters distinctions between "home" and "abroad," "home front" and "battle front." It becomes as well a way of reckoning one's place in an altered world in which, as Iain Chambers writes: "Travel, in both its metaphorical and physical reaches, can no longer be considered as something that confirms the premises of our initial departure, and thus concludes in a confirmation, a domestication of the difference and the detour, a homecoming."[5]

Critical discussion of twentieth-century travel narrative has all but ignored its engagement with war. Given the extent and particularly inhuman nature of modernity's wars – aerial, urban, global, genocidal – this surprises. Given the history of scholarship on travel literature, however, it does not.[6] Bernard Schweizer's *Radicals on the Road* makes initial steps toward bridging this gap by mapping a 1930s revision of the travel narrative into a means of engaging with the political crises of an unstable world in rapid transition. The writers he analyzes disagreed politically: George Orwell was a socialist, Evelyn Waugh a conservative with fascist sympathies; Graham Greene "wavered between his bourgeois instincts and his liberal, left-wing sympathies," whereas Rebecca West "maintained strong feminist and liberationist convictions."[7] Together, however, they altered the genre by making it deliberately political and self-consciously literary. As these writers and others take modernity's grimmest ends – civilization's decline, total war, and aggressive globalization – as their recurring subject, their strategy of combining travel, firsthand political witness, and both intellectual and affective response becomes a distinctive aspect of the genre. Although the literary travel book as narrative-of-crisis may have been new in the thirties (or the late twenties, with the first Western narratives about the new Soviet Union), it doesn't end with *Black Lamb and Grey Falcon* (1941) or reappear later only fleetingly.[8] Such concerns – already visible in *Seven Pillars*, *Forbidden Journey*, and *Journey to a War* – intensify in travel narratives published in the decades since the Second World War, from Stephen Spender's *European Witness* (1946) to Rory Stewart's *The Places In Between* (2004). They inflect travel narratives as different from one another as Richard Wright's *Pagan Spain* (1957) and Joan Didion's *Salvador* (1983). They reshape leisure travel too, through "dark tourism" to sites associated with genocide, war, and assassination.[9] By the century's end, as Graham Huggan argues, travel writing is "inextricably connected with the multiple ways in which tourism *engages* with, not *escapes* from, the unstable conditions of global modernity," and the multiple media through which it does so.[10] The travel narrative's evolution as a provocative means for responding intellectually and subjectively to political crisis and war continues in the twenty-first century, where it shapes travel narratives compelled by Western responses to 9/11.

Global modernity's complex crises pose a considerable challenge for writers who would comprehend the history of the present and represent it in narrative. In the twentieth century, the urgent necessity to write war struggles in unprecedented ways with what Margot Norris calls "art's incommensurability to war – its inability to respond with adequate and appropriate gravity, scale, and meaningfulness."[11] To read travel narrative's engagement with war requires understanding the ways that modernity's invention of "wartime" and "total war" pushes to the limit narrative's capacity to account for history, represent experience, and offer witness. In *War at a Distance: Romanticism and the Making of Modern Wartime* (2009), Mary Favret persuasively argues that modernity produces a new concept of wartime as an "affecting experience" that disorients observers as well as combatants. For Favret, "wartime" identifies war as not a finite occurrence, but a mode of being: "wartime translates war from the realm of sublime event to an underlying situation or condition of modernity."[12] With historian David Bell, Favret identifies the ongoing wars of the Napoleonic era as the first to produce this experience and first that aimed to be comprehensive and final. "The idea of a last war," she observes, "is always the idea of a world war, a war on behalf of the world (conceived as civilization, or humanity) that nevertheless threatens the end of the world, apocalypse, or a new world." For the Romantics, Favret argues, unending "war at a distance" brought uncertainty in "[h]ow time and knowledge were registered in daily life" at home and "with that uncertainty came a sense of disturbing affective responses, including numbness, dizziness, anxiety, or a sense of being overwhelmed."[13] Their experience of war's capacity to be all-encompassing in affect prefigures the intense anguish that modernists experience when altered technology and ethics bring the escalated violence of battlefield chaos directly home.[14] The aerial bombing of cities and civilian internment extend total war's reach, collapsing most remaining distinctions between observers and combatants, spectators and witnesses.

In *Ulysses* Stephen Dedalus famously declares, "History ... is a nightmare from which I am trying to awake."[15] Joyce's character echoes a concern that haunts travel narratives written following the First World War: what will be the fate of the West? Spengler's *The Decline of the West* (1918, 1922), the most influential statement from "the anti-linear-progress camp," reached a broad post-war audience by audaciously promising to reveal "the secret of world-history itself."[16] For Thomas Mann, Spengler's "stark and catastrophic" title caught the interest of a generation "most acutely conscious that the world and our time are facing portentous change":

> We read avidly. Not for diversion or distraction, but for truth's sake and the arming of our minds.... boundaries between science and art have been obliterated; fresh blood flows through the ideas and reanimates the form, producing a type of book which rules to-day – a product which might be called a novel of the intellect.[17]

Spengler had immediate influence because he offered a compelling narrative to explain a chaotic world. Writers of different political convictions read Spengler: Auden, Maillart, and West, as well as Eliot and Yeats.[18] Waugh wryly acknowledges his popularity when he jokingly packs "two or three solemn books, such as Spengler's Decline of the West," for a Mediterranean cruise.[19] As Northrup Frye explains, *Decline* "outlines one of the mythical shapes in which history reaches everybody except professional historians ... a vision of history which is very close to being a work of literature."[20] Scholars dismissed his work, but Spengler's broad assertions about cultural decline in the machine age, which included familiar notions of the Orient as essentially static, influenced even those who rejected his conclusions and hoped he was wrong.[21] For *Decline* proposed that the nightmare of history could be comprehended in a simple narrative. Frye explains: "Everybody thinks in terms of a 'Western' culture to which Europeans and Americans belong ... everybody realizes that some crucial change in our way of life took place around Napoleon's time.... The decline, or aging, of the West is as much a part of our mental outlook today as the electron or the dinosaur, and in that sense we are all Spenglerians."[22] In 1940, F. Scott Fitzgerald would write of Spengler: "I don't think I ever quite recovered from him. He and Marx are the only modern philosophers that still manage to make sense in this horrible mess."[23] Yet, as John Farrenkopf observes, there remain two "ultimately unreconcilable" Spenglers: "the nostalgic agrarian conservative" who "laments the setting of the sun upon Western culture" and "the resolute modernist" who "accepts the decline of Western *Kultur*. For it heralds the dawn … of a titanic age."[24] Spengler's real significance lies not in his answers, but in his having articulated the era's urgent questions.

Whether the nightmare of history can indeed "make sense" haunts travel narrative long after Spengler's stark answers fall from view.[25] In *Black Lamb*, West characterizes contemporary European civilization as a mysterious "labyrinth in which, to my surprise, I had found myself immured."[26] In 1934, radio news of the assassination of King Alexander of Yugoslavia in Marseille shocks her profoundly, though she lies safely in a hospital bed in London. Certain that history and geopolitics link his violent fate with her own future, she decides she must travel:

> I had to admit that I quite simply and flatly knew nothing at all about the south-eastern corner of Europe; and since there proceeds steadily from that place a stream of events which are a source of danger to me, which indeed for four years threatened my safety and during that time deprived me for ever of many benefits, that is to say I know nothing of my own destiny.
>
> That is a calamity…. We must learn to know the nature of the advantage which the universe has over us, which in my case seems to lie in the Balkan Peninsula. It was only two or three days distant, yet I had never troubled to go that short journey which might explain to me how I shall die, and why. (21–22)

Echoing Maillart's thoughts about Turkestan, West hopes to find the Balkans "a land where everything was comprehensible, where the mode of life was so honest that it put an end to perplexity" (1). The narrative she produces about her journeys in the late 1930s interweaves a travel account with extended essay on modernity. Its chapters overflow with reflections on nearly every aspect of modern European history: from racial ideology to American ascendancy, religious intrigue to technology; romanticism about love and death to analysis of good and evil. West ends her narrative with an anguished epilogue written in wartime. Total war, she concludes, threatens to destroy England, Yugoslavia, and – more importantly – the human capacity to make sense of history:

> History … could be like the delirium of a madman, at once meaningless and yet charged with a dreadful meaning; and there existed a new agent to

face this character of our age and intensify it … the aeroplane. It was the dictators' perfect tool. For by raining bombs on the great cities it could gratify the desire of the mass to murder the mass; and by that same act it would destroy the political and economic centres of ancient states with pasts that told a long continuous story, and thus make an assault on mind, tradition, and what makes the settled hearth…. this was the gibbering phase of our human cycle. (1114)

While West's text is exceptional in its complexity, her use of travel narrative to understand the "dreadful" history of the violent present marks a crucial trajectory along which the genre evolves from the crises of the thirties to those of the twenty-first century.

The calamitous wartime of total war muddies conventional distinctions between witnesses who bear immediate knowledge and spectators who watch from a distance, reporters who experience war as it happens and travelers who view its prelude or aftermath. *Black Lamb* ends in anxious urgency because West's premonition has proved prescient: obligated to bear witness to tragedy elsewhere, she experiences wartime even as she writes. In *Writing War*, Norris argues that altered ethics and technologies make twentieth-century total war "ontologically discontinuous with other wars" in ways that exacerbate its disorienting effects. As annihilating civilian populations through genocide or aerial bombing becomes a tactic, civilian casualties become the norm, from 15 percent of fatalities in 1914–1918 to 65 percent in 1939–1945; for many, war becomes a collective, unending condition literally as well as affectively.[27] Yet because "modern discourses of war fail to acknowledge this changed ethical condition" in which civilian slaughter is deemed permissible, Norris argues, art – specifically, literature – bears the responsibility of attesting to wartime experience that fundamentally violates "Western civilized pretentions."[28] By the late 1930s the metropolis, no longer a scene of safety, figures as a target. Writers perceive themselves to be on the brink of wartime: West imagines bombs falling in London when she hears of Alexander's assassination; Virginia Woolf responds to the horror of Franco's bombing of civilians with *Three Guineas*; E. M. Forster writes to Christopher Isherwood – "journeying to a war" in China – of his "extraordinary dreams" of "aerial bombardment."[29] In 1939, reporter Martha Gellhorn would write of the "stunned and unbelieving" people of Helsinki: "For the first time in history they heard the sound of bombs falling on their city. This is the modern way of declaring war."[30] The metropolis becomes the scene of war, its ruins – as Spender would write of Cologne and Berlin in 1945, Peter Maass of Sarajevo in the early 1990s – the sign of civilization's failure.

Wartime intensifies the ethical obligations attendant on those who travel and represent. It compounds the critical consciousness that Anke Gleber finds in flânerie with the moral imperatives of witness. "Because war is a world-unmaking event," Norris explains, "a reality-deconstructing and defamiliarizing activity, one of the challenges of war writing is how to make its inherent epistemological disorientation, its sense of experienced 'unreality,' real."[31] "Epistemological disorientation" identifies the critical juncture at which travel narrative, with its commitment to subjective observation, and war reporting, with its ambition to document the truth of events, meet. For writers who travel to experience wartime, the obligation to witness results in narratives of crisis that recount the abiding disorientation that unfathomable violence produces in narrator and subjects alike. Wartime compels writers and readers to ask what differences obtain between observing and witnessing, between narrative and testimony. Who may claim to be not merely an "observer" but a "witness," and who must? Who may tell whose experiences, how; which stories matter, to whom, why; and which means of representing war constitute truth?

Recent scholarship on "war writing" expansively includes disparate written and visual texts that take war and its consequences as themes, though the literary genres of fiction, poetry, and memoir continue to take precedence.[32] Scholarship on war reporting as a distinctive practice that requires travel to the scene of war and firsthand observation deals more with its history than its discursive practices.[33] To the degree that critical distinctions between travel narrative and war reporting have obtained, they have rested chiefly on what Spender in *European Witness* calls "the material" (ix). Traveling to experience unfamiliar societies and places or see the remnants of old empires in emergent nations has generally been considered the stuff of travel narrative (Gertrude Bell, Colin Thubron). Travelling to witness places in the midst of insurrection or civil war or tell stories of heroism amidst civilization's collapse has been considered the substance of war reporting (Martha Gellhorn, Philip Gourevitch). Encyclopedic hybrid texts that pose genre conundrums have seldom been discussed in these terms (T. E. Lawrence, Rebecca West); others have simply been deemed journalism about current events (Joe Sacco). The unsurprising effect has been to privilege some kinds of texts in critical discussion, exclude others categorically, and seldom bridge the divide. By artificially separating "wartime" and "travel" despite modernity's "total war," such distinctions occlude similarities among narratives that deal with both.[34]

Thinking through what narratives of travel to the scene of war have in common – whether originally published or analyzed as "travel narrative," "war reporting," or something else – helps to identify unwritten premises about genre that have constrained critical analysis of the cultural work such narratives do. It also helps to articulate the ways that travel narrative evolves as the nature of wartime alters. The shared concerns are striking:

- traveling – through economic and political privilege – to unfamiliar, sometimes dangerous, places
- providing "information, ... descriptions of scenery, ... accounts of personalities and ... general reflections"[35] – and also comment, analysis, speculation
- getting to know local civilians and using individual vignettes to signify complex cultural and geopolitical events
- explaining contemporary observations and local particulars in larger historical and geographical contexts
- including subjective reflection and artifice in a narrative that explicitly takes reporting the truth about peoples and places as its purpose
- examining cultural differences – and peoples assumed to be "strangers" – as well as internecine conflicts
- coming to terms with the ethical obligations of spectatorship, the role of witness to violence
- pushing narrative strategies to the limit to write the inarticulable and represent the incomprehensible

While scholarship on travel narrative has examined many of these concerns, it has just begun to notice the last two – the ethics of witness and the attempt to narrate the incomprehensible.[36] The necessity and impossibility of "the writing of the disaster," in Maurice's Blanchot's phrase, has been the province of work on the representation of genocide and trauma.[37] Yet the travel narrative's greatest presumption has been its confidence in the privileged vantage points of European spectators. Critical analyses using colonial discourse theory have certainly troubled this assumption; narratives representing travel in wartime destabilize it further. They must confront the profound disparity between what the witness to total war sees firsthand and the narrative strategies available to represent it. Gellhorn comments frankly on the ethical ache: "These articles are in no way adequate descriptions of the indescribable misery of war. War was always worse than I knew how to say – always."[38] Blanchot echoes, citing notes Salmen Lewental buried near a crematorium as his testament: "The truth was always more atrocious, more tragic than what will be said about it."[39]

Writers caught in the labyrinth of history travel to the scene of war hoping to make sense of events that are, in West's words, "at once meaningless and yet charged with a dreadful meaning" (1114). The narratives of such journeys call attention to travelers who deliberately understand their role to be not merely that of spectator, but that of witness. Narratives such as *Black Lamb*, *European Witness*, and Philip Gourevitch's *We Wish to Inform You That Tomorrow We Will Be Killed with Our Families* (1998) accomplish the usual tasks of describing what the traveler sees and narrating subjective response without difficulty. But they struggle with the burden of witnessing. What does a witness know – or claim to understand – that a spectator does not? What obligations attach to the writing of war? To write about the meaning of violence they must risk failure that bears ethical consequence: "one must just write, in uncertainty and in necessity."[40] What does it mean to travel in order to witness a nightmare version of the civilized world? To "journey to a war" voluntarily is to risk sounding cavalier (as Auden and Isherwood may) or bombastic (as West can) or presumptuous (as Spender might) or implausible. It is to have the audacity to invoke the ethical obligations attendant on testimony when one is not, truly, oneself a refugee.[41] Writing in 1945, Waugh would declare there was "no room" for elective wandering amidst "the great army of men and women without papers, without official existence, the refugees and deserters, who drift everywhere today between the barbed wire."[42] Finding something distasteful in using travel to write the history of the present, he misses the larger point. Displacement was not new, though the term "displaced persons" was. What was new was the scale of civilian displacement within Europe. New as well was the sense that total war posed an incomprehensible threat to the survival of civilization, and thus incurred in observers an ethical obligation to attempt to understand, to represent, to witness. Seeing this collapse of civilization firsthand anguishes West and makes Spender ill. It repeats in Cambodia, in Rwanda, in Bosnia.

Wartime chaos compounds both the difficulty and the stakes of representing human experience. Since the nineteenth century (which saw the Napoleonic wars and, in the Crimea, the invention of war reporting), European observers had been increasingly concerned with the necessity of representing war and its consequences. In an essay about writing *War and Peace*, Leo Tolstoy traces the divergence of actual, remembered, and reported experience:

> Make a round of all the troops right after a battle, or even on the second or third day, before the reports have been written, and ask any of the soldiers and senior and junior officers what the battle was like: you will be told what all these people experienced and saw, and you will form a sublime, complex, infinitely varied and grim, indistinct impression; and

> from no one – least of all from the commander in chief – will you learn what the whole affair was like. But in two or three days the reports begin to be handed in. Talkers begin to narrate how things they did not see took place; finally a general report is compiled and the general opinion of the army is formed according to this report. Everyone is relieved to exchange his own doubts and questions for this false, but clear and always flattering presentation. A month or two later, question a person who took part in the battle, and already you will not sense the raw, vital material that used to be there, but he will narrate according to the reports.[43]

As Tolstoy's account demonstrates, the experience *of* experience occurs through narrative, addressed to oneself (reflection, memory) or to others (reports, memoirs). In fact, Gary Saul Morson argues, "[p]erception itself makes use of the same mechanisms of regularization: to a certain extent, we perceive only what is more or less amenable to memory, and so introduce order not present in the actual event.... [f]rom each recollection to the next, still more distortions are introduced into events to make them fit the shape of narratives we have heard and can easily remember."[44] The human reliance on narrative to make sense of experience affects not only what can be remembered, but what can even be perceived.

Here, Mikhail Bakhtin's understanding of experience can help to account for the difficulty of writing about modern war's unspeakable events and subjective meanings, which "reside elsewhere than in facticity."[45] In his analysis, experience forms human subjects, who bear the responsibility of its meaning:

> I remember my own lived experience in an ... active manner not from the aspect of its factually existing content (taken in isolation), but from the aspect of its to-be-attained meaning and object.... [I]n so doing, I renew the still-to-be-achieved character of every one of my experiences, I collect all of my experiences, collect all of myself *not* in the past, but in the future that confronts me eternally as a future yet-to-be. My own unity, for myself, ... confronts me eternally as a unity-yet-to-be.[46]

Experience's meaning involves relation: between self and others; between past, present, and future; between narrator, reader, and text; between competing discourses available for representing event and memory. In ordinary circumstances – Bakhtin's example is the Bildungsroman – character evolves "against the immobile background of the world, ready-made and basically quite stable"; in such texts "the world" functions as a thing, "an immobile orientation point for the developing man." In the narratives he most values, however, both character and world are in transition: the world "as an experience" is unpredictable, and the character "emerges *along with the world*" and "is forced to become a new and unprecedented type of human being."[47] In such circumstances, social consensus has fractured to the extent that what counts as experience and whose experience counts are uncertain, debatable, and unresolvable.[48] Ken Hirschkop points out that this analysis is one of four "attempts to make history ... representable" that Bakhtin produces "between 1937 and 1944, when European history was outdoing itself in the creation of inconceivable, unrepresentable horror." Representability matters, Hirschkop argues, because narrative "serves two masters, ethics and aesthetics" and thus has its meaning in the dialogue that ensues between author/narrator and responding other.[49]

To write about one's travel through a world in chaos is to grapple directly with the limits of narratability. When disruption of the social order troubles the already complex relation between experience and narrative, coherence and comprehensibility become next to impossible. Literary scholars have considered these limits primarily through "trauma" and "testimony," concepts that emphasize the violent effect of experience on the individual and the cultural expectation that an individual's narrative will have probative value. As Leigh Gilmore writes, "contemporary self-representational texts about trauma ... confront how the limits of autobiography, multiple and sprawling as they are, might conspire to prevent some self-representational stories from being told at all if they were subjected to a literal truth test of evaluated by certain objective measures." The narratives she discusses as limit-cases "refus[e] ... autobiography's form and the judgments it imports" at the risk of unintelligibility and incoherence.[50] In so doing, Gilmore concludes, they open the possibility of finding a way to narrate something unprecedented that can be reached no other way. Narratives of travel to the scene of war thus may best be understood as occurring in the critical space that lies between individual "trauma" and probative "testimony." Though their narrators experience wartime and may observe horrors they can barely describe, neither preserving singular stories nor documenting events is their primary concern. Instead, by juxtaposing the unsteady "emergence" of individuals with the extreme transformation of the world, travelers' subjective perceptions with victims' stories, local observation with larger histories, such travel narratives argue that the violence of modern civilized societies must be recognized and understood as *collective* experience.[51]

The texts discussed in this chapter demonstrate modern and postmodern wartime to be a shared catastrophe that entangles narrators and subjects, witnesses and witnessed, in a labyrinth that may be inexplicable. To narrate the experiences that take place in such conditions is not only to attempt to represent their significance but stands also as an ethical act, an attempt to explain and thus to respond.

Black Lamb and Grey Falcon

In late 1941, West published *Black Lamb and Grey Falcon: A Journey through Yugoslavia*, a monumental work that reviewer Katherine Woods promptly called "not only the magnification and intensification of the travel book form, but, one may say, its apotheosis."[52] The narrative folds episodes from three different journeys made in 1936–1938 into a single Easter journey set in 1937 in which West and her husband travel the length of Yugoslavia, guided by a government official she calls Constantine and accompanied for a while by his wife, called Gerda.[53] The recent history of violence in the Balkans and the prospect of war across Europe haunt the narrative from its dedication "To my friends in Yugoslavia, who are now all dead or enslaved," to its final image of the citizens of Marseille spontaneously honoring Yugoslavia's resistance against Germany in 1941 by leaving flowers at the scene of Alexander's assassination (v). Although the text's primary divisions mime those of the nation (Croatia, Dalmatia, Herzegovina, Bosnia, Serbia, Macedonia, Montenegro), the prologue and epilogue frame the journey as an urgent, personal attempt to divine connections between events in the Balkans and in Britain. West, who opens the narrative by declaring that she travels to learn how and why she shall die, closes it by describing the first eighteen months of the new world war, in which air raids kill many thousands of civilians in London and Belgrade. Her narrative persona is at once "inspired prophetess," opinionated traveler, and anguished witness.[54] Exhaustive in scope, *Black Lamb* overflows with minute details of traveling by train and automobile, thorough depictions of landscapes and towns, portraits of historical figures, comic anecdotes and melancholy encounters, endless debates on philosophy and politics, enthralled accounts of assassinations and battles, and stark reflections on the meaninglessness of modern life and likelihood of purposeless death. At half a million words, it is roughly twice the length of *Seven Pillars*. Even Clifton Fadiman, who lauded West's book for being "as astonishing as it is brilliant" and compared it to Lawrence's, noted that "it must be candidly confessed that not many readers will want to read its every page."[55]

Like *Seven Pillars*, *Black Lamb* has received surprisingly little attention in major scholarship on modernism, travel narrative, or war writing.[56] The text's length, the writer's gender, and literary studies' relative inattention to the Second World War help to explain this, but a more significant explanation lies in the text's many contradictions. Though *Black Lamb* explicitly invokes the travel genre's familiar conventions, the narrator regularly suspends the onward movement of the journey for lengthy digressions into history and politics and sets aside chronology for geography and theme. The narrative freely subordinates literal accuracy to literary advantage, uses "my husband" strategically as discursive foil, and in general "has a strong fictional component, which is never more pronounced than when it appears to be straightforwardly autobiographical."[57] West's persona is that of a modern citizen seeking answers to the "perplexity" of modern life (1), yet her narrative is filled with contradictory political and philosophical claims that perplex readers. She vehemently rejects imperialism and its master-narratives, which she blames for the violent history of the Balkans and fears in their current manifestation, the virulent fascism of Nazi Germany. To counter them, however, she embraces an aggressive nationalism that relies on what Loretta Stec identifies as "a nostalgic logic of gender domination."[58] West writes in an authoritative, resolute voice that may be read as feminist while engaging forcefully with matters of urgent geopolitical and ethical consequence in which gender is not her primary concern.[59]

To analyze *Black Lamb* requires asking what complex relations obtain among the narrative's disparate strands and thinking through their contradictions without necessarily resolving them. Although West, like Lawrence, uses the travel genre to provide a narrative thread for philosophical speculation and political advocacy, she lacks his advantage of hindsight because she writes deep in the midst of the wartime that she travels to understand. The imperative to witness in the present requires that she risk both accuracy and coherence to write from experience *in medias res*. Her metacritical concern with how to make sense – how to narrate – runs through *Black Lamb*. "I had come to Yugoslavia because I knew that the past has made the present," West writes, "and I wanted to see how the process works" (54). To understand requires giving history vivid narrative form:

> As we grow older and see the ends of stories as well as their beginnings, we realize that to the people who take part in them it is almost of greater importance that they should be stories, that they should form a recognizable pattern, than that they should be happy or tragic.... Art is not a plaything, but a necessity, and its essence, form, is not a decorative adjustment, but a cup into which life can be poured and lifted to the lips and be tasted. If one's own existence has no form, if its events do not come handily to mind and disclose their significance, we feel about ourselves as if we were

reading a bad book. We can all of us judge the truth of this, for hardly any of us manage to avoid some periods when the main theme of our lives is obscured by details. (55)

Black Lamb handles the challenge of forming recognizable patterns in the midst of wartime uncertainty through broad dichotomies: creation and destruction, comedy and tragedy, self and society, good and evil, masculine and feminine, love and death. West characterizes complex historical events in terms of a Manichean agon in which the world is "a field for moral effort" where those on the side of "virtue and reason" seek to recover the good that has been lost to the side of "vice and brutishness" (172). Thus, Schweizer argues, "[i]n West's thinking, Eros is aligned with freedom and felicitous social arrangements bordering on utopia, while Thanatos is always associated with defeatism and destruction, and ultimately with dystopian gloom"; their relation is at once dialectical and paradoxical.[60] This strategy of understanding the world through dichotomies offers the possibility of clarity at the price of polemic.[61]

At the same time as dichotomous thinking helps West chart her way through history, her narrative demonstrates its limitations. This occurs most obviously in scenes where West's persona interprets her observations in sweeping hyperbole, which "my husband" tempers. Their exchange over an inaccurate guidebook illustrates: West "peevishly" declares the text "'so wildly wrong that it seems probable that not only can she [the "imbecile ... bedridden" author] never have visited any of these particular cities, but that she can have seen no scenery at all, urban or rural.' 'I think,' said my husband, 'that that is perhaps something of an over-statement'" (200). More substantially, it occurs in West's attempt to create a figure to stand for what she has learned: the black lamb she sees sacrificed at Kosovo, an image of violent sacrifice of the innocent, and the grey falcon that appears to Tsar Lazar in Serbian myth, an image of self-sacrifice in the name of freedom. This attempt to encapsulate history falters because the meanings West attributes to the images, and thus the juxtaposition, shift as she travels and writes. For as Schweizer notes, "the raw data of personal experience" does not fit neatly into the clear patterns that politics – and stories – require. In using both images despite their contradiction, *Black Lamb* is simultaneously "a celebration of dualistic thinking and its ultimate subversion."[62] David Farley observes that West seeks to depict not only events but "the process of [her] own understanding"; to do so, she risks showing how she "refines her ideas through a process that precludes either the priority of the eye or the mind, of either the concrete or the abstract, of either the deductive or the inductive."[63] In the epilogue, West "reinterprets" the myth of the grey falcon to serve new, nationalist ends in contemporary wartime.[64] She explains how it might be found apposite:

> An artist is goaded into creation … by his need to resolve some important conflict, to find out where the truth lies among divergent opinions on a vital issue. His work, therefore, is often a palimpsest on which are superimposed several incompatible views about his subject; and it may be that which is expressed with the greatest intensity, which his deeper nature finds the truest, is not that which has determined the narrative form he has given to it. The poem of the Tsar Lazar and the grey falcon tells a story which celebrates the death-wish; but its hidden meaning pulses with life. (1145)

West's defense of literary complexity – or, put more baldly, of contradiction and evolving interpretation – certainly reads as a defense of her own palimpsest as well.

West casts *Black Lamb* as an account of an Easter journey motivated by her narrator's passionate wish to understand a place that is "more wonderful than I can tell you" because "there is much we" – "the whole of the West" – "have not got which the people in the Balkans have got in quantity" (22–23). Much of the narrative deals with Yugoslavia's rural communities and distant history, in which West sees a vitality and capacity for meaning that are absent in modern life. The rejection of British "soulless monotony" and consequent "idealization" of a place "where a crucial proximity to spiritual truth has been retained" that typify interwar Anglophone narratives about the Balkans echo through many scenes.[65] West finds the Orthodox Easter services in Skoplje to be "the very consummation of the picturesque," and "more than that, there is true Easter, the recognition of the difference between winter and summer, between cold and heat, between darkness and light, between death and life, between minus and plus" (636, 637). She particularly admires a weather-worn woman a few years older than she who "had been born during the calamitous end of Turkish maladministration, with its cycles of insurrection and massacre, and its social chaos":

> She had far less of anything, of personal possessions, of security, of care in childbirth, than any Western woman can imagine. But she had two possessions which any Western woman might envy. She had strength, the terrible stony strength of Macedonia; she was begotten and born of stocks who could mock all bullets save those which went through the heart … who could survive malaria and plague…. And cupped in her destitution as in the hollow of a boulder there are the last drops of the Byzantine tradition. (637, 638)

In the Macedonian woman's solemn visage West finds a counter to her own "revulsion from the horror of history, and a dread that it might really be witless enough to repeat itself" (643). The assurance is provisional, ambiguous, and of her own design: though the woman "made no spectacular declaration that man is to be saved," West reads in her attitude confirmation that "this Easter would end with no more fatality than any other" and "death may last five hundred years yet not be death" (644). In Yugoslavia, she finds both a sourcebook for explaining violent history and antidotes by which it might be overcome.[66]

Black Lamb's overarching narrative, to which the Easter journey is subordinate, is that of metropolitan crisis in a time of global war. West's most compelling, shocking insights come in her understanding of London and modern civilization as sites of danger from which escape is impossible. The lengthy prologue and epilogue, where she explains her rationale for traveling and the gravity of her themes, occur primarily in London. The narrative opens on a train to Yugoslavia in 1937 but immediately returns to peacetime London in 1934. West lies in a nursing-home recuperating from an operation done "in the new miraculous way" (1). Bored, she listens to the radio, realizing "how uninteresting life could be and how perverse human appetite." The new technology brings trivia, music, and serious news: one evening West "turn[s] the wrong knob" and hears "how the King of Yugoslavia had been assassinated in the streets of Marseille that morning." Her thoughts turn immediately to the geopolitical consequences: "We had passed into another phase of the mystery we are enacting here on earth, and I knew that it might be agonizing. . . . It appeared to me inevitable that war must follow." Knowing that civilians will be targeted when war comes, she envisions not battlefields but destruction at home:

> I imagined myself widowed and childless ... for I knew that in the next war we women would have scarcely any need to fear bereavement, since air raids unpreceded by declaration of war would send us and our loved ones to the next world in the breachless unity of scrambled eggs. (2)

Technology brings dreadful news that presages mechanized destruction to come.[67] Hearing the news, she "look[s] at my radio fearfully," for Alexander's is the latest in a series of political assassinations that threaten civil existence: "all these earlier killings had either hastened doom towards me or prefigured it" (14). West explicitly links the violence of assassination on a city street with that of urban air-raids: the former leads to the latter; king and civilian are equally vulnerable.

Paul Saint-Amour, drawing on Lewis Mumford's *The Culture of Cities* (1938), characterizes the context in which West writes: the "war capital" or "war metropolis." Once aerial bombardment becomes a standard tactic of modern war, anticipation of destruction to come haunts urban existence.

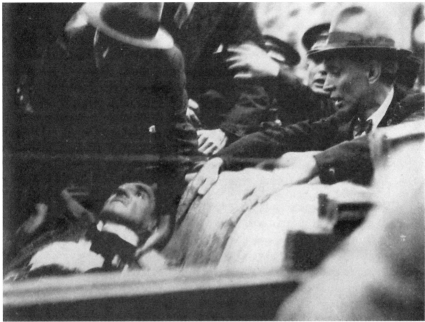

EXCLUSIVE NEWS AGENCY, LONDON

DEATH OF ALEXANDER KARAGEORGEVITCH, KING OF YUGOSLAVIA,
Marseille, October 9, 1934

Illustration 6. Photo of the death of Alexander Karageorgevitch, from West's *Black Lamb and Grey Falcon.*

Saint-Amour traces such premonitory anxiety in interwar culture, where it surfaces everywhere from the Hague Convention's inclusion of new technologies – the airplane, the radio – in international laws of warfare to novels by Woolf and Alexander Döblin.[68] Technology makes West's experience of Alexander's assassination disturbingly intimate: after hearing the news over the radio, she arranges to view it on film as soon as she leaves the nursing home.[69] She watches the newsreel privately, repeatedly, as though viewing its "extraordinary detail" might provide mastery over events, or at least comprehension (14). But the dead king lying in the car – West reproduces a photo adjacent – proves indecipherable: "he is as I was after the anaesthetic. He does not know that anything has happened" (16) (see Illustration 6). Though certain the assassination signals modernity's crisis and portends catastrophe to come, West finds it incomprehensible – "no matter how often I saw this picture" – without traveling to see the history of the present for herself (17). Saint-Amour reads the modernist encyclopedic

novel as a response to the condition of the war metropolis, an attempt at a
vantage point from which to comprehend the labyrinth. He explains:

> Of course no single origin or logic can explain the ravenously inclusive,
> even encyclopedic, projects of *Mrs. Dalloway* or *Berlin Alexanderplatz* or –
> a precursor both novels share – Joyce's *Ulysses*. But the co-presence in all
> three of an all-encompassing cartographic gaze with a sense of the urban
> object's radical vulnerability suggests the emergence of a new sub-genre of
> the city novel in the wake of the Great War: the novel of the total-war
> metropolis. Put another way, to write seriously of the city after the first
> bombs had fallen on civilians was necessarily to write of the city in and as
> a state of total war.[70]

Black Lamb – itself "ravenously inclusive" – demonstrates the total-war
sensibility that Saint-Amour describes. Like other modernist encyclopedic
texts, it ambitiously attempts to write the whole world.[71] Although its use of
travel narrative differentiates it from these city novels, *Black Lamb* frames a
journey in Yugoslavia, a place where each person "has faced the prospect of
violent death at least once," with a narrative of London as the scene of total
war, explicitly subordinating the journey to modernity as wartime (637).

   As West sits on a boulder overlooking a key battleground between
Serbia and Bulgaria in the last war, she reflects that firsthand observation
can provide only a portion of the comprehension that she seeks. Layers of
competing histories and geographies resist narration:

> What is Kaimakshalan? A mountain in Macedonia, but where is Macedonia
> since the Peace Treaty? This part of it is called South Serbia. And where is
> that, in Czechoslovakia, or in Bulgaria? And what has happened here? The
> answer is too long, as long indeed, as this book, which hardly anybody will
> read by reason of its length. Here is the calamity of our modern life, we
> cannot know all the things which it is necessary for our survival that we
> should know. This battlefield is deprived of its essence in the minds of men,
> because of their fears and ignorances; it cannot even establish itself as a fact,
> because it is crowded out by a plethora of facts. (773)

To understand the history of the present, West insists, one must identify
its production through the irreversible temporality of modernity: "what
has happened" links inextricably to what is "necessary for our survival"
in the future. Filled with what Adam Piette calls the echolalia by which
war zones are "haunted by the chronotopes of other wars," *Black Lamb*
reads the past through its overwhelming concern with "anticipated catastrophe."[72] West explains in the epilogue:

> I resolved to put on paper what a typical Englishwoman felt and thought
> in the late nineteen-thirties when, already convinced of the inevitability of

the second Anglo-German war, she had been able to follow the dark waters of that event back to its source.... I was obliged to write a long and complicated history, and to swell that with an account of myself and the people who went with me on my travels, since it was my aim to show the past side by side with the present it created. (1089)

By showing past and present "side by side," *Black Lamb* narrates the wartime already underway, anticipating the global warfare that erupts as West writes. This commingling of past, present, and future occurs most obviously in the difficult jostling between West's persona and those of her companions, whose conversations play out the contemporary significance of places they visit. It appears most pointedly, however, in scenes about gruesome death. "[N]ightmare touches" of violence haunt her: when the king and queen of Serbia were murdered in 1903, "their naked bodies [were] thrown out of their bedroom into the garden," his right hand severed (11). In Herzegovina and Bosnia, acquaintances show West photographs of peasants executed by the Austrians in 1914 in retaliation for the assassination of Franz Ferdinand. The Serb peasants look "grotesque" and wear "an expression of astonishment" (280). "[G]hastly pictures of the terror" in which "hundreds of Bosnian peasants who had barely heard of [the assassination] were put to death" disorient her:

> There were several photographs of the fields ... where these mass-executions took place, each showing the summer day thronged as if there were a garden-party going on, with the difference that every single face was marked with the extremity of agony or brutality. The interest and strangeness of the pictures were so great that I swung loose from what I was and for a moment looked about me, lost as one is sometimes when one wakes in a train or in an unfamiliar hotel; it might have been that we were all dead and that I was looking at some records of the death struggle of our race. (417)[73]

In 1903, the murders of Serbian royalty had seemed "an irrelevant horror"; decades later, West understands that when "the red light of violence shone out" then, it not only presaged but produced the future: "the whole of the modern world fell with them" (10–11).

In the litany of death that precipitates West's journey, 1934 marks "a new phase in the genius of murder which has shaped our recent history," for in quick succession fascists in Vienna carry out "a systematic battue of the Social Democrats," Hitler eliminates political enemies in a "Blood Bath" "by killing without trial and without warning about twelve hundred people, many of whom loved and trusted him," and Alexander is murdered (1110–1111). Wartime now involves casual murder of European civilians at home as well as political assassination: its ordinariness shocks. West remembers the chauffeur who drives them on their visits to Vienna, whose offhand comments reveal that he had willingly driven one of the Viennese fascists "from massacre to massacre" (1110). Repulsed, she declares: "The chauffeur's behavior can be judged only if one imagines a Cockney taxi-man cheerfully spending some days driving about a ruffian who was making it his business to assault by bombardment and machine-gun the tenants of all London County Council flats, men, women, and children alike" (1110–1111). The culminating nightmare of this "new phase" in which mass slaughters mass is aerial bombardment, "the dictators' perfect tool," for which West feels England failed adequately to prepare (1114). *Black Lamb* closes with a dramatic third-person report of Yugoslavia's resistance in 1941 – and the grim toll of 24,000 dead in Belgrade after four days of German bombing (1146).

For West, writing during total war is a desperate, urgent, ethical act. Her topic is Yugoslavia, her theme survival. *Black Lamb* ambitiously makes the travel narrative a means of witnessing the collective history of the present, the labyrinth of modernity that imperils London and civiliza-tion, threatening extinction. It thus has much in common with the work of other modernists who sought to make sense of their complex, fragile world through what Michael André Bernstein calls "a new kind of ency-clopedic masterpiece." Modernists attempt to do this, he observes, at a crucial moment when heterogeneity prevails and consensus has collapsed:

> One could accept ... the abstract principle of a *Gesamtkunstwerk*, but since there was no longer cultural agreement about what constituted a coherent totality in the first place, each artist was compelled to work out his own, particular, and thus necessarily idiosyncratic selection.... [T]he text must not only select its *materia poetica* from a range of possibilities and with an absence of generic guidelines hitherto unthinkable, but it must also do so in such a way as to make that selection appear simultaneously inevitable and complete.[74]

The writer who would create the modernist masterpiece must boldly claim to produce a *summa* of a heterogeneous, fluid world. The ethical possi-bilities are striking, the aesthetic risks substantial. Without framing, the narrative that attempts to represent heteroglossia may read as artless tran-scription or undifferentiated chaos; with it, it may read as aesthetic perfor-mance or subjective montage. The great modernist narratives inhabit this boundary, to which *Black Lamb* aspires. For West, the ethical obligations of witness require her to comprehend particular details on the ground and the larger cultural narratives of which they are a part. This Bernstein calls "perhaps the most riveting feature of the modernist masterpiece":

it "shuttles continuously between a totalizing project it intermittently recognizes as inaccessible, if not outright paranoid, and a contradictory attentiveness to the particular moment and the purely local, contingent realization," between the encyclopedic and the essayistic, "the lure of the whole" and "absorption in the immediate and local."[75] In the wartime metropolis such shuttling requires, as Saint-Amour argues of *Mrs. Dalloway*, a "narratorial gaze" that combines "the massively interconnective and totalizing gaze" of aerial war with "paradoxically, the opposite – a gaze that wants to 'travel the spider's thread of attachment'... between people, places, things, and beliefs in order to point up the fragility of their interdependence, the susceptibility of the whole social matrix to trauma if even a small part of it is assaulted or destroyed."[76] Through traveling these threads, West seeks not only to trace the "twists and turns" of the labyrinth but, possibly, to imagine a way out (1089).

West's narrator last appears in person as a witness of the war metropolis, watching the people of London as she and "my husband" stroll on summer evenings in the rose garden of Regent's Park, the sky "curiously starred with the silver elephantines of the balloon barrage" (1129). All dread "a form of attack more horrible than had ever before been directed against the common man," but when the Blitz comes, they endure:

> bombs dropped; many were maimed and killed, and made homeless, and all knew the humiliating pain of fear. Then they began to laugh. Among the roses, when safety was theirs for a word, they had not even smiled. Now ... though their eyes were glassy with horror, they joked from sunset, when the sirens unfurled their long flag of sound, till dawn, when the light showed them the annihilation of dear and familiar things. But they were not merely stoical. They worked, they fought like soldiers. ...
>
> It could not have been predicted that aerial warfare, the weapon of the undifferentiated mass against the undifferentiated mass, should utterly defeat its users by transforming those who suffer it to the most glorious of individuals. This ... at one stroke regenerated the town-dweller ... and lent him the innocence of the front-line soldier. (1130–1131)

In Marina MacKay's words, this "profoundly Churchillian" passage signals West's own complicated position as a subject in wartime who seeks to "impos[e] creative meaningfulness on ... political confusion."[77] It must be juxtaposed with West's statement on the necessity of writing *Black Lamb*:

> This has seemed to me at times an unendurably horrible book to have to write, with its record of pain and violence and bloodshed, carried on for so long by such diverse peoples; and perhaps the most horrible thing about it is that, in order to carry out my intention and show the past in relation to

the present it begot, I have to end it while there rages round me vileness
equal to that which I describe. (1126)

Yet narrating her travels through the history of the wartime present serves
a larger purpose. For West, an ethical imperative attaches to the privilege
to travel and to narrate. If human beings cannot change, she writes, "it
would be good for all of us to die" (1126). But through "the re-living of
experience" that is art, West hopes feverishly that they can: in the night-
time sky that features two bursts, "the huge red star of light that is a high-
explosive bomb" and the "small white star of light" that is the work of art,
it is the former that "withers," the latter that can have permanence (1127).

European Witness

Spender introduces *European Witness* by placing his narrative of a journey
through the devastated cities of Germany in the travel genre:

> This book is a Travel Book of a conventional kind. It is written from jour-
> nals made on journeys through Germany in July and August, and again in
> September and October; and through France in May, August and October
> in 1945.
>
> It consists of the information, the descriptions of scenery, the accounts of
> personalities and the general reflections which are usual in Travel Books.
> Any unusualness in it lies in the material itself, that is to say, in the interest,
> and the novelty of Germany after the collapse of the Nazi regime. (ix)

Spender's official status guarantees access to extraordinary sights: assigned
by the Allied Control Commission to review the state of German intellectual life and assess conditions for reopening libraries, he carries "a document stating *to those whom it might concern* that I might speak freely with
German civilians in pursuance of my duties (this was in the days of non-
fraternization)" (3).[78] *European Witness*, however, is subjective travel narrative, not official government report: not only does Spender alter names
of real people, in some instances he "invent[s] characters or incidents in
order to convey some impression which could not be conveyed more
directly," for the "general picture of what I saw in Germany in 1945 ...
counts, not the isolated incidents" (ix). The dust jacket for the English
edition promises a travel narrative of "penetrating sympathy" and "critical judgment" filled with "impressions of devastated Rhineland cities,"
"conversations with their leading citizens," meetings with "[a] fascinating
variety of British characters," and "contrasting contacts with Russians,
Americans and Displaced Persons." The jacket text for the American

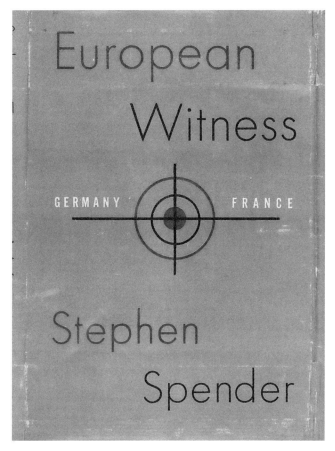

Illustration 7. Dust jacket of the American edition of Spender's *European Witness*.

edition, foreshadowing the Cold War, ominously declares the book "a valuable and essential evocation of Europe today – completely divorced from the shallow thinking on the subject which is so prevalent – and so dangerous – at the present time." Its cover features a disquieting image: black cross-hairs above a red target, the continent viewed abstractly from a bomber flying south, *European Witness* as a testament of cities and civilians ruined in war (see Illustration 7).

As Spender was writing *European Witness*, Waugh was preparing *When the Going Was Good*. Spender's explicit invocation of the travel genre in a narrative about war-torn Germany startles, particularly in juxtaposition with Waugh's book, which announces the genre's demise. Waugh's preface doubles as an elegy for an era of privileged travel – before "the shades of the prison-house" closed – and the sort of book it produced. Detecting a betrayal of that era's spirit in his own writing about wartime Abyssinia, he resolves to restore it: his anthology collects his earlier travel narratives, deletes passages of "historical summary and political argument," and presents "all that I wish to preserve."[79] "I do not expect to see many travel books in the near future," he declares, for

> [t]here is no room for tourists in a world of 'displaced persons.' ... others, not I, gifted with the art of pleasing public authorities may get themselves dispatched abroad to promote 'Cultural Relations'; the very young, perhaps, may set out like the *Wandervogels* of the Weimar period: lean, lawless, aimless couples with rucksacks, joining the great army of men and women without papers, without official existence, the refugees and deserters, who drift everywhere today between the barbed wire. I shall not, by my own wish, be among them.

Waugh asserts and entangles several distinctions: between the travel of men of privilege and the wandering of the displaced and disreputable; between authorized and constrained mobility; and between the proper stuff of travel books ("charm and wit") and the writing of "disaster."[80] He elects a conservative stand and opts out; Spender, to whom he might allude here, opts in.[81] Though both *When the Going Was Good* and *European Witness* appeared in 1946, scholarship on travel narrative mentions the former often, the latter seldom. Yet it is Spender's work, which provocatively depicts the world in transition that Waugh finds incompatible, that demonstrates the genre's evolution to meet new cultural needs at modernity's end.

In a narrative that follows many conventions, Spender describes landscapes, events, and encounters with individual strangers; generalizes about nations and national character; and befriends locals, at times using his privileged status to help them out. Yet at every turn he reminds the reader that although the form may be conventional, the journey is not. The roads are "almost impassable," the sight on either side "heaps of ruins" (147). He traverses once-familiar cities and landscapes now damaged beyond recognition and meets people no longer themselves: he travels through the violent aftermath of war. Cologne, the first major city he sees, shocks him. In an apocalyptic postscript to modernist city texts, Spender writes of an obliterated metropolis ghosted by its former self:

> Through the street of Cologne thousands of people trudge all day long. These are crowds who a few years ago were shop-gazing in their city, or waiting to go to the cinema or to the opera, or stopping taxis. They are

the same people who once were the ordinary inhabitants of a great city when by what now seems an unbelievable magical feat of reconstruction in time, this putrescent corpse-city was the hub of the Rhineland, with a great shopping centre, acres of plate-glass, restaurants, a massive business street containing the head offices of many banks and firms, an excellent opera, theatres, cinemas, lights in the streets at night.

Now it requires a real effort of the imagination to think back to that Cologne which I knew well ten years ago. Everything has gone. In this the destruction of Germany is quite different even from the worst that has happened in England (though not different from Poland and from parts of Russia).... The external destruction is so great that it cannot be healed and the surrounding life of the rest of the country cannot flow into and resuscitate the city which is not only battered but also dismembered and cut off.... The ruin of the city is reflected in the internal ruin of its inhabitants who, instead of being lives that can form a scar over the city's wounds, are parasites sucking at a dead carcase, digging among the ruins for hidden food, doing business at their black market near the cathedral – the commerce of destruction instead of production. (14–15)

Cologne is all but unrecognizable, its inhabitants reduced from citizens of the metropolis to parasites on its corpse. As he travels, Spender "often feels haunted by the ghost of a tremendous noise," for in shattered cities it "is impossible not to imagine the rocking explosions, the hammering of the sky upon the earth, which must have caused all this" (16). His driver maneuvers along roads bordered by refugees and "covered with glass and rubble," through countryside littered with wrecked tanks, graves, and "great aluminum corpses of crashed aeroplanes" (147, 220). As they work their way toward the center of Berlin, Spender observes that "Life only continues at the edges of the German cities. The centre is broken and blackened" (233).

The abrupt moment of destruction from above haunts Spender because it seems to sever history absolutely. To remember the modern city of cinemas, street lights, and taxis seems delusional. In Cologne, he finds that "magical feat of reconstruction" nearly impossible, but in Berlin nostalgia overshadows him. As they drive toward the center of the ruined city, Spender's narrative detours into a long reminiscence of Weimar Berlin: a city that seemed "realer" than any other, "the *reductio ad absurdum* of the contemporary situation" (236). He remembers the bed-sitting rooms he rented; the Café am Zoo, where he wrote; the "very smart bar and restaurant" guarded by "one of two extremely handsome page boys"; and the brazen nightclubs "notorious because there was nothing secret about them." None of it remains: "the whole of this settled, elaborated life where the roads were like polished grooves and rails along which everyone who moved knew his or her destination, whether for good or for bad, had gone. The contours which I saw through the darkness were torn, ragged edges" (238). By the time he reaches the heart of the city – skeletal and exposed – he realizes "that everything was like this, that an enormous shroud of sameness has blurred and covered the whole face of Berlin and that nothing which I knew existed any longer" (239). Wartime has utterly obliterated the city that memory had carefully preserved.

In her postwar study *Pleasure of Ruins*, Rose Macaulay distinguishes between ruins whose "weathered patina of age" and strange beauty draw European travelers and "new ruins," which are "stark and bare, vegetation-less and creatureless; blackened and torn, they smell of fire and mortality." Their ruin still raw, they draw only horrified observers. Majestic buildings just destroyed resemble "murdered bodies"; bombed cities produce "resentful sadness."[82] The destruction permeates the observer: Spender explains that bodies decaying in the rubble and mounds of rotting garbage produce "a persistent smell which never le[aves] one alone" (24). Most shockingly, the ruins he sees are inhabited: the masses trudging amidst them without apparent aim are "the same people" who once gazed in shop windows, dined in restaurants, and moved purposefully through the streets. Spender's visceral reaction pervades his description of the thousands who inhabit Cologne's ruins: "quite dissociated" from the city, they resemble "a tribe of wanderers who have discovered a ruined city in a desert and who are camping there, living in the cellars and hunting amongst the ruins for the booty, relics of a dead civilization" (15). Their existence is "a base mechanical kind of life like that of insects," or "rats in the cellars, or bats wheeling around the towers" of the ruined cathedral (17). Against this nihilistic nightmare, Spender's traveling to witness the condition of intellectual life and imagine the future of libraries seems absurd.

Throughout, *European Witness* subordinates Spender's official mission to his subjective responses and disrupts temporality and geography for effect. The narrative begins with Spender at the headquarters of the Twenty-first Army Group in a requisitioned nineteenth-century spa in Westphalia; it ends with him in the shelter of a dead dictator in the devastated heart of Berlin. The first section, "Rhineland Journey," is dated July and August 1945. The second consolidates three sojourns in France (May, August, and October) into a single "French Interlude" to offer respite and perspective. The third, "Journeys through the British Zone," is dated September and October 1945. The dates place his account in time, but *European Witness* proceeds more by juxtaposition than by itinerary. Within the first section, for example, the chapter describing the life of refugees in ruined Cologne is followed by a chapter about visiting university professors in their comfortable, undamaged suburb of Bonn overlooking the Rhine, just twenty-five miles away. In the third section, he intersperses his reflections on what he's reading with stories about what he's doing. Midway through *European Witness* Spender explains that subjective interest, not official importance, drives his narrative. In "French Interlude" he describes a party of left-wing intellectuals at which he sees the surrealist Tristan Tzara, who later uses "grotesque" in replying to a minor error he makes in print. The recollection occasions Spender's preemptive defense of his method:

> Here is an opportunity to explain that in a certain sense this book is much nearer to being a romance than an official report. I am not trying to do justice to things in their order of importance.... My point of view is really that since I have my own pen, my own paper, my own ink and my own typewriter, I write about what interests me rather than about what ought to interest me. As a matter of fact, in this lies my only chance of interesting my reader. I might even invent a few "grotesques" if that suited my purpose. (117–118)

Later, stuck in Bonn because of car trouble, Spender looks up Rudi Bach, a young German boy whose life he had saved by obtaining penicillin. Although compassion figures in his account of their earlier exchanges, his motives now are literary: he wants "to write up the sequel." His actions, he explains, are "dictated partly by the desire of my Journal to achieve its own investigations through the agency of me, partly by the whims of my motor car and the intrigues of my driver" (156).

Spender's odd suggestion that his narrative directs his agency hints at the impossibility of the ethical task to which he has set himself: bearing witness of the present state of life in Germany. No single vantage point suffices for comprehending the consequences of a dozen years of Nazi rule and half-dozen of war, or the chaos of a defeated nation broken into occupied zones. In *Writing War*, Norris argues that "the generic difficulties of presenting the effects and experiences of mass warfare are aggravated by the inadequacy of fictional traditions to address the fundamental destabilizations of entire populations." The strategy of "exteriorizing the horror, representing it as seen but inadequately incorporated into the viewing eye" fails, for in "straddling the thin line between voyeurism and witness" it favors the decadence of the former over the affective obligation of the latter. Thus, she explains, many narratives – fictional and nonfictional – make "synecdochic use of the 'vignette'" to provide "'representative' figures for elucidating the war experience."[83] In a ruined world, sense seems to cohere only in the immediate present and only at

the level of the anecdote, so Spender oscillates between his own experiences and vignettes in which individuals tell him their stories in their own
voices. Chapter titles announce synedoche: "Polish Displaced Persons,"
"A Student," "Interpreter," "Concentration Camp Inmate." In several
Germans recount their wartime relation to Nazism. The student, "very
anxious to please" Spender, makes "doubly revealing" remarks about race
and says he opposed the Nazis but remained a party member to cover
himself (30). He is the first of many Spender meets who doubt the news
reports of atrocities at Belsen and Buchenwald. The interpreter – recom-
mended for his sincerity – turns out to be a rabid anti-Semite who denies
party membership yet is "quite sure that the Führer knew nothing about
what was going on" at the extermination camps (37). Frau Bach, "the most
unctuous type of respectable pious hausfrau," complains that the occupiers requisition the houses of non-Nazis before those of party members
and declares that "[s]ome of the worst Nazis have been clever enough to
avoid being Party members, but everyone knew who these were" (158).
Professors in Bonn who opposed Hitler demonstrate a parochialism of
thought that Spender attributes to years of intellectual isolation; the
Düsseldorf librarian, whose mayor identifies him as "no Nazi, although he
had been a member of the Party," explains his vigorous efforts to combat
"the nazification of German literature" (151, 154). These vignettes demonstrate the difficulty of a question – how to distinguish who or what is
Nazi? – that drives Spender's journey.[84]

The most understated, fragile vignettes in *European Witness* depict a
recently released concentration camp inmate and several refugees from
Nazi work camps who are Displaced Persons, or DPs, "the slaves who were
now worse off than slaves, having been freed to become a mass whom
no one wanted" (73).[85] The inmate, who had been a left-wing student,
describes his capricious treatment at the hands of the Gestapo and SS to
Spender and the university librarian. Although his rhetoric initially strikes
Spender as banal – he wants to write a book about his experiences titled
"Human Beasts" – the "curious details" he gradually reveals have the ring
of truth and make his story "difficult not to believe" (41, 42). The first
DPs Spender meets, six Polish peasant men sitting listlessly in a park, survived genocide at home only to be forced into slave labor in the Third
Reich. Their anger at their treatment by the Nazis is palpable but hard
to voice to "a stranger, coming from an island": they speak in bursts, followed by silences (26). When Spender asks about their origins, the oldest
explains: "Thirty thousand people were murdered in the town which we
came from. The town was burned down and many people we knew were

hanged on trees." His son, who escaped with him, adds that they "know nothing" of his mother and sister; the others have all "lost their relatives" (27). The moment demonstrates both the power of the individual anecdote and its limits. The men's stark story explains the profound apathy on their faces, which Spender professes wanting to understand. Yet he identifies neither the men nor their town by name; nothing distinguishes them as real rather than invented. Their particular traumatic experiences of death, dislocation, and forced labor quickly disappear into the sheer scale of the ruined world around them. As Norris explains, although the vignette "reduces the scale and magnitude of modern war violence sufficiently to retrieve an imaginable community of victims available to empathy and identification," it does so at the price of producing "deracinated figures."[86] In Spender's narrative, the Polish men remain "displaced," for they cohere only as types of a larger horror which he has seen "in the faces of the desperate young men of the demobilized Reichswehr, also in those of the French repatriated prisoners, and in those of other men and women labeled Displaced Persons" (29). Behind their visage lies internal ruin, "the fires which burned the cities of Europe still smouldering in the minds of men. This is a state of mind which glows beyond despair, beyond the destruction of our civilization" (28).

Having witnessed the extent of the war's ruin, Spender attests that the physical destruction and internal trauma he has seen must be of collective concern. The destruction in Cologne is "*serious* in more senses than one," he realizes, precisely because it reveals the defining shape of modernity: "a climax of deliberate effort, an achievement of our civilization, the most striking result of co-operation between nations in the twentieth century" (16). John Xiros Cooper argues that traveling in ruined Germany shocked Spender and other liberal British intellectuals because it exposed the "abyss of moral nihilism into which the Nazis *and* the Allies had all been swept."[87] Thus for Spender, "Germany" becomes synecdoche for a condition of despair that afflicts both Occupiers and Occupied, between whom relations can only be venal or violent, never mutual or free. This realization enervates him, producing a "violent home-sickness accompanied by a sensation of panic that I would never get out of Germany" (55). In a key chapter, "Nausea,"[88] he explains that his vertigo comes from

> the sense not just of a temporary condition around me in Germany which could be remedied by programmes of Reconstruction, but by the realization of a real potentiality ... of the ruin of Germany to become the ruins of the whole of Europe: of the people of Brussels and Paris, London and New York, to become herds wandering in their thousands across a continent....

> It was the sense as I walked along the streets of Bonn with a wind blow-
> ing putrescent dust of ruins as stinging as pepper into my nostrils, that the
> whole of our civilization was protected by such eggshell walls which could
> be blown down in a day. (62)

After months of travel in "a fantastic landscape of ruin and destruction, its
men and women as ruined as the land they inhabit," Spender imagines the
end of the world as easily as its survival.[89] The nations now inhabit perpetual wartime, all countries attached to a single time-bomb that is "likely
to explode" unless they collectively find a way to refuse chaos (92). In the
moment of modernity in which the only "unifying symbol" is the new
horror of the atomic bomb, *European Witness* asks whether the potential
for global ruin can be reversed (95).[90]

For long stretches, Spender subordinates depiction of people and places
to speculation on the ethical imperative that Europe faces:

> There is an Either-Or choice before men to-day which in the past was only
> real to religious thinkers whose minds saw life as an eternity where there
> was a separation of humanity into the good and the evil, heaven or hell,
> on the day of Judgment. But to-day we are confronted with the choice of
> making a heaven or a hell of the world in which we live, and the whole of
> civilization will be bound by whichever fate we choose. Moreover, it seems
> that we have to make the choice: we have to decide one way or the other;
> we cannot abdicate from the position of having to choose. (88)

What he witnesses most surely in this fractured narrative, as does West in
her encyclopedic text, comes to be the obligation that rests on him by virtue of his vantage point. Like *Black Lamb*, *European Witness* ends with an
assertion of hope, though neither narrator nor narrative has found a certain way out of the labyrinth. In its last scene, Spender and his wife walk
through the ruins of Berlin. For the first time since the introduction, he
returns to the language of tourism: "The Reichstag and the Chancellory
are already sights for sightseers.... They are the scenes of a collapse so
complete that it already has the remoteness of all final disasters"; "one
goes to the ruins with the same sense of wonder, the same straining of the
imagination, as one goes to the Colosseum at Rome." Tour guides stand
ready to "show you where Hitler stood, and contemptuously repeat what
he said": for a few cigarettes, one can buy an Iron Cross or fragments of the
Führer's desk (240). The present is already being packaged for the future.[91]
In that moment, at what once was the seat of Nazi power, Spender too
looks to the future. Having indicted the world of which he is a part, he
turns to distinguishing between good and evil.[92] Here, he attests, "Satan
was incarnated." Taking away pieces of Hitler's desk as "unholy relics," he

declares that "the only answer to this past and this present is a conscious … determination to make our society walk in paths of light" (245, 246).

Narratives of the "shattered present": *Love Thy Neighbor, We Wish to Inform You That Tomorrow We Will Be Killed with Our Families,* and *Palestine*

The "necessary reimagining of the world"[93] that follows the Second World War results not only from the dismantling of European empires but also from a deepened sense of the ethical crises of Western civilization in late modernity. For what Spender poses as a stark Either-Or endures longer and more chaotically than anyone might briefly have hoped in 1945. The aftermath of the global war at mid-century includes the establishment of the United Nations, the creation of international tribunals to judge crimes against humanity, and the irruption of little wars, year in and year out, around the globe. The decades of conflict called the Cold War coincide with the emergence of a compelling new literature about the experience of systematic violence against civilians, a practice identified by new term: "genocide."[94] When Gellhorn saw the "accursed cemetery prison" Dachau in May 1945, she wrote: "Nothing about war was ever as insanely wicked as these starved and outraged, naked nameless dead." "[S]urely," she concluded, "this war was made to abolish Dachau, and all the other places like Dachau, and everything that Dachau stood for, and to abolish it forever."[95] Yet twenty years later, during the war in Vietnam, she would add: "Tragically, the greatest war of the world, to date, spawned almost ceaseless little wars; the business is still unfinished."[96] In the increasingly globalized world of the second half of the century, as Favret suggests, "war" and "the everyday" coincide in both practice and theory: the postmodern condition is one of perpetual wartime.[97]

Black Lamb and *European Witness* anticipate new kinds of narrative that appear later in the century as writers travel to make sense of the chaos of postmodern history and write of wartime that never ends. Postmodern wartime seldom resembles an unambiguous Either-Or, but rather a labyrinthine moral ambiguity that challenges understanding. Fred Inglis describes the difficulty American writers have had representing the "ideological cacophony" they observe after the collapse of the Cold War's tidy rhetoric of good and evil:

> Diagnosticians of the shattered present overrate the tidy past. But it is clear that the way in which human clusters define and antagonize one another is once more on the move, and that journalists presently lack a ready political

narrative within which to situate stories, explain action and find meaning. The break-up of the former Yugoslavia, the attempted secessions of parts of Indonesia and Sri Lanka, the inexplicable civil wars of central Africa, above all the hideous destruction of the New York World Trade center, all offer recent examples of political news which journalists struggled helplessly to explain: they could only describe what they saw.[98]

Yet description alone does not suffice, for narrative is the necessary means for making war intelligible. As Svend Erik Larsen argues, it is specifically through narration, or *la mise en discours*, that literature "makes an event out of the war – with a place, a beginning and an ending that the war does not have in itself, and which we subsequently project on the real events." Narrative "*constitutes* a relation between war and landscape"; it "offers a perspective on the relationship at the same time that it constructs a specific version of it."[99] *How* it does so is of critical importance, for no single vantage point allows full comprehension of war's insanity, and – to echo Gellhorn – war is "always worse" than one knows how to say. To attest to trauma and to understand why and how civilian bloodshed and genocide happen in a global, metropolitan world, many writers draw on the travel narrative, with its "concern for witness and event."[100] In such texts, writers who travel to report stories of tragedy elsewhere do more than convey "news": they use the stance of the subjective, mobile observer to provide a narrative thread for chaos, a vantage point through which the relation between war and event can cohere. Here travel narrative and war reporting meld in a reflective, investigative, literary narration of violent crisis that might be called the "narrative of the shattered present."

This strategy works compellingly in late twentieth-century narratives about travel through war and genocide, for in these narratives writers' sense of ethical obligation motivates their understanding of complex violent events as matters of collective concern in a post-atomic world. Although the traveler may not experience acts of violence firsthand, he or she can attest firsthand to their consequences and the condition of wartime. More productive than the question of whether such narrators are technically observers or witnesses may be the question of what stories they can be positioned to tell that others cannot.[101] The most formative element in these texts may well be the travel narrative's awareness of subjectivity's advantages and limitations, which allows the recognition that to constitute a perspective on war is to construct a version of it that makes some kinds of knowledge possible while precluding others. In travel narratives about war and genocide, this concern appears in the trajectory by which the traveler narrates the process of "coming to understand" both wartime events and his or her own ethical relation to them, however distant and unfathomable they initially appear. This concern animates the anecdote with which Woolf begins *Three Guineas*, in which she views "gruesome" photographs of death and destruction in Spain while at home in England. In so doing, Sarah Cole observes, she foregrounds "the disjunction between her own comfortable domestic position and the ripped-apart world of the people in the photographs, victims of fascist bombs." Rather than reprinting the photographs for readers, Woolf narrates the subjective process of viewing and responding. Thus, Cole explains, she presents war as an event of urgent concern though understanding is inevitably mediated: "It is only with that combination of immediacy and distance, Woolf believes, that we can begin to change our whole attitude towards militarism, war, violence, and patriarchal authority – those conditions which, in her view, have always been the enemy of humankind."[102] Only in simultaneous recognition of one's implication in violent events and one's own security can ethical comprehension of modernity's failure fully occur.[103]

Three texts of the 1990s by writers from the United States serve to demonstrate travel narrative's capacity for depicting a "shattered present" of genocide and perpetual wartime: Maass's *Love Thy Neighbor: A Story of War* (1996), about Bosnia; Gourevitch's *We Wish to Inform You That Tomorrow We Will Be Killed with Our Families* (1998), about Rwanda; and Joe Sacco's *Palestine* (1993–1996; collected 2001).[104] Each aims to convey war's catastrophic rupturing of civil order and civilian life and to elicit an affective response from readers whose own privileged location compounds the difficulty of representing as well as the urgency of understanding such extreme experiences. West asserted forcefully that a labyrinth connected events in Yugoslavia with life in Britain and could cite the Great War as evidence; Spender hardly needed to persuade his readers that the condition of Europe affected them. Narratives about genocide and wartime in Bosnia, Rwanda, and Palestine for postmodern American readers, however, require strategies that convincingly represent events there as shared matters of concern in which they are already implicated. (When the decade opened, the United States had little distinctive connection with Yugoslavia, lacked France or Britain's colonial history in Africa, and by public policy was firmly pro-Israel on Palestinian matters.) To this end, these narratives directly invoke readers with a frankness that startles in contrast with Spender and West. Maass and Gourevitch use the second person in their titles and quickly address readers directly. "When you grow up in America, you don't really learn how foul humans can smell, just as you don't learn about the smell of death," writes Maass.[105] "I'm telling you this here, at the outset, because this is a book about how people imagine themselves and one another – a book about how we imagine our world," explains Gourevitch (6).[106] Sacco, who uses graphic narrative, invites the reader in through his persona, who appears on many pages and allows access to his thoughts: readers simultaneously see what he sees, watch him observing, and glimpse his response – but only partially, for his ever-present glasses obscure his eyes. *Palestine* opens with Sacco having a tourist's response to Cairo traffic: "CRAZEEE!" He takes a break by "hanging with the hotel receptionists"; when one pounds a table saying "I WOULD SMASH ISRAEL!" he responds silently, "Hoo boy! I'm in the Middle East!"[107]

In differing ways, these narratives use the subjective, mobile observer of the travel genre to write about wartime. The through-line of *Love Thy Neighbor* is less "a story of war" than the story of Maass's own struggle to understand the horrors he reports. Sent to Bosnia to cover the war, he is skeptical when he first hears a refugee's story: "I wrote it down in my notebook but I didn't believe it. How could she have been on the run with two children for forty-five days? ... The year was 1992, not 1942, and Bosnia had smooth roads and fast cars with antilock braking systems and double-overhead cam engines. What was going on?" (5). He initially answers the question that refugee stories "posed about human beings – how could they do such monstrous things?" by clinging to the "comforting explanation" that the violence is "an antimodern and anti-Western phenomenon – an exception." Yet he must soon abandon this notion, for "even in its wrecked state, you learn very quickly that [Bosnia] was a relatively sophisticated place before the war" and many of the perpetrators of "ethnic cleansing" "were lawyers and engineers who, in peacetime, wore ties to work and had Sony televisions" (14).[108] Maass's narrative becomes a quest to comprehend why and how the "wild beast" of evil persists within civilization (15). To this end he listens to the last wish of Muharem Kržić, a Bosnian Muslim leader who wants to smuggle his wife's and daughter's diplomas out of Banja Luka, and seeks out Nedret Mujkanović, a surgery intern who spends nine months saving lives in besieged Srebrenica, where he must perform "hundreds of amputations without anesthetic" (243).

The narrative proceeds by Maass recounting experiences, then stepping back to frame events for American readers. (Though it begins with his arrival and ends with his departure, the order is not strictly chronological, and Maass comes and goes between Bosnia and Belgrade.) In 1992, he travels to Prijedor with other journalists, determined to see a Serbian gulag before its master, an anesthesiologist turned warlord, conceals all evidence of concentration camps. Led by an "unsavory" local official, they take a "Potemkinized tour" (39). Maass narrates his shock:

> I never thought that one day I would talk to a skeleton. That's what I did at Trnopolje. I walked through the gates and couldn't quite believe what I saw. There, right in front of me, were men who looked like survivors of Auschwitz. I remember thinking that they walked surprisingly well for people without muscle or flesh. I was surprised at the mere fact that they could still talk. Imagine, talking skeletons! As I spoke to one of them, I looked at his arm and realized that I could grab hold of it and snap it into two pieces like a brittle twig. I could do the same with his legs. I saw dozens of other walking skeletons of that sort. I could break all of their arms, all of their legs. Snap. Snap. Snap. (41)

After describing the horrific scene, he addresses American skeptics who ask whether the camps were "really" as bad as reported: "Yes, I visited them, and yes, they were as bad as you could imagine. Didn't you see the images on television? Don't you believe what you see?" (41). He writes of his own affective response, at times nakedly. During a three-hour interview of Mujkanović, "at several points … I had to look away and not listen, and tell myself to hold on" (243). Maass sees the consequences of violence on the streets and in hospitals, where he interviews patients while trying to keep his eyes from focusing on "the soiled bandages sticking onto their wounds … or the rows of metal rods poking out from their shattered limbs" and keep his breathing even (133). But he stops short at "the horrors of the morgue," and so sees only one of the "100,000 human beings … turned into corpses": "what I feared was not the disgust of seeing a boy without a head, but the memory I would have of it for the rest of my life" (135, 134).

By narrating not only what he learns and observes but also his visceral responses, Maass offers a mix of distance and immediacy that echoes Woolf. What finally makes him "spiritually sick" is the awful juxtaposition of his interview with Mujkanović and the public speech that "William Jefferson Clinton, perhaps the only person in the world who could turn things around," gives at the dedication of the U.S. Holocaust Memorial Museum in 1993 (243). Clinton's remarks on the obligations of witness hypocritically belie his refusal to act on the testimony of those who have seen the violence in Bosnia firsthand. Exhausted and determined that his work remain ethically engaged and not drift into cynical "horror porn," Maass decides he must leave Bosnia to regain critical perspective (247). Two years later, as he finishes *Love Thy Neighbor*, he explains the entanglement of observer and observed: his book

is about war, about Bosnia, about politics and hatred and demagogues and
heroes and cowards and me and … I think it is about the wild beast, which
is … a spirit of evil that exists in all animals, all peoples, all societies.…
Why should Bosnia matter to those of us fortunate enough not to live
there? Here is my answer: Bosnia can teach us about the wild beast, and
therefore about ourselves, and our destinies (273).

His epilogue on the fragility of civilized human relations echoes the moral
imperative of his title.

Maass leaves Bosnia in the midst of the war, with thousands dead and
displaced, many yet to die. Gourevitch arrives in Rwanda in 1995, a year
after the government-provoked Hutu slaughter of 800,000 Tutsi citizens in three months. In the latest atrocity, Tutsis have just killed 2,000
Hutus at the Kibeho camp for IDPs – "internally displaced persons."
The narrative of *We Wish to Inform You* moves among multiple threads as
Gourevitch reports events of the genocide through the stories of Rwandans
he meets – particularly those of Odette Nyiramilimo, a physician, and
Paul Rusesabagina, manager of the Hôtel des Mille Collines – travels to
scenes of mass murder, and observes as Rwandans attempt to found a new
civil order with ineffectual help from the United Nations. The massacre
of IDPs demonstrates the difficulty of ending the evil of genocide, perhaps the impossibility of ever exiting the condition of wartime: "Nobody
had any idea how to close [the camps] peacefully; in fact, nobody really
seemed to believe that was possible" (187). Odette "was three when this
history of the genocide began" and her family's house was burnt by men
with machetes (63). She is older than forty in 1997, when more than 300
Tutsis are murdered by Hutu Power terrorists the same month that U.S.
Secretary of State Madeleine Albright publicly declares: "We, the international community, should have been more active in the early stages of the
atrocities in Rwanda in 1994, and called them what they were – genocide"
(350). Gourevitch's own reflections center on the relation among individual stories, the mind-numbing totals of "the most efficient mass killing
since the atomic bombings of Hiroshima and Nagasaki," and two abstrac-
tions as unfathomable as they are crucial: "genocide" and "justice" (3).

Early in the narrative – but relatively late in his time in Rwanda –
Gourevitch and two Canadian military officers travel by UN helicop-
ter to visit the Roman Catholic church at Nyarubuye. Many thousands
who sought sanctuary were slaughtered there in 1994, and afterward their
bodies deliberately kept unburied as a stark memorial. The dead "did not
smell," Gourevitch observes, and many of their bones "lay scattered away
from the bodies, dismembered by the killers, or by scavengers – birds,

dogs, bugs. The more complete figures looked a lot like people, which they were once" (15). Why had he come to see them, "so intimately exposed"? "I had felt compelled to come to Nyarubuye: to be stuck with them – not with their experience, but with the experience of looking at them. They had been killed there, and they were dead there" (16). The most unsettling moment comes when an officer inadvertently steps on a skull and breaks it; Gourevitch, angered at this violation, then hears "another crunch.... I had stepped on one too" (20).[109] Later in the narrative – but earlier in time – Gourevitch and Alexandre, a Greek UN Human Rights monitor who had been at the Kibeho massacre, discuss the ethical obligation of the living to the dead. Gourevitch, who doubts "the necessity of seeing the victims in order fully to confront the crime," speculates about the line between voyeurism and witness: "The aesthetic assault of the macabre creates excitement and emotion, but does the spectacle really serve our understanding of the wrong? ... Even as we look at atrocity, we find ways to regard it as unreal. And the more we look, the more we become inured to – not informed by – what we are seeing" (196).[110] But Alexandre, haunted by the fact that he had to walk upon the dead to rescue orphaned children from piles of bodies, disagrees: "I experienced Kibeho as a movie. It *was* unreal. Only afterward, looking at my photographs – then it became real" (196). In the horrific moment, meaning is inchoate; Alexandre's comprehension of traumatic experience comes through narrating his actions in witnessing the massacre and saving children and "his own passage from a sense of unreality during the events to the reality of his pictures" (197).

For Gourevitch, the brute fact of Nyarubuye and Kibeho, where "[y]ou couldn't walk for all the dead," becomes synecdoche for the crime at which "the mind balks," the crime of genocide, of "wanting to make a people extinct" (201, 202). He leaves Rwanda exhausted but returns often, driven to understand the incomprehensible, hoping to glimpse the possibility of a way out of genocide's perpetual wartime. "Carefully balancing personal response, extensive interviews, historical research, and vivid descriptions," Peter Hulme concludes, "Gourevitch manages – against all odds – to produce a life-affirming book" about events of inarticulable horror.[111] To do so, he must face a cruel truth: justice can never be obtained. He paraphrases a politician who tells him that "a true genocide and a true justice are incompatible," for then killing will never end – and, despite tribunals and reconciliation ceremonies, it doesn't (249). Gourevitch ends his narrative with a last story of martyrdom, in which he finds "some courage": when Hutu Power *génocidaires* attack boarding schools in 1997, the schoolchildren refuse their orders to divide themselves as Hutus and Tutsis. Instead of choosing to live by turning on each other, they elect "to call themselves Rwandans," dying for a future others will inherit (353).

Like Maass and Gourevitch, Sacco uses his own "coming to understand" to link disparate stories and competing points of view in *Palestine*, a narrative about his travels in the Occupied Territories during the first intifada. Originally published in serial form, *Palestine* comprises nine chapters with more than four dozen episodes. Sacco's candid depiction of journalistic ego reveals the complex position of privileged narrator especially well. Early on, he grabs taxis with thoughts of himself as Lawrence of Arabia or Dan Rather and saunters through Nablus with attitude, seeking Palestinians to tell him their stories. It is a game to obtain "real life adaptation of all those affidavits I've been reading" and get "up close and almost personal." When a man asks, "You write something about us?" Sacco thinks quickly of success: "Of course of course! ... I will alert the world to your suffering! Watch your local comic-book store.... Mission accomplished!" (10). Similar thoughts – slightly tempered by experience – preoccupy Sacco as he and Sameh, a volunteer social worker, traverse Jabalia, a huge refugee camp in Gaza:

> I'm blinking fast, snapping mental pictures and thinking. "This'll make a great couple of pages in the comic" – a weird scene of a pitching car with the rain going torrential while Sameh strains to see over his shoulder into the dark and fumbles with the gears to back us out of another washed-out path ... and that's me next to him and this is my happiest moment.... I've made it, you understand ... here I am, brushing up against the Palestinian experience, a goddamn adventure cartoonist who hasn't changed his clothes in days, who's stepped over a few dead rats ... who's bullshitted with the boys and nodded knowingly at their horrible narratives ... and I'm pinching myself in a car in the dark in a flood, giddy from the ferocity outside, thinking, "Throw it at me baby, I can take it," but I've got the window rolled up tight...

Awash in reverie as he plans his adventure tale, he almost forgets the risks Sameh takes to show him the violence of occupation: "Sameh, on the other hand, is unaware of the moment's magnificence.... He's stressing ... he hasn't got a license ... also, we've got a forbidden video on board" (208). Later, sobered after one of "the guys" tells him "the last time I showed a journalist around, I spent two years in prison," Sacco sheds his bravado for anxiety about the curfew they are violating and the illicit video in his hand (210).

Here, as in his next book, *Safe Area Goražde* (2000), Sacco "portrays himself both visually and anecdotally as an ambiguous figure whose instinct[s] for self-preservation and gratification sometimes outweigh his ability to be an ethical witness."[112] In some situations, he acts like an outsider "raised a suburban schoolboy," such as when he insists that men who were forcefully interrogated "indulge" him by demonstrating the Shin Bet's techniques, for he knows torture only through wax museums and childhood cruelty to animals (94). In others, he deliberately plays the role of one who understands, such as when he talks with feminists to get "the lowdown on the Palestinian women's movement" – "we're all on the same wave-length" – and then meets with refugee women to "get some handle" on their wearing of the hijab (133, 137, 138). Sacco ends that episode by reflecting that listening to religious women "throws me for a loop, and I see the gulf between us … I've forgotten what it's like to *want* to have faith" (140). Yet immediately following he places a one-page episode, "Still One of the Boys," in which he jokes with Palestinian men about polygamy, laughing so hard tears come to his eyes (141).[113] In such scenes, Sacco archly depicts the traveling observer's vacillation between using people for his own ends and understanding their stories with genuine empathy.

Sacco effectively uses graphic narrative's juxtaposition of text and image to challenge official discourse that obscures the realities of quotidian Palestinian life. The episode "Return" contains a brief history of Zionism and juxtaposes the story of an American Jew, Dave, with the story of an elderly Palestinian man. American and Palestinian appear up close on opposing pages, each talking about "home." Dave initially found it "kinda funny … getting into my heritage" but now thinks "*this* feels like home to me" (11). The man, a refugee since fleeing his home in 1948, had "returned, as it were," decades later to view "my land … where my house was"; to his horror he found a highway cutting through bare landscape, "no sign that we ever lived there" (14, 15). "Refugeland" criticizes the UN relief agency for giving bus tours of Jabaliya that underplay the "open sewage and omniscient I[sraeli] D[efense] F[orce] towers" by ending on "an upbeat note" of progress – a star deaf child at a rehab center who has learned to read lips (149). "Moderate Pressure" recounts the story of Ghassan, whose arrest on suspicion of belonging to an illegal organization takes him from his "middle class living room" into the "parallel universe" of "people strapped to chairs, sleep deprivation … other things happening for 'reasons of national security' … to combat 'terrorist activity'" (102). A black border marks each page, demarcating the nightmare world that engulfs him (see Illustration 8). Ghassan is shackled in painful positions for hours, a bag on his head as

Illustration 8. "Moderate Pressure," panels from Sacco's *Palestine*.

Illustration 8. (*continued*)

loud music blasts nonstop. "After four days without sleep, I began to have hallucinations" (109). Sacco decreases the panel size, echoing the bound man's heightened sense of claustrophobia.[114] Ghassan's nightmare visions of family members appear in succession: his daughter and brother dead on the floor, his father and uncle in coffins, his mother in a hospital bed, then, days later, his daughter again, dead in a urine-soaked confinement cell. When an Israeli judge finally orders his release after nineteen days, he and his attorney climb wordlessly into a car and drive away. The last panel, which fills a half-page, shows a busy urban street where secular Jews and Hasidim coexist peacefully with apparently unaware of the apparatus of torture undergirding their alternate reality.

In "The Bucket," Sacco addresses the disparity between what he can depict through vignettes and what he cannot. Each story is just "a teardrop in the bucket": the six olive trees that one anguished man was forced to cut on his land figure more than 120,000 that were destroyed during the first four years of the intifada; one old woman's story of soldiers bulldozing her house represents nearly 1,250 houses demolished; a panel that depicts two men bleeding to death after being shot by a Jewish settler who goes free is followed by a statement about forty others (62). Sacco is an engaged observer who travels without predetermined conclusions; in Edward Said's words, "Joe is there to be in Palestine, and only that – in effect to spend as much time as he can sharing, if not finally living the life that Palestinians are condemned to lead."[115] Like other narratives that use vignettes for indirect witness, *Palestine* asserts as a principle of faith that one privileged to hear others' stories has an ethical obligation – that each teardrop in the bucket does matter. Near the end of Sacco's narrative, a refugee woman in Gaza who has lost two sons and her husband to intifada and inadequate medical care tells him her story; it brings Sameh, who translates, to tears. She ends with a question that is an indictment: "She asks, what good is it to talk to you? ... We don't want money, she says, we want our land, our humanity. Aren't we people too? ... How are words going to change things?" (242–243). In the moment, asked whether his work has meaning, Sacco doesn't know what to say. *Palestine* is his impassioned response. It ends in uncertainty, the comic book artist a passenger on an Israeli bus lost in Gaza, backing away from Palestinian boys with stones.

At the end of the conventional travel book, the narrator returns home, renewed and perhaps enlightened. At the end of the war memoir, the narrator returns home, scarred but alive. Narratives of travel through the scene of perpetual wartime, however, necessarily end *in medias res*.

For wartime, as Kate McLoughlin argues, "reconfigures time as well as space": having a "special property of *open-endedness* or *endinglessness*," it "demands a bespoke narratology, or even, given the importance to it of (lack of) endings, a bespoke eschatology or theology."[116] Thus its narratives end with narrators still immured in the labyrinth of modernity, hoping that the act of attesting to what they have witnessed might help to open a future yet-to-be.

CHAPTER 6

The Allure of Authenticity

On the third pass, I find our house. It has been converted into a
community health clinic, a big Red Cross sign out front.

My heart dips at the sight of it. The front of the building has been
demolished and rebuilt farther back to make room for motorbike
parking. I peek inside. There have been some major structural modi-
fications. The head nurse greets me at the door. When I tell her that
my family once lived here, she expresses concern that I might be
one of those Viet-kieu returning to reclaim properties the government or squatters seized. I assure here I am only here for my childhood memories. Sighing relief, she tours me through the clinic.
The building seems new, small, strange. There is nothing left of my
youth. After fifteen minutes, she returns to work, leaving me milling
about the house trying to – as she puts it – *"visit the humble life that
came before."*

Andrew X. Pham (1999)[1]

In the globalized world of the twentieth century – consequent modernity's transformations and wartime's dislocations – transience and rupture replace stasis and continuity as the norm. The common notion that
modernity diminishes authenticity understands these profound changes
as a story of loss. By separating human beings from identities, places of
origin, and modes of being that have been and properly should be their
own – so the argument goes – modernization and globalization produce
new forms of life, for which a new term appears: "inauthentic."[2] Several
entangled premises comprise this view: that rural life is more natural than
urban life, that origin determines identity, that security lies in continuity,
that rootedness is preferable to diaspora, that the agrarian past was more
genuine than the global present, that history rather than futurity grounds
life's meaning. In the nineteenth century, Marx diagnoses the condition of alienation; in the twentieth century, existentialist philosophers
respond to alienation's effects with a clarion call for authentic modes of

being, sometimes figured as pre-modern. Theodor Adorno thus criticizes existentialism's "jargon of authenticity":

> Past forms of societalization, prior to the division of labor, are surreptitiously adopted as if they were eternal. Their reflection falls upon later conditions which have already been victimized by progressive rationalization, and in contrast to those the earlier states seem the more human. That which authentics ... call with gusto the image of man, they locate in a zone in which it is no longer permitted to ask from where those conditions emerged; neither can one ask what was done to the subjugated at any particular time, with the transition from nomadic life to settledness.[3]

Once some kinds of experience are deemed inauthentic, those now esteemed as "authentic" acquire new value (for they appear endangered) and nostalgic patina (for they conjure the past). The advent of the postmodern era of simulation accelerates the demand for the authentic, as Jean Baudrillard famously argues: "There is a plethora of myths of origin and of signs of reality – a plethora of truth, of secondary objectivity, and authenticity. Escalation of the true, of lived experience.... Panic-stricken production of the real and of the referential."[4] Modernity, in short, may be understood as a complex condition that produces the pursuit of representations and circumstances it romanticizes as authentic even as it makes them scarce, postmodernity as the historical condition that follows, in which authenticity can no longer be recovered but only fashioned anew.[5]

Travel's claim to provide firsthand experience of the world thus acquires a new urgency: moderns and postmoderns travel to observe and participate in authentic life. (Through ethnography, photography, and museum-building, they also seek to preserve whatever remains.[6]) The desire for authenticity motivates travel even as "tourist" becomes "a derisive label for someone who seems content with his obviously inauthentic experiences," as sociologist Dean MacCannell has argued.[7] Erik Cohen's phenomenological analysis of touristic experience distinguishes five modes. The first two designate travel symptomatic of modern societies generally: "recreational" and "diversionary."[8] In the third, "experiential," tourists seek, as MacCannell explains, "to see life as it is really lived"; they hope to achieve "an *authentic* and *demystified* experience of an aspect of some society or other person."[9] In the most serious modes, which Cohen calls "experimental" and "existential," journeying "takes up a new and heightened significance," for the traveler seeks to "sample" others' authentic life, or even undertake a life-changing pilgrimage "from chaos into another cosmos, from meaninglessness to authentic existence."[10] Such travelers envision authentic existence as the opposite of tourism: it involves being so fully in place, so engaged in the present, that the fragmentation modern subjects experience as anxious self-consciousness or malaise dissipates. To claim authenticity for oneself is to situate oneself in the world.

Travel narratives concerned with authenticity demonstrate each of Cohen's last three modes, often intermixed. Most commonly, the narrator casts the journey as an attempt to transcend the conditions of (post) modernity to obtain the knowledge and experience necessary to distinguish genuine from spurious. This understanding of travel's meliorative potential rests on the conviction that experience can confirm the truth of things. In her analysis "The Evidence of Experience," Joan W. Scott cites Raymond Williams' account of "experience" as referring to both "subjective testimony as immediate, true, and authentic" and "social conditions, institutions, forms of belief or perception" external to individuals, to which they react. Confident in the authority of the former, subjects take it to be "the ground for all (subsequent) reasoning and analysis" and thus the basis for comprehension of the latter.[11] By pledging to represent the narrator's real experience, depict places so vividly that readers may travel vicariously, and translate difference into comprehensibility, such travel narratives promise to guarantee the authentic. They reiterate the allure of the notion that experience signifies, that it bears "epistemic authority."[12]

Notions of authenticity thus attach to every aspect of travel and its representation: travelers' experiences, places and peoples observed, and narratives written. Authenticity becomes the avowed purpose of both journey and narrative. But whose authenticity, determined how, by whom, for what purposes, remains subjective and contestable. Ethnographers and travelers like Ella Maillart concern themselves most with ways of life that might disappear: the Bedouin in Arabia, the "real" Russia threatened by Soviet collectivization. Others, especially later in the century, care most that their own travel be authentic: autonomous, unique flânerie in a world of mass reproduction. As discussed in Chapter 4 – and as Adorno observes – nostalgia often provides the language and images through which travelers imagine a world in which meaning is certain, even as it fails to reverse the temporality of modernity or guarantee authenticity.[13] Many travelers seek authenticity to ameliorate their experiences of wartime chaos, secularization, and diaspora. In response to abrupt transformations and the consequent collapse of old forms of meaning, they seek to mitigate transience or repair anomie through travel to sites of familial or national origin: the rural village, the place one's great-grandfather was born, the landscapes that gave birth to mythic figures. This seeking of authenticity for oneself or, by metonymy, the nation is a distinctive development in the travel genre. In the years following the First World War, for example, H. V. Morton travels by car through England, Scotland, Ireland, and Wales "in search of" places that maintained "individuality" and villages where "the national spirit can thrive in peace."[14] Many wartime refugees who become American citizens, such as Eva Hoffman and Andrew X. Pham, travel back to their first homelands seeking to make sense of their families, their persistent dislocation, and themselves. Others seek authenticity through pilgrimage to sites credited with significance that might prove uncompromised even in the era of simulation: they trek to Lhasa, go on haj to Mecca, climb sacred Buddhist mountains, or – in one of the more overdetermined journeys possible – retrace the steps of Jesus. In such narratives, travelers vexed by modernity's irreversible transformations and the condition of postmodernity create new versions of affiliation and meaning.

Like the narratives of perpetual wartime analyzed in Chapter 5, travel narratives concerned with authenticity cast the narrator as subjective witness. But the purpose of witnessing differs, for here narrative serves to demonstrate that the traveler's own experience has distinctive, meliorating value. In her analysis of travel tropes, Caren Kaplan identifies the modernist strategy of resisting modernity's "commodifications" through "celebration of 'experience.'"[15] In counterpoint to stories of alienation, travel narrative simultaneously performs and tells the story of performing the authentic. The performance produces the meaning it promises to chronicle; it makes elusive experience concrete and ineffable meaning real. Susan Stewart explains:

> Narrative is "about" closure; the boundaries of events form the ideological basis for the interpretation of their significance. Indeed, without narrative, without the organization of experience, the event cannot come to be. This organization is … an establishing of the causality implicit in temporality, but narrative closure is offered outside the temporality of our everyday lives. It … is performed with self-consciousness, with a manipulation of point of view within its own story time, the context of its performance.[16]

Travel narratives concerned with authenticity require more explicit closure than narratives of travel through perpetual wartime, which necessarily end *in medias res*, for here narrative constitutes the journey as authentic event and confirms its abiding value. Laced with evidence of the conditions they would ameliorate, such narratives close by creating a provisional authenticity, grounded in the immediacy of the event, that might be viable for the future. When Morton travels through Palestine "in the steps of the Master" in the 1930s, for instance, he seeks genuine traces of Jesus amidst the trappings of tourism and signs of British rule. His narrative, which evidences his skepticism, nonetheless attests to the meaningfulness of his journey by ending with Mary Magdalene meeting the resurrected Christ, an event Morton makes immediate by telling it as though he were an eyewitness.

Yet celebrating experience through narrative incurs a paradox, for it makes explicit the fact that language and memory mediate access to the event. Stewart identifies the contradictory assumptions upon which our understanding of experience rests:

> Although narrative offers transcendence, it lacks authenticity, for its experience is *other*. The printed word suffers doubly from this lack, for not only has it lost the authenticity of lived experience – it has lost the authenticity of authorial voice as well. Who is speaking? It is the voice of abstraction.... In this outline of experience we can see a simultaneous and contradictory set of assumptions. First, the assumption that immediate lived experience is more "real," bearing within itself an authenticity which cannot be transferred to mediated experience; yet second, the assumption that the mediated experience known through language and the temporality of narrative can offer pattern and insight by virtue of its capacity for transcendence.[17]

Travel narrative that takes authenticity as its subject faces this conundrum at every turn, for its claim lies in its fidelity to experience. Yet apprehension of experience is tenuous and disputable, for relations between occurrence, perception, narration, and reception are anything but straightforward and pristine. That an experience offers purchase on the authentic is not a certain fact but a claim about meaning: the scene that sates one traveler's longings shatters another's preconceptions, and one person's homeland is another's occupied territory. Experience, as Scott explains, "is at once always already an interpretation and something that needs to be interpreted. What counts as experience is neither self-evident nor straightforward; it is always contested, and always therefore political."[18] Claims about its meaning are contingent and situated, as Trinh T. Minh-ha explains in writing about identity:

> Despite our desperate, eternal attempt to separate, contain, and mend, categories always leak. Of all the layers that form the open (never finite) totality of "I," which is to be filtered out as superfluous, fake, corrupt, and

which is to be called pure, true, real, genuine, original, authentic? Which, indeed, since all interchange, revolving in an endless process? (According to the context in which they operate, the superfluous can become real; the authentic can prove fake; and so on.) *Authenticity* as a need to rely on an "undisputed origin," is prey to an obsessive *fear*: that of *losing a connection*.[19]

Authenticity cannot be guaranteed, for it is a complex performance that occurs within cultural and geopolitical contexts that are at once mutable and fragile.

Narratives about travelers seeking "the Holy Land" in Palestine cast the politics of authenticity in sharp relief. Western travel in the Levant proliferated rapidly after the end of the Crimean War, and the development of package tours coincided with secularism's growing influence and higher criticism's challenge to the Bible's presumed historicity.[20] For some, Palestine was one of many stops on a grand tour; for others, it was the ultimate devotional destination. However such travelers' motives may mix religious and secular interest, the conventions of pilgrimage – the practice of demonstrating one's own faith and memorializing that of others through travel to sacred sites – influence their narratives. The pilgrim travels in earnestness, seeking to discover the real (though collectors of relics and memorabilia, pilgrims seldom foreground their material and imperial ambitions). The pilgrim seeks not merely to observe, but to experience an already known authentic and thus become its witness. Mary Baine Campbell explains:

> [T]he Christian pilgrim is looking for the past, but it is a past made up of singular events and personalities, individual epiphanies, incarnations, and martyrdoms. Places are referred to as "witnesses" of those events and people, and pilgrims in turn are witnesses of those places as events....
>
> The agendum of the pilgrim-traveler is an agendum of moments of perception ... the pilgrim-traveler's written account of the journey is a testimony to the achievement of such perceptions.[21]

Both Christian pilgrimage and devotional travel more generally presume that only believers can understand sacred places authentically, for they know the true history through which to perceive them.

The traveler prepared to know the authentic recognizes no slippage between signifier and signified. Simply being in the right place, in the right state of mind, text in hand provides the "plethora ... of signs of reality" that Baudrillard describes. For nineteenth-century travelers prepared to read "sacred geography," Hilton Obenzinger explains, "the Bible was more than a guidebook; it became the Holy Land itself – and the scenery of the living Palestine was continually adjusted to the textualized necessities of biblical narrative: the traveler always stepped into its pages."[22] Because it sets high stakes for travel as authentic experience, devotional travel is vulnerable to every promise of the real. Mark Twain – here postmodern before his time – satirizes this susceptibility in *The Innocents Abroad, or, The New Pilgrims' Progress: Being Some Account of the Steamship Quaker City's Pleasure Excursion to Europe and the Holy Land* (1869).[23] But whereas Twain questions the very notion of authenticity, most nineteenth- and early twentieth-century travel narratives about Palestine sought earnestly to divine the holiness of places. Frank DeHass's popular 1880s tome *Buried Cities Recovered; Or, Explorations in Bible Lands*, is representative. To one traveling "with the Bible as a guide-book," DeHass writes:

> The events of the remote past seem to have occurred but yesterday. Christ appears everywhere present, and you can almost fancy you hear his voice, saying, "Lo, I am with you alway." The narratives of the New Testament become living realities, and so striking is the harmony between the text of Scripture and the landscape, and so wonderfully do they accord, the very scenery is like a new gospel, or fresh revelation from God.[24]

In such narratives, Palestine's contemporary reality as a region within the Ottoman Empire is but a transient condition; its genuine existence lies in a transcendent identity as the Holy Land, an idea that rightly belongs to Christendom and the West.

John Finley's *A Pilgrim in Palestine: Being an Account of Journeys on Foot by the First American Pilgrim after General Allenby's Recovery of the Holy Land* (1919) demonstrates the geopolitics of the notion "Holy Land" unusually well. An American who headed the Red Cross in Palestine, Finley unabashedly celebrates Britain for "making it possible for Christendom to walk again in its holy places free of the Turk" – and free of Germans. He depicts Allenby's entry into Jerusalem in 1917 as "the greatest event of all the centuries of the Christian era since the first" and declares him "the real Deliverer of the Holy Land."[25] Finley goes so far as to identify Allenby as the Restorer prophesied in the book of Isaiah and devise a fanciful etymology by which his name, in Arabic, means "God-prophet."[26] Subordinating geography, history, and language to his own logic, Finley finds Palestine's primary significance in its role as proof-text for the victors' version of Christianity. Once the land has been secured by British forces, he journeys by foot, looking past the ruins left by battle to view the landscape of belief firsthand. At the end, he turns to the politics of the present. Writing as the global powers meet in postwar negotiations at Versailles, he calls for Palestine to be made an international territory, not an Arab state or

Jewish homeland. Although he would welcome "every earth-child who turns toward its holy hills with a pure heart and with clean hands," Finley argues that the West must restore Palestine reverently after "centuries of misrule and oppression" and enhance it as a symbol of "the supreme international planetary whole."²⁷ Finley's Christian dreams for how Palestine's history should be venerated differ profoundly from those of the Muslims and Jews whom Joe Sacco meets more than seventy years later, but their convictions about the authenticity of their claims are surprisingly similar.

Narratives of travel in search of authenticity respond to the century's perpetual transformations and dislocations in disparate ways, depending on cultural context and narrative purpose, as the texts discussed in this chapter demonstrate. The authentic that Morton seeks in the British Isles and Palestine lies in preserving particular ways of life and versions of history: he casts his objectives in cultural terms, largely ignoring the actual political contexts in which he writes. Although the persona of his narratives proves vague and inconstant, the terms of his investment in authenticity anticipate the more existential longing evident in travel narrative later in the century. For Pham, in contrast, travel serves as a way of amending an entanglement in his origins that has so impeded his ability to inhabit the present fully that it has done him harm. The authenticity he seeks lies in bridging between the past and the present to claim an identity fully his own. For others, authenticity lies in the present moment and its potential for the future. Thus Rosemary Mahoney, who finds traditional religiosity alien, joins contemporary pilgrims as a postmodern observer, seeking at once to understand their perception of the authentic and, critically, to articulate her own. In an "age of authenticity" in which, as Pericles Lewis argues, "the kinds of experience that formerly had been the province of organized religion to channel and explain shifted to belong, in large part, to private life and idiosyncratic expression," travel narrative, like the novel, serves as a means of working out, confirming, and creating authentic meaning.²⁸ For each of these travelers, narrative becomes the ultimate souvenir, in the sense described by Stewart: the souvenir serves "to authenticate a past or otherwise remote experience" in the present, for the future; its referent is "the intimate and direct experience of contact," or authenticity itself.²⁹

In Search of series and *In the Steps of the Master*

In *A Shrinking Island*, Jed Esty revises the influential view of modernist literature as primarily metropolitan and cosmopolitan with an account of late modernism's concern for national culture. In counterpoint to "international modernism and imperial Englishness," both of which "tend to subsume national, ethnic, or regional particularisms," he describes a "reorientation" of English culture that begins around 1930 in the work of both "popular writers and established modernists." In an inward turn, England "was refigured as the object of its own imperial discourse, its own touristic imagination, its own historical affections, its own documentary gaze, its own primitivizing fantasies ... and its own myths of origin."[30] Esty cites Morton's *In Search of England* (1927), which inaugurated a "self-discovery" trend of "popular books dedicated to the quest for authentic rural life in England" that fed a burgeoning domestic industry that would come to be known as heritage tourism.[31] The nine travel narratives that Morton would publish over the next decade demonstrate both modernism's inward turn and its imperial reach, even as signs of the empire's eventual contraction appeared. A journalist whose first success came reporting the discovery of Tutankhamen's tomb, Morton published newspaper columns while traveling and then promptly incorporated them into narratives presented as continuous, solitary journeys.[32] Having "found a voice" as "the perfect, modest English amateur" in his books about the British Isles, he later "adapted the formula in order to cater to the religious market."[33] He found considerable commercial success: *In Search of England* saw twenty-nine editions in sixteen years and *In the Steps of the Master* (1934) sold 210,000 copies in just two years.[34] His narratives about the British Isles and Palestine reveal both authenticity's allure in a mutable world and the artifice that his preferred versions of it require.

Morton frames *In Search of England* with familiar conventions, some reversed: it opens with a narrator who is anxious to escape "the black depths of misery," but rather than being in dismal London he's in Palestine, where he has succumbed to "a wave of home-sickness" and "solemnly cursed every moment I had spent wandering foolishly about the world."[35] Though he's a city dweller, a pastoral scene fills his imagination – a village at dusk, church bells ringing as the sun sets. "Why did I not think of St. Paul's Cathedral or Piccadilly?" he asks. "I have learnt since that this vision of mine is a common one to exiles all over the world: we think of home, we long for home, but we see something greater – *we see England*" (2).[36] This *England* grounds history and offers a "vitality older than London," for in it lie "the germs of all we are and all we have become: our manufacturing cities belong to the last century and a half; our villages stand with their roots in the Heptarchy" (3, 2). Once he returns, he hears "the road calling me" and sets out by motor-car to "see what lies off the beaten track" (3). In the narrative that follows, he drives through England, heading west to Cornwall, north through Glastonbury and Shrewsbury to Hadrian's Wall, south to Norwich, and on to Stratford and Warwick. The journey ends with the narrator arriving, as he envisioned in Palestine, in an unnamed "little hamlet, untouched by modern ideas, in spite of the wireless and the charabanc," where the last "real big sensation was in 1066" (266, 270). In what Michael Bartholomew aptly describes as the "culminating, immaculately stage-managed episode of the search," Morton's narrator sups with the elderly vicar of the "brilliantly conceived, imaginary village."[37] "We are far from the pain of cities, the complexities," the vicar says in the twilight. "Life is reduced here to a simple common denominator" (267). In the last scene, the narrator observes the annual harvest festival in this place out of time and confirms its value: "'Well,' smiled the vicar, as he walked towards me between the yew trees, 'that, I am afraid, is all we have.' 'You have England,' I said" (272).

In the five years following *In Search of England*, Morton published several more books about the British Isles, identifying three by title as continuing his search for distinctive national cultures. In each he combines the narrative of a journey with descriptions of scenery, anecdotes about meeting locals, and imaginative retellings of historical events. Morton's persona while traveling "in search of" Scotland, Ireland, and Wales is that of an Englishman steeped in history and literature who is curious to see firsthand what he knows only vicariously. Although his personality never comes quite into focus, he often opines pointedly. He delights in the autonomy of the motor-car, which allows access to remote areas that have been ignored since the advent of railway tourism, and the spontaneity of traveling alone. People who "look more or less sane as individuals," he declares with satisfaction after describing solitary travel in the Snowdon district of Wales, "appear incredibly stupid when seated in a charabanc."[38] He cares particularly to experience "individuality," for the "fearful standardization of this age is making one place so like another that there will be no point soon in leaving home."[39] Thus he celebrates Ireland's future as a nation "not dehumanized by industrialism"[40] and commends the people of Wales for "living a healthy, self-contained life" in which they are "bound together by the same local interests" rather than "depend[ing] on outside and alien influences" such as cinemas, dance-halls, and "multiple stores."[41] Morton imagines the people about whom he writes thriving because they live a communal village life rather than the metropolitan autonomy that he prefers for himself.[42] The contradiction escapes him.

National myths and nostalgic visions overwrite the landscape before the narrator's eyes. In Scotland, "The Border is Scott, Ayr is Burns, Edinburgh is Mary, the Highlands are Prince Charlie, and the Trossachs and Loch Lomond are Rob Roy" (279). Driving past Moray Firth into Inverness on an unusually sunny day, he has "a queer feeling of unreality" because he sees not the "real Scotland" known from poetry, with "mist, wind, rain, the cry of whaups, and the slow clouds above damp moorland," but a "railway poster ... come true!" (190–191). In Ireland, he admires the "delicious slowness of life" and through it envisions an England of which only traces remain:

> Ireland is a country of vivid personalities, as England ... before life was influenced by standardization. The only remaining characters in England now are the old farmers and labourers in remote places. They will soon pass away and leave the stage to sons who look alike and think alike, who use the same advertised razors and shaving-soap, who buy the same cars, take in the same newspapers, and manipulate the same wireless sets. The individuality of an Irish crowd is stimulating. It is full of vitality. It is full of originality. (64, 57–58)

In Connemara, where life is "tribal and epic," his romanticism reaches a fever pitch when he longingly observes a young woman raking seaweed along the coast (223). Finding her "sensational in her complete unconsciousness of sex," he declares: "Here, within twenty-four hours of London, was a primitive woman" (186). Yet though he savors being in isolated places where it seems "difficult to believe in London," he feels "alien and alone" when surrounded entirely by people speaking Gaelic or Welsh.[43] In Caernarvon on a market day, he theatrically imagines himself back in the Middle Ages, surrounded by people "speaking Ancient Briton" who – because he cannot understand them – seem "much more foreign, even more dangerous, than Frenchmen or Italians. I might have been a Roman spy in a British town of the first century – a member of Claudius Caesar's C.I.D." (115, 116). Near the end of his journey in Wales, however, he must return to the present when he learns that the rural world of handicrafts that he has sought now occupies the "Bygones Gallery" of the National Museum (268).

Even as Morton seeks to promulgate conservative, "cardinal British national myths," his narratives bear significant evidence of the modernity against which those myths pose a defense.[44] Some early readers missed this when they found his British Isles so idealized that they "suggested that [he] had not actually visited some of the places he described" but rather written "undisturbed by British contemporary reality."[45] Bartholomew explains that *In Search of England* rests on the premise that "the skilful, inspired narrator" will find his way from the "inauthentic, bogus version of England" to "the elusive, *real* England."[46] Certain in advance what constitutes authenticity, he deliberately tours only the land of his imagination, leaving London behind, acknowledging Manchester only as "an ominous grey haze in the sky," seeing "no trace of that monster" Birmingham, and finding consolation for the grimy mill towns of Lancashire in the claim that they are "a mere speck in the amazing greenness of England" (180, 181). This selectivity makes narrative closure easy.[47] However, Morton's narrator sets himself to a more difficult task in Scotland, Ireland, and Wales; here modernity enters more pointedly. The difference manifests itself in what he chooses to see and value en route. Rather than setting out certain he knows what will distinguish the genuine from the false, as in England, he now travels to discover the authentic nature of each place, from which he will devise the "commanding concept" of national character that his narrative requires.[48] His journeys require that he include major cities and modern industry. He visits Edinburgh and Glasgow, Dublin and Cardiff – and writes admiringly of the workings of the "once world-famous naval base of Rosyth," a Glasgow shipyard, a Welsh steelworks, and a "chain of mining towns" that "have never made peace with the landscape."[49] The resulting narratives abruptly juxtapose modern scenes and pastoral descriptions, making little effort to synthesize them. Scotland, Ireland, and Wales appear as places flush with stereotypes that fail to cohere as national wholes – or, to the degree they do, do so as places marked by wartime or modernization.

The most revealing appearances of modernity in Morton's narratives about the British Isles come from war and women, and though his narrator frames them as anecdotes, they suggest an irremediably modern world that exceeds his control. Newly-constructed war memorials mark the landscape, posing a challenge for a patriotic narrator most interested in a pre-industrial past. He can skirt past them in England and Ireland, but their prominence makes them unavoidable in Scotland. He effusively admires the Galashiels memorial as "the most imaginative I have seen," for it depicts a timeless figure of a horseman with sword and lance rather than a soldier in "steel helmet" with rifle, thus linking the recent dead with "the symbol of all Border men who have gone a-roving for hearth and home" (33, 34). As C. R. Perry explains, the memorial encompasses the history that Morton venerates: "a man-fashioned environment of ancient churches, romantic castles, and picturesque cottages in which national history and development provided the organizing schema."[50] When he praises it in a local pub, an ex-soldier turned traveling salesman recounts, "in crude, naked sentences, full of army slang and war profanity, a story that made me see Vimy Ridge in the wet spring of '16, the chalk hells of trenches ... the tangled mass of wire" (34). Although the narrator casts this as a moment of conviviality, the conversation a celebration of Scots' loyalty, the man's story has precisely the historical specificity that the memorial effaces.[51] Later, in Edinburgh, the narrator finds himself "inarticulate" with reverence before Scotland's new National War Shrine, which rises high above the city as "a requiem and a hymn of praise" (62, 60). Awed by its aesthetic harmony, he finds it "cosmic in its conception and still personal in its appeal" (59). Yet its remarkable windows, "full of the Gothic spirit," show "subjects never before interpreted in glass": "land girls gathering a war harvest," "a woman machinist ... in the grim reality of a shell factory," "anti-aircraft guns defending a city from Zeppelin," and "minesweepers at sea." Taken with the sight before him, the narrator declares: "There is no aspect of war forgotten in these windows." But a few lines later an acknowledgement slips out: "There is nothing here of the beastliness and horror of war" (61). The shrine has no depictions of the "chalk hells of trenches," no profane stories from Vimy Ridge.

The oddest anecdotes involve young women whom Morton's narrator finds physically attractive but thematically disruptive. They appear and reappear in the series: the "beautiful maiden" who drives recklessly, "magazine-cover" and "careless" American girls on horseback, confident yet lovely "Amazons" from Birmingham who lack poetry and hike on their own.[52] He remarks their beauty cavalierly but quickly finds their persons disappointing, for they are modern women who share neither his love of history nor his concern for authenticity. In Scotland, at the ruins of Melrose Abbey, he spies "a remarkably long, slim leg" of "authentic beauty" on a wall; it belongs to an American college "girl" who has lost her guidebook. Offering to be her guide, he proffers a cigarette and tells the story of Robert the Bruce's heart, which she finds "perfectly horrible." The narrator finds her "a perfect flower of the New World. All this was to her improbable and unreal. She was slightly contemptuous" (29). For a moment, he finds their exchange "rather stimulating," for instead of having inaccurate notions of the past she has none: "This brain was beautifully free from history" (29, 30). Yet when her father appears and the narrator recognizes a kindred spirit, he promptly resumes his romantic investment in the past. The father travels on a "sentimental journey" to "find his roots," a longing for origins that the narrator finds genuine and admirable. Sure that "deep down in him his Scots blood was stirring," the narrator declares it "a pity" that the man could not have left his disinterested daughter behind. He hopes that he finds what he seeks, for "I liked him" (31). In Connemara, Morton's narrator supposes that the young Irish woman he encounters is herself authentically primitive. As he stares, certain that "[t]hose fine legs had never known, or wished to know, the feel of silk," he longs to paint or sculpt her, then imagines "a man in flight from the artificiality of sophisticated women ... who loved her simplicity ... and her magnificent ignorance" taking her into "the modern world" (187). Speaking with the young woman, however, shatters his illusions.[53] When he sees her again, talking with an older woman, and asks to take her photograph, their conversation quickly reveals that she already dwells in the modern world. To his disappointment she blushes "with a kind of hoydenish coyness," dreams of material possessions, and speaks English. When he seeks to restore his vision of pastoral innocence by saying he'll return someday and see her again by the sea, "looking like a queen in a story," the savvy older woman, who has lived in cities, calls him on his daydream: "and if you're a good girl the gentleman will take you away with him" (189). Morton's narrator wants women to accede to his romantic conceits about national character, but instead they disturb them, so he motors on alone.[54]

Morton's change in subject from national to spiritual homelands in *In the Steps of the Master* requires a shift in narrative strategy, for in Palestine a distinct set of "historical affections" and "myths of origin" obtain.[55] Although he casts each journey in terms of a longing for authenticity, what constitutes the authentic – and more importantly, what threatens it – now differs significantly. In the logic underlying Morton's narratives, authenticity in the British Isles has to do with national culture, which he wants to savor before it is extinguished by "modern ideas," standardization, and lack of reverence for history.[56] In Palestine, however, authenticity lies in Christian history as properly understood, which he intends to reconfirm in the face of competing forms of piety and contending versions of historical truth. To find the Holy Land he seeks, he must read past cultural and political realities – the importuning of Arab salesmen, the traces left by Allenby's troops, and the signs of Jewish immigration under the British Mandate – to the Palestine that he already believes to be real. Morton explicitly casts the narrative as "the thoughts that come to a man as he travels through Palestine with the New Testament in his hands," imagining himself in Jesus's footsteps.[57] Yet even as he seeks out "the steps of the master," in a place so overdetermined he must also acknowledge others' versions of history, if only to subordinate them to his own. The narrator puts it this way: "The Christian, who naturally regards Jerusalem only as the scene of the Crucifixion and the Resurrection, is apt to forget that to the Jew it is still the city of Jehovah, and to the Moslem it is the most sacred spot on earth outside Mecca." The "Holy City ... become a thrice-holy city" figures the problem of authenticity, for he finds it "full of a feeling of spiritual barriers and frontiers" and "a violence of mind instead of the violence of physical action which characterizes all modern cities" (46).

Travel in Palestine poses a new challenge that Morton's familiar narrative persona quickly conquers. Although the Mandate allows British visitors relative autonomy and decrees English an official language, as a foreigner fluent in neither Arabic nor Hebrew he must manage as best he can. The first anecdote after he checks into his hotel in Jerusalem introduces these themes: "I went straight out to find my way to the Church of the Holy Sepulchre. I had been studying a street plan of Jerusalem for weeks, and wondered whether I could find my way alone through the twisting lanes of the old city" (5–6). Accustomed to making his way with ease, the narrator confesses his distress at finding "the real Jerusalem" – filled with "donkeys and camels and men selling oranges" and blasphemous Turks eager to guide him – to be "very different from the clear street plan that I knew by heart!" (6). The noisy crowds at the Jaffa Gate present "a perfect microcosm of the East, and I looked at it with the delight of a child at a Christmas circus," but the "bright chaos" of the Old City quickly disorients him (6, 8). Lost in the cacophony, he ends up on desolate side streets, thinking that "anyone who ventures alone into these lanes without a knowledge of Arabic deserves a knife in the back" (8). When he chances upon the Via Dolorosa he is at once relieved to be back on course, "ashamed" by his irreverence, and startled to see "a real road with men and women and animals upon it" (8, 9). Having handled this initial venture, he resumes his typical confidence by explaining that such disparate thoughts typify travel in this place: "At home one always thinks of Jesus in heaven, on the right hand of God the Father, but in Jerusalem one thinks of Him walking the dusty white roads, and one's intelligence is perpetually rejecting or accepting certain places that tradition associates with His manhood" (9). To experience Palestine, one must navigate constantly between the imagined Holy Land and the immediate present.

The devotional traveler in Palestine must also differentiate assiduously between the genuine and the spurious to obtain the "moments of perception" that pilgrims seek.[58] Nowhere is this more evident than in the Church of the Holy Sepulchre, which rests on Calvary, "the holiest place on earth":

I looked round, hoping to be able to detect some sign of its former aspect, but that has been obliterated for ever beneath the suffocating trappings of piety....

When the crowd thinned, I approached nearer.... [A]Greek priest ... beckoned me to come near the altar and pointed out a silver disc edged with candle grease and, below it, a hole in the rock in which, he whispered to me, the Cross of our Lord was fixed. The pilgrims came up, weeping and praying, to touch the rock with trembling fingers; and I went away wishing that we might have known this place only in our hearts. (49–50)

On the long walk from Jerusalem to Bethlehem, Morton's narrator reflects on the contradictions that inevitably interfere when modern men and women seek to experience the Holy Land:

... travel in Palestine is different from travel in any other part of the world because Palestine exists already in our imagination before we start out. From our earliest years it begins to form in our minds side by side with fairyland, so that it is often difficult to tell where one begins and the other ends. Therefore the Palestine of reality is always in conflict with the imaginary Palestine, so violently at times that many people cannot relinquish this Palestine of the imagination without a feeling of bereavement. That is why some people go away disillusioned from the Holy Land. They are unable, or unwilling, to reconcile the real with the ideal.

Any truthful account of travel in Palestine must mention this conflict. Every day you hear travellers say, as they visit some place: "I never imagined it quite like that," or "I always thought of it in a different way." (112)

The narrator's own reluctance to reconcile real and imagined persists throughout his journey. From the hill above it, he declares, Nazareth "is exactly as one likes to imagine it": "snow-white houses," "spear like cypresses," and "terraces of figs and olive trees." But the inhabitants, whose concerns lie in the present, disrupt his reverie, and their interactions produce no insight, for he meets only "waspish children" crying "Baksheesh" and "unpleasant persons" selling postcards. "It may be childish to be furious," he writes, "because one's picture of Nazareth is spoilt by a horde of noisy people, and because arrival in one of the few towns on earth which should be holy is made horrible by every kind of mean huckster trading on the sacredness of the place.... I don't think so. There are some places in this world which should be grave and quiet and lovely" (166).[59] Here he identifies what Cohen calls the "ultimate problem" for the existential traveler: "is the 'true' life at the centre indeed commensurable to his high hopes and expectations? ... Jerusalem may be the Holy City, but ordinary human life in Jerusalem is far from holy. The pilgrim or the existential tourist 'ascends' spiritually to the ideal centre, but he necessarily arrives at the geographical one."[60] Not surprisingly, Morton comes to prefer natural settings – the Mount of Olives or the Sea of Galilee – where shrines and competing sects don't impede the view. There he can *know* that he literally walks where Jesus once walked.[61]

Yet, whereas *In the Steps of the Master* takes the concerns of the pilgrim-traveler seriously, the narrator's own journey turns out to be less existential than it might first appear. Though he frames his story as that of a would-be pilgrim, he demonstrates himself to be a skeptic who finds Christian claims about holy sites unconvincing and knows that his "own private little vision" of Bethlehem, "edged with gilt," derives from Christmas cards (112). More traditionalist than believer, he advises trusting feeling over "a certain school of scriptural criticism," for "I cannot help feeling that over sixteen hundred years of firm tradition are more reliable than any theory, not matter how plausible" (73, 57). A seasoned traveler interested in archaeology and antiquities, he is more at home with knowledge than piety. In fact, he seems to admire the "real happiness" he sees in the eyes of a Bulgarian pilgrim who weeps at Christ's tomb precisely because he has not experienced it himself: "Never in all my life have I beheld peace and contentment written so clearly on a human face" (12).[62] *In the Steps of the Master* slides unevenly between the devotional and the documentary, sometimes shifting back and forth in a single paragraph. It is as though Morton cannot decide which version of his persona to adopt or which conventions to heed. Of first seeing David's Tower, he writes, "I saw it with the emotion which any relic of the time of Christ must inspire, whether the observer be a devout Christian or merely a devout historian. Those huge yellow stones at the base of the tower existed in the Jerusalem of the Crucifixion. Perhaps He saw them" (6). The "studied ambiguity" of this passage reappears throughout the text: "Without seeming deliberately evasive, he manages never fully to declare himself."[63] The narrator disdains the "fashion" of thinking that the Old Testament is a collection of fables and exhorts readers not to "imagine that men like Saul and David never existed." But the affirmation that follows is ethnographic, not devotional: "Not only did they exist, but to-day there are men whose lives and outlook are exactly the same. You meet them on every road. The Bible is a most accurate guide to the life of modern Palestine" (148).[64]

The narrator's preoccupation with authenticity informs the narrative at every step as he seeks to articulate what he views as the proper version of Palestine's convoluted history, that of Christianity.[65] To make his own narrative cohere, he must subordinate competing histories that privilege Islam and Judaism. At such moments he minces few words: the Dome of the Rock is "one of the most startling places I have ever seen," he declares, not for the "exquisite" beauty visible to others but because "shining like a spectre through this great shrine of Islam, is a reflection of the Temple of Herod" (75, 78, 75). Declaring that "the hundreds of books and guide-books on Jerusalem have neglected what I consider to be the most significant thing" about the Dome of the Rock, he sets the story straight: it marks "the ghost of the Temple in whose courtyards Jesus preached" (75). To see the place as he wishes, he looks past the literal sights before him to the imagined moment: "all the time I found myself looking not at the present-day Moslem sanctuary but at the older Jewish temple which it has replaced," where Zacharias, father of the John the Baptist, had his vision (76).[66] Were it possible, he would travel in the steps of Jesus chronologically, but "the fragmentary nature of the Gospel narratives presents a rather perplexing problem" (110). Constant reminders of modernity disturb his passage as well, like the "notice-board which absurdly pins this region to reality: 'Bethlehem Municipal Boundary,' it says. 'Drive slowly'" (118).

At the end of *In the Steps of the Master*, Morton follows through on his original purpose of attesting to the authenticity of Christian history by recounting Jesus's crucifixion and resurrection. This dominant theme is surely what his initial audience found affirming.[67] Yet a less obvious thread that runs through the narrative reveals another familiar theme, that of the fate of Western civilization in later modernity. The one history Morton does not subordinate to that of Christianity is that of the British Empire. Instead, *In the Steps of the Master* works out an affiliation that forever links the fortunes of Britain and Palestine. From the moment he arrives in Jerusalem, the narrator traces a parallel between the role of the Roman Empire at the time of Jesus and the contemporary role of Britain. "His Majesty's High Commissioner" is "the lineal successor in office of Pontius Pilate," each representing an empire that will determine Palestine's future: "Rome drove out the Jews; Britain is bringing them back" (99).[68] In his account, Rome matters chiefly for its role in Christian history: he buys a tile bearing the mark of the Tenth Legion, which, in destroying the temple, had "fulfilled the prophecy of Christ"; speculates that the legion's auxiliary troops included ancient Britons; and observes that Jesus, in choosing Galilee, had elected to live "upon one of the main highways of the Roman Empire" (22, 221). The narrator turns the parallel between

Britain and Rome into a defense of civilization against barbarism as he watches Bedouin dance feverishly near Petra:

> I ... wondered whether anything like this dance would ever take place in Trafalgar Square or the Place de la Concorde. One has the feeling in Palestine that the civilization that crashed into ruin was very like our own. One has more in common with the fallen pillars of Jerash than with the finest Moslem mosque. Our world, imperfect as it is, is still a Christian world and has its roots in Christianity. Everything that is against Christianity, no matter how trivial it may appear, is a spy from the forces of savagery which have always waited ready with drawn knives to dance among the ruins. (311)

To begin Holy Week, he attends an Anglican service in the British War Cemetery on the Mount of Olives, where more than 2,000 soldiers and airmen lie amidst hedges of rosemary, English flowers, and Flanders poppies. One can see Calvary to the west, and a photograph in the text confirms that the cemetery's cross "rises over the graves as the banner of St. George might have stood above a company of Crusaders" (see Illustration 9). Melding the interests of Britain and Palestine as one, the narrator declares: "It was good to hear English prayers in a spot sacred to the British race" (324).

Recalling his initial surprise at finding the Via Dolorosa to be ordinary, Morton's narrator announces that the authenticity that matters lies not in the place but in the experience of it: it may not matter whether it is "the actual road or a memorial to the actual road. What is important is that men and women who have walked upon it have met there the vision of Christ" (9). For the unwavering logic of Morton's travel narratives about the British Isles and Palestine is that authenticity remains within reach if one approaches the world in the right state of mind. To sustain it requires an appropriation of history: preserving the real England, confirming the Christian account. An anecdote set in Galilee reiterates this. Morton, the middle-aged English travel writer, meets a middle-aged Australian traveling around the world who types long letters home. The man's typing disrupts Morton's reverie as he looks at the sun-lit sea, but once they talk he finds his "zest for life" delightful:

> Everything was, to him, exciting and superlative. "I am always ready for adventures," he said. Genuine enthusiasm carries with it an entirely spurious atmosphere of originality. Yet is that true? The man was really blazing a trail through all the well-worn paths of the world: he was blazing it through the terrific jungle of his own enthusiasm. I admired him because

BRITISH WAR CEMETERY, JERUSALEM

Illustration 9. Photo of the British War Cemetery in Jerusalem, from Morton's
In the Steps of the Master.

he was so genuinely in love with the world. He had absolutely no shred of cynicism. (217)

By this point in the narrative – and in Morton's career – the persona of *In Search of England* has become jaded, his writing inconstant for its contradictions.[69] In questions that reflect his own state of mind, he asks the man whether he is "disappointed in travel" or finds the world "as wonderful" as he'd anticipated (216). But his new acquaintance, an exaggerated echo of an earlier Morton, finds travel so wonderful that he's devised a way to enliven his daily letters to his wife. He fictionalizes, narrating in present tense "so that she can feel that she is with me" rowing across Galilee or standing atop the Great Pyramid in Egypt. Through artifice, he makes experience and narrative "more vivid and real" (215).

Catfish and Mandala

The geopolitical upheavals consequent to twentieth-century wartime and the dissolution of empires make displacement a common phenomenon: "migration, expatriation and exile [become] the norm, rootedness the exception."[70] Travel and authenticity occupy crucial roles in the considerable body of narrative literature that examines the subjective experiences of immigrants, exiles, refugees, and displaced persons. In many narratives, the place of origin signifies a plenitude that one desires or has half forgotten, and journeying back offers the possibility of bridging the gap between the origin as imagined and the present that actually is. Baudrillard, writing of the value postmodernity places on authenticity, identifies a similar desire: "We require a visible past, a visible continuum, a visible myth of origin, which reassures us about our end. Because finally we have never believed in them."[71] In such narratives, travel shimmers as the possibility of proving authenticity and thus making fragile identities whole. Travel promises the evidence of experience: through immersing oneself in a place, one can see, smell, taste, touch, hear – and thus claim it for oneself. Although Morton dismisses most Americans he meets in the British Isles as crass, disinterested tourists, he admires those who travel in search of their origins because they share his belief in origins' meliorative effect. To *be* English, in this logic, is to be *at home in* England, to be Scottish, in Scotland: descendants of emigrants who are cognizant of their "Englishness" or their Scottish "blood" necessarily feel the pull of their place of origin. Though "there are none of our family here now" except in cemeteries, the American man he meets in Scotland says: "It is just fine to be here at last" (31). Morton finds this longing congenial, for his own rejection of cosmopolitanism and modernization as inauthentic comes in tandem with his celebration of a "common racial heritage" that must be sustained and kept vital.[72] He credits Americans' tendency to undertake such "sentimental journeys" as the "most lovable trait" in their character precisely because it involves setting aside the modernity and orientation toward the future for which they are known in favor of the cultural inheritance he values.[73]

Morton's depiction of affluent Americans who travel "home" to the British Isles in the interwar years foreshadows a new kind of travel narrative that emerges much later in the century: the narrative of a journey to the place of origin in hopes of mitigating dislocation and thus finding – or creating – authenticity for oneself. But the privileged instances of travel to discover ancestral origins that Morton describes are touched with sentimental historical feeling more than existential need.[74] They threaten neither the questing American nor the English narrator, for one's sense of authenticity confirms rather than impinges on the other's. Each prospers, and neither is at war. Such journeys may annoy moderns who dwell only in the present or locals skeptical of city folk, but they deeply discomfit no one. The American with the leisure to travel to his grandparents' place of origin has only faint, secondhand memory of impoverished emigration; the Englishman placid and secure in his own land intuits nothing of rootlessness. On the surface, little is at stake for either one. Neither knows the anxiety of the refugee; neither can imagine the possibility of having no home to which he can return. The insularity they share belies the times in which they live, for the next global war approaches, and profound cultural upheaval accelerates.[75]

Literal diaspora and displacement intensify the alienation, fragmentation, unresolved longing, and figurative homelessness common in modernist and postmodern literature. In these circumstances the narrative of travel to one's place of origin takes on an existential urgency unimaginable to Morton's Americans, for such journeys seek to ameliorate damage, to repair fractured identities through the restorative experience that the very concept of the authentic promises. Though elsewhere perceptive about the postmodern preoccupation with authenticity, Baudrillard romantically misreads the United States as a site of freedom from the weight of history: "America ducks the question of origins," he declares; it "lives in a perpetual present" and "has no identity problem."[76] Yet the vantage point from the United States – or Canada, or Australia – suggests otherwise. For it is in such nations, to which many emigrate from the ruins and genocide of Europe in mid-century and the endless "little wars" that follow, that a distinctively postmodern concern with authenticity becomes most visible, in late-century narratives of journeys to homes lost and now imagined, to countries destroyed by war and holocaust, and to places transformed. In these narratives America, far from being free of the past, is a place longing for origins, a nation of hyphenates uncertain what constitutes authentic identity, a new homeland haunted by the stories of immigrants who come as refugees displaced by politics, poverty, and war.[77]

Rather than traveling to escape into adventure, these narrators travel to locate themselves and their half-remembered histories. Rather than seeking respite from home, they hope to lay claim to authenticity in order to lay homelessness to rest. Some return to abandoned childhood home-lands, such as Pham, bicycling through Vietnam in *Catfish and Mandala* (1999), Hoffman, visiting post-Communist Poland in *Exit into History* (1993), and Andrew Riemer, whose *Inside Outside* (1992) recounts a jour-ney from his home in Sydney to the Budapest he remembers only in ruins. Others, driven by what Marianne Hirsch calls the "postmemory" of later generations, travel to understand their own entanglement in the histories of parents or ancestors who were exiles, emigrés, or convict laborers: Alan Cheuse in *Fall Out of Heaven* (1987), Mary Morris in *Wall to Wall: From Beijing to Berlin by Rail* (1991), Christopher Koch in *The Many-Coloured Land* (2002).[78] And following the most tenuous thread of all, Rebecca Solnit, longtime resident of "hybrid California, world capital of amnesia," descendant of Irish Catholics and Russian Jews, opts to claim Irish citi-zenship though she knows "almost nothing" of "this unknown country" that becomes, legally, "mine."[79] Postmemory, as Hirsch explains, because it lacks direct connection, works "through an imaginative investment and creation."[80]

Pham's *Catfish and Mandala: A Two-Wheeled Voyage through the Landscape and Memory of Vietnam* narrates an urgent personal journey toward authenticity with particular eloquence and frankness. A simple chronology of Pham's earlier life, which emerges in fragments over the course of the narrative, reveals the complexity of his situation.[81] Second of six children of a college-educated propaganda officer and his resourceful wife, Pham experiences village life and wartime Saigon as a boy. At the war's end his father is incarcerated in Minh Luong Prison, a reeducation camp, and later the whole family flees Vietnam in an overloaded fishing boat. The refugees reach the United States when Pham is ten and settle in northern California, where cultural dislocation strains family relations to the point of rupture. Pushed to excel by his hard-working parents, Pham completes a degree in aerospace engineering and secures a good job but soon finds himself adrift and decides to be a freelance writer: "Do the American thing, chase your dream, follow your heart" (28). He is shaken deeply by the life and death of his older sibling Chi, who after fleeing the family as an adolescent girl "reverted to her true self" and became a man named Minh (297). Years later, Minh returns to the family, broke and lonely after losing his wife, but his desolation leads to suicide. The nar-rative opens when Pham, twenty-seven, flees the scene of Minh's suicide, abandons his work, and escapes from obligation on a long bicycle trip in Mexico.

A month into Mexico, Pham splits a bottle of tequila with Tyle, another man who has fled family in the States to wander. They share stories at a desert campsite, one a self-identified Vietnamese American who hates being asked where he's from "originally," the other a veteran with a "Viking face" who is haunted by what he did in Vietnam in his youth (6, 9). The ex-soldier asks the ex-refugee for forgiveness, and Pham thinks:

> All my life, I've looked at you sideways, wondering if you were wondering if my brothers had killed your brothers in the war that made no sense except for the one act of sowing me here – my gain – in your bed, this strange rich-poor, generous-cruel land. I move through your world, a careful visitor, respectful and mindful, hoping for but not believing in the day when I become native. I am the rootless one, yet still the beneficiary of all of your and all of their sufferings. Then why, of us two, am I the savior, and you the sinner? (8–9)

Pham, who cannot resolve the guilt Tyle cannot escape, resolves to journey to Vietnam. He knows the common motives for such visits well: "to prove to ourselves that we are no longer Vietnamese but Vietnamese Americans," "to show through our material success that we, the once pitiful exiles, are now the victors," to "gloat at our conquerors," and, above all, "because we are lost" (7–8). The chapter title gestures toward the trajectory ahead: "Exile-Pilgrim" (5).[82] Several months later, he rides north from San Jose "on a disintegrating shoestring budget," having told his family he will tour the West Coast but knowing that he will go on to Vietnam on a journey he must make alone, seeking "the reasons I need to find before I can mend the mess that is my life" (29).

Pham's journey to make sense of his fractured life begins in a state close to existential despair. Life in a postmodern American society taken with identity politics and fearful of its own cosmopolitan heterogeneity has left him a mess. American in education, sensibility, and taste, with a Vietnamese sense of obligation that extends to polite lying, he remains acutely conscious of his vulnerability to "big-boned, fair-skinned white Americans" who presume the nation to be theirs (25). He makes the decision to cycle into his future – "so American, pioneering, courageous, romantic, self-indulgent" – in the face of years of being characterized a "good Oriental" at work and assaulted as he cycles by passers-by who throw refuse at him and yell "Hey, Jap!" or "Go home, Chink!" (29, 25, 37, 328). Although his father has always cautioned him to work hard and be compliant, Pham decides "I can't be his Vietnamese American. I see their groveling humility, concessions given before quarters are asked.... So, what the hell, I have to do something unethnic. I have to go. Make

Illustration 10. Photo of Andrew X. Pham, from Pham's *Catfish and Mandala.*

my pilgrimage" (26). Traveling by bicycle serves his purposes because it forces him into the vulnerability of life on the street, though it cannot protect him from being seen as an affluent Viet-kieu, or "foreign Vietnamese" (see Illustration 10). (Relatives in Saigon try to dissuade him from biking to Hanoi, for it is dangerous and his gear reveals him to be foreign.) A method "particularly suitable for the stubborn masochist," it also makes literal the arduousness of Pham's journey into his own authentic way of being Vietnamese American (33). He knows the stakes of identity are high, for he cannot forget the disturbing comment that having become "too American" – or was it remaining "too Vietnamese"? – drove his sister to suicide.[83]

For the postmodern traveler who left home as a refugee and returns to the scene of wartime, journeying requires a reckoning with the violent history of the present as remembered by its survivors. No simple return is possible, for too much that is too difficult intervenes, and the stakes over which interpretation will prevail are too high. Pham's narrative plays out the troubled entanglement of past and present by juxtaposing scenes in the present with scenes recalled or imagined from the past. The chapter just before he arrives in Saigon depicts events leading up to the family's departure two decades earlier. He remembers the penultimate moment of exhilaration as they walk barefoot toward the sea, almost imagining they could "simply walk out of Vietnam and right into America, beautiful free America" – then recalls that he naively thought nothing of danger ahead (61). His return in peacetime proves surprisingly disconcerting, for looking down from the plane he sees "[n]othing familiar in the bombed-out darkness," not even "the red tracers of bullets ripping the night sky," and feels an "unnameable apprehension" that he is too exhausted to handle after weeks spent biking up the West Coast and through Japan. Tossing back "yet another lowball," he knows both what he wants and what he needs: "Here's to you, Saigon. I've come for my memories. Give me reconciliation" (62).[84]

Memory proves a poor guide, for while disparate details from the past flood Pham's mind, some painfully, others sentimentally, he can locate almost none of them in the present. He "can't place" the distant cousin who calls him by his Vietnamese name, An, at the airport and knows his grandaunt only "from pictures"; in their Saigon neighborhood, one woman recalls his father but "no one remembers me or I them" (67, 100). Of the places he recalls best, only one remains "exactly as I remember it": the aging divan on which he slept in his childhood home (181). Yet finding it provides none of nostalgia's prelapsarian solace, for it evokes cruel images: his father, "visage terrible to behold," canes Chi "in a cloud of blind wrath" though neighbors "clamored for mercy," continuing furiously through her howls until the last cane shatters and An spirits her to safety with their grandmother (56). All else has been altered beyond recognition. "Nothing looks familiar" at Minh Luong, where his father and other prisoners cleared landmines by hand, and their grandmother's house, a refuge where he spent "lazy summer days," is now a "hovel," its once-lush star-fruit tree nearly dead (161, 182, 181).[85] Despite the "bitter bile of finding a world I don't remember," Pham presses on, testing what he recalls against what he observes, hoping to find something to allow him to "come full circle" (102, 143). He tracks the road near the coastline repeatedly, "looking for the precise spot where my family had staged our escape, but it is hopeless. The landmarks are all gone" (186–187). Truong, an old soldier turned motorbike-taxi driver who drives him around Minh Luong, advises: "Forget this place. Go see the world.... Everything has changed. Your roots here have turned to dust. Nothing here to bind you" (161). Truong's street wisdom is right: after seeing the remains of his grandmother's house, Pham realizes that where he sought roots "[t]here is only ash." "In this Vietnamese muck, I am too American," he reflects. "Too refined, too removed from my *que*, my birth village. The sight of my roots repulses me. And this shames me deeply" (183).

Pham's hope to reconcile the fragments of his life into an identity that will cohere authentically proves to be the most difficult aspect of his journey, which continues for many weeks after he recognizes his revulsion. Some emigrants and exiles "find themselves" by affiliation through a shared history, familiar place, or sense of common ethnicity, though it requires suppressing some elements of their lives to write others large. Solnit unravels the fantasy in the "roots" metaphor: "you can find yourself in origins, though you may have to choose an arbitrary point – a great-grandmother, an ancestral home, the Irish Cliffs of Moher – and beyond that you can lose yourself in origins."[86] This might work for her in Ireland, whose tourist industry depends heavily on "reverse immigrants" wanting to see "where their ancestors came from," for there "[t]he animosity between American tourists and hosts that exists in other parts of the world seems largely absent."[87] It cannot work for Pham, though he is native, for at every turn people he meets contest whatever claim to identity his traveling seems meant to confirm. In post-civil war Vietnam, violent history remains too raw to allow a capacious sense of national identity. To those resident in the United States the "uncentered" younger Viet-kieu are "mat goch – lost roots," but to those resident in Vietnam "Viet-kieu are the lottery winners," to be envied (63, 183). The term that differentiates those who fled often feels like an epithet: Pham, who comes "searching for truths, hoping for redeeming grace," finds many who expect Viet-kieu to be benefactors, some who despise them as traitors, none who truly claim them as they are (102).

At the beginning of his journey, Pham seeks only Vietnamese company in restaurants and on the road, hoping to "meet as many of them as I can, to learn all our differences and similarities" (284). Though he introduces himself as Vietnamese and speaks the language fluently, his physical presence seems to refute his words: his haircut looks Korean, his stature evidences years of good nutrition, and his voice carries a difference. Because his American sensibilities extend to his digestive system, the local microbes he cannot avoid and unfamiliar delicacies he eats to be polite or prove himself make him ill much of the journey.[88] More than one drunk – suspecting that Pham deceives him – angrily disputes his claim, "Really, I'm Vietnamese" (174). When he reaches Hanoi, Pham tables his search to "bum around ... with Australians, French, Danes, Brits, Germans, and Americans just soaking up the culture," relieved to be with "friends of similar spirit, all non-Asian, not one of them Vietnamese" (225, 226). He enjoys Hanoi as a Westerner: bar-hopping, boat tours, motorcycle expeditions in the countryside, gawking at Ho Chi Minh's spectral body. He "thrive[s] on the camaraderie and the adventurous spirit of the other Western tourists," whose company ameliorates the loneliness he experiences when cycling; it's a restorative interlude that he needs badly (284). Eventually, after one too many bad experiences with Vietnamese he meets in his travels, he stops correcting people who insist he is Korean or Japanese or "half-and-half." Whatever confirmation of authenticity he obtains will have to come from himself, not from external recognition.

In a narrative that interlaces past and present, proceeding by juxtaposition, Pham's narrator gives his experiences on the road the effect of releasing stories from the past with which he must come to terms. Uncle Tu, an old man who once fought for the North, invites him to share his modest, well-tended hut for a few days, and rather than resenting Pham's Viet-kieu life he responds with an "insatiable appetite for details about the rest of the world" (265). When Pham awakens with a high fever, Uncle Tu treats him with folk remedies like a kindly grandfather, ignoring his skepticism. They talk about the war, and when Pham describes Tyle's debilitating guilt, Uncle Tu insists that they were all boys back then. Now, he declares, *"[t]here is nothing to forgive.... [H]e is welcome here"* (267). Their encounter allows Pham to rethink prior experiences with the former Vietnamese officers he knows – a girlfriend's father, his own father. Later, he writes about sightseeing with an Australian woman who "is so openly enamoured of the people, choosing to overlook their foibles much more readily than I do," that "[i]n her company, I like the country more" (293). In the following chapter, he finally tells his family's most painful story, that of Chi's years as a runaway, return as Minh, and suicide – the story of the sibling to whom he dedicates his narrative, the story he has avoided. Telling it frankly, which Chi could not do until too late, seems to release Pham from some of the weight of the past.[89] A few chapters later, he recounts two moments when his family's deep reticence breaks: his first candid conversation with his younger brother Huy, who comes out to him after graduating from college, and the late-night talk in which his father confesses that to beat Chi in "the Vietnamese way," as his own father had taught by beating him, was "wrong" and "abusive" (320, 321). Pham interprets the exchanges differently. "[T]alking plainly" with his brother feels good, but his father's honesty worries him, for though he has been "forever forced to rewrite his paradigm, even if only to survive," his father remains "an intellectual, the quintessential Vietnamese" who may find the guilt of admission unbearable (318, 322, 321). Pham's compassionate response to his father names their affiliation and their difference: "He wasn't American, not like me" (321).

At the clinic that occupies the building once their Saigon home, Pham chides himself for "banking on a stupid Hollywood ending" that would "make everything all right and justify all the hardships I have gone through" (98). Because rootedness has been the talisman of the authenticity he desires, he has imagined that finding his past will make him whole in the present. But Vietnam and Pham have changed irrevocably: too much has happened, and he is too fragmented, for going back to resolve his alienation. What he needs, instead, is a way to "fasten" disparate but "terribly vivid" memories "in a continuity that I can comprehend" in the present, for the future (98). At one point he wonders wearily which plotline will prevail: will the journey he imagined "a pilgrimage" prove to be "a farce"? (110). The answer proves elusive; he reaches neither the confirmation that pilgrimage guarantees nor the restoration of order that concludes farce. But his narrative ends by suggesting the lineaments of a more existential sense of identity with which he can live. Having rejected illusions that authenticity comes through restoring the past or proving himself to someone else, he concludes that it lies in knowing how to live in the present, by comprehending complexity as his own and moving forward.[90] He ends his journey disappointed he cannot convince himself that the Vietnamese belief that "white Americans are to Viet-kieu as Viet-kieu are to Vietnamese, each one a level above the next, respectively" is "entirely true or false" (329). But he decides not to be bound by that logic, and thus to live freed from its weight. He imagines being a chameleon, with "no center, no truer sense of self than what he is in the instant," and wishes he could tell Tyle that "a pure desire that things might have been different, a wish of wellness for the survivors," allows one to move authentically forward, for "our truths change with time.... No was. Only is" (339).[91] As the plane home nears San Francisco, his seatmate, an older immigrant from Vietnam, asks Pham whether this is America. Pham offers him a portion of his own new-found freedom for the future by smiling, American-style, and saying: "'Yes, Brother.... Welcome home'" (342).

The Singular Pilgrim

To understand travel narrative in the last century requires considering both authenticity's allure and the particular circumstances in which the longing for it occurs. Authenticity matters when it appears threatened or doomed by transformation, fragmentation, or loss. In travel narrative, to sustain it often requires reconciling an old version of history with present experience or creating a new version for the future: not reiterating what was, but coming to terms with what is. For twentieth-century travelers, the notion that the authentic may survive promises that the plenitude of meaning it signals may still occur, that one can indeed make one's way through the labyrinth of modernity toward a future-yet-to-be. Philosopher Peter Kivy articulates a novel way of thinking about authenticity, one surprisingly congenial to Pham's conclusion of "No was. Only is." Kivy identifies four notions of authenticity in musical performance. Three involve faithfulness to history – to composer intention, original performance, period instruments – and the fourth, fidelity to the present. The last, which Kivy calls "personal authenticity," consists of "faithfulness to the performer's own self, original, not derivative or an aping of someone else's way of playing."[92] This authenticity locates itself in creation in the present, not in reverence toward the past; its characteristics include sincerity, assertion of emotion, and improvisation. The personally authentic performer, Kivy writes, works "as she sees it, in the circumstances in which she finds herself.... If there is a kind of charlatanism about her, it is that of the conjurer and the magician, not of the dealer in snake oil or the phony evangelist."[93] In locating authenticity not in allegiance to what came before but in performance rooted in present being, Kivy provocatively offers an avenue for thinking about the existential traveler who seeks authenticity not by recreating a particular past but by situating him- or herself in the mutable world.

In *The Singular Pilgrim: Travels on Sacred Ground* (2003), Mahoney undertakes a series of journeys in order to understand why humans in cosmopolitan postmodern societies continue to feel "the need to leave the place they know and travel great distances to envision or experience God at a previously ordained site."[94] An American raised on her great-aunt's stories of Irish revolutionaries, Mahoney obtained Irish citizenship at fifteen and later spent a year in Ireland, finding contemporary society familiar yet alien and savoring her mobility as "a foreigner" who "didn't have to obey their rules, didn't have to be watched or reined in."[95] A skeptic who has left the Catholicism of her youth behind, she begins *Singular Pilgrim* uncertain where she stands. Her travels take her to the shrine at Lourdes and the trail to Santiago de Compostela, through Walsingham in Norfolk and on pilgrimage to Lough Derg in Ireland, and to two places over-written with religious meaning, Varanasi and "the Holy Land." *Singular Pilgrim* consists of discrete episodes in which Mahoney's persona narrates her experiences in different places (like Iyer's *Video Night*), interweaving events from her childhood and adult life as they impinge on the present (as Pham does in *Catfish and Mandala*). Her own uncertain relation to belief provides the thematic through-line, the "longer journey" of which these are selected episodes (6).[96] Her meditation on that journey, *Singular Pilgrim* takes authenticity as its subject in unusual ways by inquiring directly into its persistent allure despite its apparent artifice.

Unlike most travel narratives concerned with authenticity, *Singular Pilgrim* begins in skepticism rather than longing: Mahoney, a postmod-ern whose experiences of "shrines and holy places ... had been strictly touristic," decides to explore "the devotions of true pilgrims, whose realm I stood apart from" (4). Her "investigation" starts from rational prem-ises and anticipates intellectual results; she does not expect to find God or have authentic religious experiences herself, but rather to gain critical insight into "the meaning of these journeys undertaken in the name of an unknowable, unseeable God" (9, 6). To "ease into" it, Mahoney starts with the Anglican National Pilgrimage at Walsingham's shrine to the Virgin Mary, a twentieth-century revival of a pre-Reformation ritual. It appears to be an uncomplicated entrée well-suited to her purposes: "The pilgrim-age was small and brief; it took place on a single day. I would not have to explain or identify myself, nor would I be expected to do anything." The otherwise unremarkable procession of Anglican clergy through a Norfolk village offers an "enticing" counter-spectacle: shouting protestors (9). What Mahoney finds proves to be a melodrama that reenacts the major conflicts of the last five centuries of Christianity: Catholics and Anglicans honor the Virgin in competing pilgrimages on succeeding days, with Protestants from Northern Ireland protesting loudly against the Anglicans for "leaning toward Rome" (39). To her surprise, being in the midst of so partisan a scene makes her want to explain herself, and when a conspiracy theorist slanders Catholicism she feels the "subtle gravitational pull" of her family's tradition (48). "For me the unsettling discovery," she observes, "was that ... [m]y religious history, slight and skewed and rejected as it was, still had the power to set me at variance with those who didn't share it" (49). Being a skeptic, she realizes, does not erase her origins.

As Mahoney learns at Walsingham, the practice of pilgrimage refuses its participants the critical distance assumed by the flâneur. Over the course of her journeys she finds self-explanation hard to avoid when others ask her why she travels among them, though she declines candor in deference to others' beliefs that she does not share. Genuinely interested in "other people's cosmic theories and philosophies of life" even as she finds them "cluttered and clubbish and obscuring," Mahoney remains "anxious about forming my own" and uncertain in purpose (124). Few among the ordinary people she meets share her skepticism or wide experience of the world, so even when in close company she travels alone. In Lourdes and on the road to Santiago she joins Catholic pilgrims, and then for a long interlude she becomes a religious tourist in India, guided through Varanasi and Hinduism by a reflective youth who shares her tenuous affiliation with tradition. In Israel and the Occupied Territories she seeks the Holy Land of the New Testament despite the distractions of military checkpoints and "tiresome … religious segregation and competition" at the shrines (332). There, she articulates something she has come to understand: pilgrimage "satisfie[s] the human need for a palpable historical reality" by allowing one to "see and touch things that were part of a story that … explained the purpose of life. If you could … touch one of those things, you could be part of the story" (274). As she rows across Galilee, it occurs to her that she's seeking to correct her perception of Jesus, "soft and awash with mythology," with "a few more facts, even if they were just sensory geographical facts," to "know what the ground felt like beneath his feet, what the sky looked like, how the night smelled, how the birds sounded" (310). Whereas the obscurity of "cosmic theories" still leaves her skeptical, the sheer physicality of travel grounds her perception of what matters, how, here and now.

Mahoney's "longer journey" progresses most clearly when she casts herself as participant rather than observer, and after feeling the gravitational pull at Walsingham she does that wherever possible. Watching a man and his sons prepare for the ritual cremation of their wife and mother at Varanasi moves her deeply, but later, as tourist boats hover while pilgrims pray at the ghats, she sees the inauthenticity of her own spectatorship: it is "undeniably voyeuristic and intrusive and even odd – all these foreigners, including me, coming to watch the Indians bathing and praying and dying," just as rude as the reverse would be were Indians to go the United States and "gawk while we prayed" and groomed (251).[97] She feels a very different sense of accomplishment when she participates in pilgrimage as purposefully as she can, even without clarity. As a priest blesses her group before they set out on the 750-kilometer walk to Santiago, she compares medieval pilgrims who "knew exactly why they were doing it" with herself, who "could not

explain why I was about to walk all the way across Spain" (87). Along the
way she savors the "self-containment, anonymity," and "pure joy" of walking alone; it clears her mind, which is troubled by a failing relationship
(96). Unlike the devout pilgrims she reads about, she "obtain[s] no spiritual ecstasy," and her serious thoughts about belief alternate with exasper-
ation about her decision to write (125). She pushes on, however, and at the
end of the trail – though her belief has not altered – she feels certain that
she has "accomplished something strange and monumental" (141).[98]

In the last episode of her narrative, Mahoney joins ninety pilgrims at
Saint Patrick's Purgatory, a shrine in the middle of Lough Derg, an Irish
lake. This pilgrimage has higher stakes than the others, for Mahoney, who
now describes her journey as one to "find belief," has become weary of
both travel and God: "It was a struggle, it was uncomfortable, and I had
felt frustrated that in my holy travels belief had not suddenly dawned
on me, that no great bolt of lightning had struck me" (367). As a site
for penitential practice, St. Patrick's Purgatory requires full engagement
in a "precisely orchestrated" regimen of fasting, walking, kneeling, and
prayer (336). Bereft at the end of her relationship, needing "comfort," and
ready to end her long journey, Mahoney determines to "fulfill each pre-
scribed step ... whether my heart was moved to or not" (367, 337). It is an
extreme step for a rational woman not given to prayer, for it requires sus-
pending the critical judgment that causes her to stumble over the creedal
phrases she cannot accept. Unexpectedly, she finds the exhausting ritual
"amazing," for reciting prayers hundreds of times has "the quality of a
meditation," with a disciplining of body and mind that produces access
to the soul (404, 389). Questions about history, doctrine, and politics
evaporate in the intensity of performance, allowing her to experience a
plenitude of meaning she had imagined impossible: "The physical body
went about in circles, with frozen feet and stinging eyes, kneeling, moving
constantly, like a wind-up toy, while within it the soul percolated, inviting
God in, inventing him" (404). The experience does not remove Mahoney
from quotidian reality: to confirm that, the book ends with her on the
bus to Dublin, listening to a woman who loves travel abroad and disdains
the art documentaries of Sister Wendy. But the practice of Lough Derg
offers "a way of framing the self in time and space" that makes more sense
to her than either revering tradition or savoring disbelief (389). By taking
performance seriously, the skeptic surprises herself by finding authenticity,
fragile and tenuous, in the present.

Because wartime and globalization shatter identities, places, and cultural
norms that had once seemed timeless, authenticity's allure escalates.

Traveling to places whose significance seems to lie outside the irreversible temporality of modernity promises the possibility of plenitude, of meaning that will endure. Such gestures often fail to achieve what they suppose they desire: Morton may imagine an essential England, but his own modernity makes his narratives contradictory, their artifice visible. But as the twentieth century turns into the twenty-first, travel narratives about literal and spiritual homelands gesture toward new versions of authenticity that come from setting aside the weight of the past and looking forward, fragments of meaning linked together in a continuity that works, ready for possible futures.

CHAPTER 7

Conclusion

For a long while I stood on the bridge that leads to the former research establishment. Far behind me to the west, scarcely to be discerned, were the gentle slopes of the inhabited land; to the north and south, in flashes of silver, gleamed the muddy bed of a dead arm of the river ... and ahead lay nothing but destruction. From a distance, the concrete shells ... in which for most of my lifetime hundreds of boffins had been at work devising new weapons systems, looked ... like the tumuli in which the mighty and powerful were buried in prehistoric times.... But the closer I came to these ruins, the more any notion of a mysterious isle of the dead receded, and the more I imagined myself amidst the remains of our own civilization after its extinction in some future catastrophe.... Where and in what time I truly was that day at Orfordness I cannot say, even now as I write these words.

W. G. Sebald (1995)[1]

This book has argued that the cultural work of the travel narrative changes profoundly in the twentieth century. Drawing on the literary strategies of modernism, writers transform a genre of nearly moribund conventions into an agile, heterogeneous means of representing complex, often violent geopolitical upheaval through subjective experience. Travel narrative shifts its focus to the subjective, immediate view from the thick of things, *in medias res*. Setting aside the conventional closure provided by a return from distant places figured as premodern to an England assumed to be constant and sure, it faces the uncertainty of a present in which both home and abroad are vulnerable to alteration before one's eyes. To write of travel in the century of perpetual wartime is to test the presumption of narrative authority against the obligations of critical observation, the privilege of storytelling against the vertiginous disorder of experience. In such texts, to narrate travel functions both as souvenir and as action; to represent is to attempt comprehension, bear witness, and compel others to see. Using first-person narration as a strategy for understanding the tumultuous history of the present, the travel narrative explores the subjective and ethical consequences of the cultural transformations consequent to war, modernization, secularization, and global media.

Scholarship on twentieth-century travel narrative has often emphasized continuity with earlier texts as part of its original task of demonstrating the genre merited critical attention. To argue that the genre has evolved significantly is not to reject those claims of continuity but rather to put them in context. In the considerable body of Anglophone travel narratives published in the twentieth century, many texts echo ideologies from the past, as Mary Louise Pratt demonstrates, or use colonial discourse with little attention to geopolitics, as Debbie Lisle argues. Many of the most innovative and ambitious, however, reinvent the genre to serve new cultural purposes in a tumultuous late modern world, as modernity fractures into postmodernity. In recognizing that what Daphna Erdinast-Vulcan calls "the contingency of our narratives in an authorless existence" requires us to "become fully responsive to and responsible for the other," they have grappled with the ethical import of the serious, perhaps unanswerable questions that representing travel now poses.[2] The travel narrative continues to be situated in the mobility and preoccupations of the first-person narrator who has the opportunity to leave his or her own location temporarily to experience existence elsewhere. Yet travel narratives dealing with war and postmodern upheaval also seek to understand the involuntary mobility and uncertain future of people whom the traveler meets en route. Rebecca West speculates whether people she met in Yugoslavia have survived the first years of war, and Stephen Spender describes wandering, dissociated persons in dead cities in Germany who appear to have neither home nor destination. Colin Thubron listens to aging workers formed by a Soviet world that is no more, and Joe Sacco travels among second- and third-generation Palestinian refugees who have no hope of return.

In books as different as H. V. Morton's and Ella Maillart's, narrators seek salve for malaise through travel in places that they imagine to be untroubled by modernity, only to demonstrate the futility of that conceit. Later texts echo the theme that travel may be more disconcerting than restorative. In *The Rings of Saturn: An English Pilgrimage* (1995), W. G. Sebald undertakes an extended walking tour of the eastern coast of England "in the hope of dispelling the emptiness that takes hold of me," yet finds that his long rural walks lead simultaneously to a "sense of freedom" and to a "paralyzing horror ... when confronted with the traces of destruction" evident "even in that remote place" (3). Traces appear everywhere: in relics and ruins of imperial industry, in a documentary about Roger Casement's report on atrocities in the Congo, in newspaper stories about ethnic violence in the Balkans, in writer Michael Hamburger's memories of wandering the ruins of Berlin "like a sleepwalker" in search of "traces of the life I had lost" (178).³ Lost walking Dunwitch Heath, Sebald panics: the horizon spins "as if I had jumped off a merry-go-round" (172). Months later he returns in a dream, still unable to "find my way out of the maze which I was convinced had been created solely for me," certain that the labyrinth pattern represents "a cross-section of my brain" (173). His paralysis proves literal, and writing is the cure: a year after he starts walking, hospitalized "in a state of almost total immobility," he "began in my thoughts to write these pages" (3–4). At its most anguished, travel narrative reveals civilization's deep instabilities and grim failures, arguing they must be of collective concern for a future to occur.

Looking back ninety years makes these dramatic changes especially clear. Narratives such as Andrew X. Pham's account of his travels through war-scarred Vietnam in the 1990s would have been unimaginable in the literary and political contexts of the 1920s, in which T. E. Lawrence wrote his strikingly modernist narrative of his wartime travels in Arabia. The kind of postcolonial, hybrid subject position Pham claims was not yet visible, and the refugee longing to travel back to a homeland lost through revolution was largely unknown: in the 1920s, travel narrative remained the all-but-exclusive province of metropolitan subjects whose race and class allowed them privileged access to the rest of the world. The familiar trope of the self-assured explorer that Peter Fleming parodies with ease in *Brazilian Adventure* allowed no room for the anguished exile seeking purposiveness. Indeed, it verged on precluding the notions that travelers might have existential concerns or travel a transformative effect on individuals, whose imperial discourse always already carried authority. Nor did the kinds of travel narrative written before the First World War anticipate that the literary travel narrative might become a mode of serious engagement with the labyrinthine modernity that anguishes Rebecca West – a world filled, in W. H. Auden's words, with "places/Where life is evil now:/ Nanking; Dachau."⁴ The self-conscious attention to relations between individuals and the irreversible temporality to which they are shackled that figure so crucially in Pham's narrative were not yet among the genre's possibilities.⁵ But the innovations that Lawrence, Auden, West, and others introduce reinvent the travel narrative as a subjective, heterogeneous literary form that serves each of their purposes – and eventually, in a later iteration, Pham's as well. The travel narratives examined here demonstrate how genres evolve in a dialogic "zone of direct contact" with disturbing, sometimes unspeakable geopolitical realities.[6] They do so in fits and starts, through a concert of strategies that Jed Esty sums as "negation, deviation, variation, and mutation."[7] The frank acknowledgment of feeling that is startlingly modernist in Lawrence and West is familiar by the century's end. Hence Rory Stewart writes of weeping when he learns of the death of his mastiff Babur, who accompanied him across Afghanistan, and Pham recounts unbearably wrenching exchanges with his father on the eve of his journey. The twentieth century altered the genre irreversibly, and it continues to evolve.

Much work yet remains on twentieth-century travel narrative. This book has argued for a new version of its history that credits modernism with a significant role and a new understanding of its concerns as critically cosmopolitan. In the course of doing so, it has cast provisional light on the role of visual images in the genre. The interrelation of text and image in travel narrative, whose long history predates much media innovation in fiction, merits further attention. Scholars and publishers alike have treated travel narratives' maps, photographs, and illustrations as expendable ephemera. Significant aspects of *Seven Pillars* and *Journey to a War* remain largely unexamined because the artwork of the former and photo commentary of the latter were silently altered or deleted in later editions, minimizing the extent of their modernist experimentation. Recent travel narratives such as Joe Sacco's graphic depictions of Palestine and Bosnia and Sebald's postmodern *The Rings of Saturn*, which intertwines text and photographs, give visual images a new prominence. In works such as these, images clearly play crucial roles that scholars must examine. This development suggests that visual images will be increasingly significant in the travel narrative in the future, as in the global media culture through which writers travel. Maillart and Fleming were surprised to come across six-week-old issues of the *Times* in Kashgar in the 1930s. Seventy years later, Stewart would come across bootleg copies of a recent British/American film in Afghanistan just six weeks after the Taliban departed Herat. Already adapted for sale in the twenty-first century, "*The Man in the Iron Mask* … had been brushed up for the Afghan market so that Leonardo DiCaprio, as Louis XIV in seventeenth-century dress, brandished a Browning 9mm."[8] Devising strategies for reading the dialogic relation of language and image may well prove critical to understanding the aesthetics, cultural politics, and ethics of travel narrative in the future.

In a new chapter written for the second edition of *Imperial Eyes*, Mary Louise Pratt speculates on the reinvention of travel narrative in the context of twenty-first-century mobility and globality. Once the "grand narrative of modernity" has "lost its grip" and "reversed diasporas" prevail, both metropole and periphery play transformed cultural roles. In this "reconfigured" world, "the normative backdrop of immobility ('home and here') against mobility ('elsewhere and away') is no longer the basis of the geo-social ordering of the world, nor the sole criterion for citizenship and belonging."[9] Pratt suggests that new geographies will be necessary to map this world; so too will new narratives. To write of travel experience in this transformed world is, in Iain Chambers's words, "to abandon the fixed geometry of sites and roots for the unstable calculations of transit. It is to embark on the unwinding and interminable path of heteronomy" and "to contemplate crossing over to the 'other' side of the authorized tale, that other side of modernity."[10] It is to read Auden and Isherwood with Sacco, West with Gourevitch, Lawrence with Pham. More importantly, it is to seek not the atavistic certainty of walking where Jesus walked, but rather the contemporary disarray of traveling to understand others as embodied, heterogeneous subjects with disparate points of view, not mere players in one's own story. It is to recognize displacement to be as normal as rootedness in an ever-mutable world of perpetual war. In the twenty-first century, travel narratives may well find in Pham's improvisational "No was. Only is." an apposite strategy for making one's way through the world without remaking the world as one's own.

Notes

Chapter 1   Introduction: Critical Paradigms and Problems

1 Rebecca West, *Black Lamb and Grey Falcon: A Journey through Yugoslavia*, 2 vols. (New York: Viking, 1941), 1088–1089.
2 West, *Black Lamb*, 733.
3 Katherine Woods, "Rebecca West's Brilliant Mosaic of Yugoslavian Travel," *New York Times*, October 26, 1941.
4 Charles Forsdick, *Travel in Twentieth-Century French and Francophone Cultures: The Persistence of Diversity* (Oxford: Oxford University Press, 2005), 1.
5 The most comprehensive overview is Peter Hulme and Tim Youngs (eds.), *The Cambridge Companion to Travel Writing* (Cambridge: Cambridge University Press, 2002). The sole scholarly survey of travel writing in Britain is Barbara Korte, *English Travel Writing from Pilgrimages to Postcolonial Explorations*, trans. Catherine Matthias (London: Macmillan, 2000). On "dark tourism," see John Lennon and Malcolm Foley, *Dark Tourism: The Attraction of Death and Disaster* (London: Continuum, 2000); on "travel," see, e.g., James Clifford, *Routes: Travel and Translation in the Late Twentieth Century* (Cambridge, MA: Harvard University Press, 1997).
6 On the reconceptualization this signifies, see, e.g., Douglas Mao and Rebecca L. Walkowitz, "The New Modernist Studies," *PMLA* 123 (2008), 737–748. Scholarship on modernist literature seldom mentions travel narrative. For instance, work on modernism and anthropology deals chiefly with fiction and ethnography; see Marc Manganaro, *Culture, 1922: The Emergence of a Concept* (Princeton, NJ: Princeton University Press, 2002); Michael North, *Reading 1922: A Return to the Scene of the Modern* (New York: Oxford University Press, 1999); and Carey J. Snyder, *British Fiction and Cross-Cultural Encounters: Ethnographic Modernism from Wells to Woolf* (New York: Palgrave Macmillan, 2008). Studies of travel writing typically refer to modernist or postmodernist contexts only briefly. Exceptions include David G. Farley, *Modernist Travel Writing: Intellectuals Abroad* (Columbia: University of Missouri Press, 2010); and Alison Russell, *Crossing Boundaries: Postmodern Travel Literature* (New York: Palgrave, 2000).
7 See, e.g., Mary Baine Campbell, *The Witness and the Other World: Exotic European Travel Writing, 400–1600* (Ithaca, NY: Cornell University Press, 1988).

8 On tourism's effect on representations of culture, see James Buzard, *The Beaten Track: European Tourism, Literature, and the Ways to 'Culture,' 1800–1918* (Oxford: Clarendon, 1993) and Peter D. Osborne, *Traveling Light: Photography, Travel and Visual Culture* (Manchester: Manchester University Press, 2000).

9 Mary Baine Campbell, "Travel Writing and Its Theory," *The Cambridge Companion to Travel Writing*, ed. Hulme and Youngs, 261.

10 Michael S. Roth, "Foucault's 'History of the Present,'" *History and Theory* **20** (1981), 43.

11 Edward W. Said, *Orientalism* (New York: Random House, 1978), 92–94.

12 Mary Louise Pratt, *Imperial Eyes: Travel Writing and Transculturation* (New York: Routledge, 1992), 5, 6, 10.

13 Mary Louise Pratt, *Imperial Eyes: Travel Writing and Transculturation*, 2d. ed. (New York: Routledge, 2008), xiii. A fuller list of distinctive contributions includes James Clifford, *The Predicament of Culture: Twentieth-Century Ethnography, Literature, and Art* (Cambridge, MA: Harvard University Press, 1988) and Caren Kaplan, *Questions of Travel: Postmodern Discourses of Displacement* (Durham, NC: Duke University Press, 1996).

14 Jerry C. Beasley, "Facts about Fiction: Two New Books on the Early History of the Novel," *The Eighteenth Century: Theory and Interpretation* **27**.1 (1986), 70.

15 Paul Fussell, *Abroad: British Literary Traveling between the Wars* (New York: Oxford University Press, 1980), vii, 203.

16 On Fussell's premises, see, e.g., Kaplan, *Questions of Travel*, 49–57.

17 Karen R. Lawrence, *Penelope Voyages: Women and Travel in the British Literary Tradition* (Ithaca, NY: Cornell University Press, 1994), 2, 18.

18 Lawrence, *Penelope Voyages*, 21.

19 Sara Mills, *Discourses of Difference: An Analysis of Women's Travel Writing and Colonialism* (London: Routledge, 1991), 199. See also Shirley Foster and Sara Mills (eds.), *An Anthology of Women's Travel Writing* (Manchester: Manchester University Press, 2002), 1–12.

20 Patrick Holland and Graham Huggan, *Tourists with Typewriters: Critical Reflections on Contemporary Travel Writing* (Ann Arbor: University of Michigan Press, 1998), x, xiii. The book's topical organization obscures some concerns posed in the preface: e.g., the analysis of gender is split, with masculine tropes discussed in one chapter, texts by women and gay men in another.

21 Holland and Huggan, *Tourists with Typewriters*, ix, x. See also Debbie Lisle, *The Global Politics of Contemporary Travel Writing* (Cambridge: Cambridge University Press, 2006), which examines best-selling books' implication in "the prevailing discursive hegemonies at work in global politics" (261).

22 Holland and Huggan, *Tourists with Typewriters*, 198.

23 Helen Carr, "Modernism and Travel (1880–1940)," *The Cambridge Companion to Travel Writing*, ed. Hulme and Youngs, 74.

24 Peter Hulme, "Travelling to Write (1940–2000)," *The Cambridge Companion to Travel Writing*, ed. Hulme and Youngs, 87, 91, 94, 93.

25 Holland and Huggan speculate on this in the postscript to *Tourists with Typewriters*, Pratt in *Imperial Eyes*, 2d ed.

26 Lisa Lowe, *Critical Terrains: French and British Orientalisms* (Ithaca, NY: Cornell University Press, 1991), 14–15, 28. While crediting *Orientalism* with a foundational role, many found its claims overly broad; Said responded in *Culture and Imperialism* (New York: Knopf, 1993). Said's work has not played a comparable role in francophone scholarship; Forsdick, *Travel*, 18.

27 Iain Chambers, "Leaky Habitats and Broken Grammar," *Travellers' Tales: Narratives of Home and Displacement*, ed. George Robertson, Melinda Mash, Lisa Tickner, Jon Bird, Barry Curtis, and Tim Putnam (London: Routledge, 1994), 245, 246.

28 On the ethics of travel in Western literature, see Syed Manzurul Islam, *The Ethics of Travel: From Marco Polo to Kafka* (Manchester: Manchester University Press, 1996).

29 Ralph Cohen, "Do Postmodern Genres Exist?" *Genre* **20** (1987), 241.

30 Hayden White, "Anomalies of Genre: The Utility of Theory and History for the Study of Literary Genres," *New Literary History* **34** (2003), 612.

31 Adena Rosemarin, *The Power of Genre* (Minneapolis: University of Minnesota Press, 1985), 46; White, "Anomalies of Genre," 605. See also *New Literary History*'s special issues on "theorizing genres," **34**.2–3 (2003).

32 Pratt, *Imperial Eyes*, 10–11.

33 David Spurr, *The Rhetoric of Empire: Colonial Discourse in Journalism, Travel Writing, and Imperial Administration* (Durham, NC: Duke University Press, 1993).

34 Percy G. Adams, *Travel Literature and the Evolution of the Novel* (Lexington: University Press of Kentucky, 1983), 283.

35 Tim Beasley-Murray, *Mikhail Bakhtin and Walter Benjamin: Experience and Form* (New York: Palgrave Macmillan, 2007), 1.

36 Scholarship on colonial discourse and travel has drawn on Bakhtin's theories infrequently; see, e.g., Graham Pechey, "On the Borders of Bakhtin: Dialogization, Decolonization," *Bakhtin and Cultural Theory*, ed. Ken Hirschkop and David Shepherd (Manchester: Manchester University Press, 1989), 39–67; and Edward M. Bruner, *Culture on Tour: Ethnographies of Travel* (Chicago: University of Chicago Press, 2005).

37 M. M. Bakhtin, *The Dialogic Imagination: Four Essays*, trans. Caryl Emerson and Michael Holquist, ed. Holquist (Austin: University of Texas Press, 1984), 259. Subsequent references cited in text by page number. Bakhtin's intellectual affiliations have been much debated; see Gary Saul Morson and Caryl Emerson, *Mikhail Bakhtin: Creation of a Prosaics* (Stanford: Stanford University Press, 1990); Michael Gardiner, *The Dialogics of Critique: M. M. Bakhtin and the Theory of Ideology* (London: Routledge, 1992); and Ken Hirschkop, *Mikhail Bakhtin: An Aesthetic for Democracy* (Oxford: Oxford University Press, 1999).

38 Beasley-Murray, *Mikhail Bakhtin*, 304.

39 Gardiner, *Dialogics*, 43.

40 Chambers, "Leaky Habitats," 246.

41 Pratt, *Imperial Eyes,* 201–208.

42 Meaghan Morris, "At Henry Parkes Motel," *Cultural Studies* **2** (1988), 35.

43 Buzard, *The Beaten Track*, 5.

44 See Clifford, *The Predicament of Culture*.

45 Fussell, *Abroad*, 8.

46 Bakhtin, *Dialogic Imagination*, 39.

47 Jed Esty, *Unseasonable Youth: Modernism, Colonialism, and the Fiction of Development* (Oxford: Oxford University Press, 2012), 18.

48 See, e.g., Pericles Lewis, *Modernism, Nationalism, and the Novel* (Cambridge: Cambridge University Press, 2000); David Adams, *Colonial Odysseys: Empire and Epic in the Modernist Novel* (Ithaca, NY: Cornell University Press, 2003); Jed Esty, *A Shrinking Island: Modernism and National Culture in England* (Princeton, NJ: Princeton University Press, 2003); and Richard Begam and Michael Valdez Moses (eds.), *Modernism and Colonialism: British and Irish Literature, 1899–1939* (Durham, NC: Duke University Press, 2007).

49 Rebecca L. Walkowitz, *Cosmopolitan Style: Modernism beyond the Nation* (New York: Columbia University Press, 2006), 2.

50 Walkowitz, *Cosmopolitan Style*, 5, 29.

51 Walkowitz, *Cosmopolitan Style*, 15, 35. For a differing account that also prefers a more complex history, see Tyrus Miller, *Late Modernism: Politics, Fiction, and the Arts between the World Wars* (Berkeley: University of California Press, 1999), which follows Charles Jencks in using "late modernism" and "post-modernism" to characterize overlapping, coexistent "responses to the legacy of modernism and its possible continuation" (9).

52 Fussell, *Abroad*, 209, 216, 224.

53 Schweizer, *Radicals*, 3–4.

54 Rob Nixon, *London Calling: V. S. Naipaul, Postcolonial Mandarin* (Oxford: Oxford University Press, 1992), 15.

55 Holland and Huggan, *Tourists with Typewriters*, 11.

56 Other transformations may feature more prominently in other traditions, e.g., francophone; see David Scott, *Semiologies of Travel: From Gautier to Baudrillard* (Cambridge: Cambridge University Press, 2004); and Forsdick, *Travel*.

57 Bakhtin, *Dialogic Imagination*, 291–292.

58 Pechey thus argues that Bakhtin's theory of discourse rejects the polarities of "othering" for "the notion of a multilingual field where the languages of colo-niser and colonised are indelibly inscribed within each other," a notion that cultural theorists and progressive writers "should seek to exploit rather than escape"; "On the Borders," 63.

59 W. H. Auden and Christopher Isherwood, *Journey to a War* (New York: Octagon Books, 1972), 43.

60 Pico Iyer, *Video Night in Kathmandu: And Other Reports from the Not-So-Far-East* (New York: Vintage, 1989), 25.

61 Holland and Huggan, *Tourists with Typewriters*, 68.

62 Holland and Huggan, *Tourists with Typewriters*, 109.

63 T. E. Lawrence, *Seven Pillars of Wisdom: A Triumph* (New York: Anchor, 1991), 549.

64 West, *Black Lamb*, 22.

65 For another account of modernity's transience precluding narrative completion, see Esty, *Unseasonable Youth*.

66 In these narratives the metaphorical "displacement" familiar in the genre becomes grimly literal. See Kaplan's *Questions of Travel*, which argues that Euro-American modernity may be understood by the narratives through which it manages history, writing in certain affiliations and displacing others. These narratives rely on concepts of home, diaspora, nomadism, and displacement that cite real circumstances yet play metaphorical roles in theory that often obscure those origins.

67 Margot Norris, *Writing War in the Twentieth Century* (Charlottesville: University Press of Virginia, 2000), 18–19, 1.

68 Fred Inglis, *People's Witness: The Journalist in Modern Politics* (New Haven: Yale University Press, 2002), 346.

69 On displacement in twentieth-century narrative, see Frances Bartkowski, *Travelers, Immigrants, Inmates: Essays in Estrangement* (Minneapolis: University of Minnesota Press, 1995).

70 Susan Stewart, *On Longing: Narratives of the Miniature, the Gigantic, the Souvenir, the Collection* (Durham, NC: Duke University Press, 1993), 23.

71 Evelyn Waugh, *When the Going Was Good* (Boston: Little, Brown, 1984), 9.

72 On mobility as both enabling and threatening, see Paul Smethurst, "Introduction," *Travel Writing, Form, and Empire: The Poetics and Politics of Mobility*, ed. Julia Kuehn and Paul Smethurst (New York: Routledge, 2009), 7–8.

Chapter 2 The Privilege – and Problem – of Narrative Authority

1 Freya Stark, *The Zodiac Arch* (New York: Harcourt, Brace & World, 1968), 132–133.

2 W. Somerset Maugham, *On a Chinese Screen* (1922; London: Heinemann, 1935), ix.

3 Paul Fussell, *Abroad: British Literary Traveling between the Wars* (New York: Oxford University Press, 1980), 203.

4 The genre's epistemological purpose persists well into the nineteenth century; see Nigel Leask, *Curiosity and the Aesthetics of Travel Writing, 1770–1840: "From an Antique Land"* (Oxford: Oxford University Press, 2002).

5 See, e.g., Tzvetan Todorov, "The Journey and Its Narratives," *The Morals of History*, trans. Alyson Waters (Minneapolis: University of Minnesota Press, 1995), 60–70. On masculinist adventure tropes, see, e.g., Graham Dawson, *Soldier Heroes: British Adventure, Empire and the Imagining of Masculinities* (London: Routledge, 1994); and Jen Hill, *White Horizon: The Arctic in the Nineteenth-Century British Imagination* (Albany: SUNY Press, 2008).

6 On "travel" versus "tourism" as "a binary opposition fundamental to and characteristic of modern culture," see James Buzard, *The Beaten Track: European Tourism, Literature, and the Ways to 'Culture,' 1800–1918* (Oxford: Clarendon, 1993), 18; on the "belatedness" of fin-de-siècle travelers, Ali Behdad, *Belated Travelers: Orientalism in the Age of Colonial Dissolution* (Durham, NC: Duke University Press, 1994).

7 Gertrude Bell, *The Desert and the Sown* (London, Virago, 1985), xix–xx.

8 Bell later wrote the British government's 1920 White Paper on Iraq; on her political role, see, e.g., Edward W. Said, *Orientalism* (New York: Random House, 1978), 223–254.

9 Bell, *The Desert*, 1.

10 Bell thus illustrates Mills's analysis of the genre as one in which "'experience' is channeled into and negotiates with pre-existent schemas which are discursive in nature" (*Discourses of Difference*, 39).

11 Surprisingly, neither Said nor Pratt cites Lukács.

12 Georg Lukács, "Narrate or Describe?" *Writer and Critic and Other Essays*, trans. and ed. Arthur Kahn (London: Merlin Press, 1970), 120, 111, 116.

13 Lukács, "Narrate or Describe?" 130, 127, 140.

14 Lukács, "Narrate or Describe?" 111, 130, 127.

15 Lukács, "Narrate or Describe?" 116.

16 Said, *Orientalism*, 239, 240.

17 Mary Louise Pratt, "Fieldwork in Common Places," *Writing Culture: The Poetics and Politics of Ethnography*, ed. James Clifford and George E. Marcus (Berkeley: University of California Press, 1986), 27–28, 55.

18 Pratt, "Fieldwork," 35, 32.

19 Said, *Orientalism*, 246; Pratt, "Fieldwork," 33.

20 The centrality of these concerns in modernism is well known; see, e.g., Tamar Katz, *Impressionist Subjects: Gender, Interiority, and Modernist Fiction in England* (Urbana: University of Illinois Press, 2000); and Pericles Lewis, *Modernism, Nationalism, and the Novel* (Cambridge: Cambridge University Press, 2000), 210–216.

21 Lewis, *Modernism, Nationalism* 4, 213.

22 Virginia Woolf, "Mr. Bennett and Mrs. Brown," *Collected Essays*, ed. Leonard Woolf (London: Hogarth, 1966–1967), I.324.

23 Aldous Huxley, *Along the Road: Notes and Essays of a Tourist* (London: Triad/Paladin, 1985), 20.

24 Simon Gikandi, *Maps of Englishness: Writing Identity in the Culture of Colonialism* (New York: Columbia University Press, 1996), 167. Allusions to *Heart of Darkness* permeate twentieth-century travel narrative.

25 Lewis, *Modernism, Nationalism*, 213.

26 Rebecca Walkowitz, *Cosmopolitan Style: Modernism beyond the Nation* (New York: Columbia University Press, 2006), 2. Jed Esty proposes that "[p]erception or perspective can refer both to local aesthetic experiments with narrative point of view and to global geopolitical and epistemological possibilities associated with life in the Age of Empire"; "The British Empire and the English

Modernist Novel," *The Cambridge Companion to the Twentieth-Century English Novel*, ed. Robert L. Caserio (Cambridge: Cambridge University Press, 2009), 23.

27 Tim Youngs, "Travelling Modernists," *The Oxford Handbook of Modernisms*, ed. Peter Brooker, Andrzej Gąsiorek, Deborah Longworth, and Andrew Thacker (Oxford: Oxford University Press, 2010), 272.

28 Colin Thubron, *Behind the Wall: A Journey through China* (New York: Atlantic Monthly Press, 1988), x.

29 Greene traveled with his cousin Barbara Greene, who published her own account, *Land Benighted* (1938).

30 Graham Greene, "Introduction," *Journey without Maps*, 2d ed. (London: Heinemann & Bodley Head, 1978), xi, xii. Cf. Katz, *Impressionist Subjects*: "Attempting to move between a subject permeated by the world and one enclosed from it, modernist impressionism also tries to move rhetorically between a subject imagined as socially specified, formed by particular places, and the possibilities of a subject that might seem to be above place, to be universal" (13).

31 "In Liberia: An Explorer Explores His Own Mind." *The Times* May 22, 1936: 19.

32 Bruce Chatwin, *The Songlines* (New York: Penguin, 1988), 4.

33 Susannah Clapp, *With Chatwin: Portrait of a Writer* (New York: Penguin, 1999), 203. See, e.g., T. E. Lawrence, *Seven Pillars of Wisdom: A Triumph* (New York: Anchor, 1991), 23; Rebecca West, *Black Lamb and Grey Falcon: A Journey through Yugoslavia*, 2 vols. (New York: Viking, 1941), 1158; and Thubron, *Behind the Wall*, x.

34 Salman Rushdie, "Travelling with Chatwin," *Imaginary Homelands: Essays and Criticism 1981–1991* (New York: Viking Penguin, 1991), 233.

35 Youngs, "Travelling Modernists," 274.

36 For instance, Andrew Hammond writes that in interwar British texts about the Balkans,

> the scientific style of objective reportage … underwent moments of considerable pre-
> cariousness as the travel writer's doubts about his or her knowledge and cultural status
> emerged and interacted with some of the more innovative poetics of the contempo-
> rary fiction. Most evidently, there was a reduction of faith in empiricism, and a fre-
> quent exchange of the confident imperial gaze for an acknowledgement of cultural
> subjectivity.

"'The Unending Revolt': Travel in an Era of Modernism," *Studies in Travel Writing* 7 (2003), 183.

37 Many writers work in both genres – e.g., Henry James, Edith Wharton, Rebecca West, Graham Greene, Rose Macaulay, Colin Thubron, Mary Morris.

38 Lewis, *Modernism, Nationalism*, 5.

39 M. M. Bakhtin, *The Dialogic Imagination: Four Essays*, trans. Caryl Emerson and Michael Holquist, ed. Holquist (Austin: University of Texas Press, 1984), 415. Subsequent references cited in text by page number.

40 Gary Saul Morson and Caryl Emerson explain that Bakhtin so favors the second line that he "often contends that characteristics present only in the second stylistic line are nevertheless definitive of the entire genre"; *Mikhail Bakhtin: Creation of a Prosaics* (Stanford: Stanford University Press, 1990), 345.

41 In Bakhtin's literary history, which does not extend to modernism, the novel's potential is most fully realized in the later nineteenth century. See Stacy Burton, "Paradoxical Relations: Bakhtin and Modernism," *Modern Language Quarterly* **61**(2000), 519–543.

42 In English translation, *Dialogic Imagination* prefers "author" and "speaker" to "narrator," which it uses all but interchangeably with "posited author" or, occasionally, to refer to the teller of an incorporated story; see 301–366.

43 Richard F. Burton, *Personal Narrative of a Pilgrimage to al-Madinah and Meccah*, memorial ed. ([1855, 1893]; New York: Dover, 1964), I:1–2.

44 Lawrence, *Seven Pillars*, 23.

45 Lawrence, *Seven Pillars*, 23–24.

46 Lawrence circulated the introductory chapter privately but withheld it from the first published text; see Chapter 4.

47 The Bildungsroman – linked historically to travel literature – figures prominently in Bakhtin's thinking; see "The *Bildungsroman* and Its Significance in the History of Realism (Toward a Historical Typology of the Novel)," *Speech Genres and Other Late Essays*, trans. Vern W. McGee, ed. Caryl Emerson and Michael Holquist (Austin: University of Texas Press, 1986), 10–59; and Bakhtin, *Dialogic Imagination*, 388–396.

48 Mary Baine Campbell, "Travel Writing and Its Theory," *The Cambridge Companion to Travel Writing*, ed. Peter Hulme and Tim Youngs (Cambridge: Cambridge University Press, 2002), 261.

49 Wlad Godzich, "Correcting Kant: Bakhtin and Intercultural Interactions," *Boundary 2* **18** (1991), 7. Cf. Graham Pechey, who argues that Bakhtin's "concepts are nothing if not precisely designed to theorise otherness, including their own"; "On the Borders of Bakhtin: Dialogization, Decolonization," *Bakhtin and Cultural Theory*, ed. Ken Hirschkop and David Shepherd (Manchester: Manchester University Press, 1989), 62.

50 Daphna Erdinast-Vulcan, "The *I* that Tells Itself: A Bakhtinian Perspective on Narrative Identity," *Narrative* **16** (2008), 9, 12. Scholars differ considerably on the relation of ethics and aesthetics in Bakhtin's work; see, e.g., Morson and Emerson's *Mikhail Bakhtin*, and Hirschkop's rejection of their analysis in his *Mikhail Bakhtin*.

51 M. M. Bakhtin, *Problems of Dostoevsky's Poetics*, trans. and ed. Caryl Emerson (Minneapolis: University of Minnesota Press, 1984), 68.

52 Anke Gleber, *The Art of Taking a Walk: Flanerie, Literature, and Film in Weimar Culture* (Princeton, NJ: Princeton University Press, 1999), 1, 23, 7.

53 See Clare Olivia Parsons, "Women Travelers and the Spectacle of Modernity," *Women's Studies* **26** (1997), 399–422; and Deborah L. Parsons, *Streetwalking the Metropolis: Women, the City and Modernity* (Oxford: Oxford University Press, 2000).

54 See, e.g., Elizabeth Wilson, "The Invisible Flâneur." *New Left Review* **191** (1992), 90–110.

55 Walter Benjamin, *The Arcades Project*, trans. Howard Eiland and Kevin McLaughlin (Cambridge, MA: Belknap/Harvard University Press, 1999), 10; *Charles Baudelaire: A Lyric Poet in the Era of High Capitalism*, trans. Harry Zohn (London: NLB, 1973), 36.

56 Gleber, *The Art*, 31–37.

57 John Urry, *The Tourist Gaze: Leisure and Travel in Contemporary Societies* (London: Sage, 1990), 5.

58 Mary Gluck, "The *Flâneur* and the Aesthetic Appropriation of Urban Culture in Mid-19th-century Paris," *Theory, Culture & Society* **20** (2003), 53; Parsons, *Streetwalking*, 4; Chris Jenks, "Watching Your Step: The History and Practice of the *Flâneur*," *Visual Culture*, ed. Jenks (London: Routledge, 1995), 148.

59 Parsons, *Streetwalking*, 4.

60 Gluck, "The *Flâneur*," 78.

61 The concept seldom appears in studies of travel narrative; an exception is Marie Williams, "The Traveller as *Flâneur*: Modernity, *Flânerie* and Bruce Chatwin's Travelogues," *Cross-Cultural Travel: Papers from the Royal Irish Academy Symposium on Literature and Travel*, ed. Jane Conroy (New York: Peter Lang, 2003), 439–448.

62 John Urry, *Consuming Places* (London: Routledge, 1995), 141.

63 Urry, *Tourist Gaze*, 138, 139. Cf. Chris Rojek and John Urry (eds.), *Touring Cultures: Transformations of Travel and Theory* (London: Routledge, 1997). On photography and tourism, see John Taylor, *A Dream of England: Landscape, Photography and the Tourist's Imagination* (Manchester: Manchester University Press, 1994).

64 John Frow, "Tourism and the Semiotics of Nostalgia," *October* **57** (1991), 142, 144.

65 Gleber, *The Art*, 131, 132.

66 Characters who long to be urbane travelers yet suspect they are but tourists populate twentieth century fiction from E. M. Forster's English men and women abroad to Paul Bowles's expatriate Americans in North Africa – and beyond.

67 Gleber, *The Art*, 41, 133.

68 Gleber, *The Art*, 133, 132.

69 Gleber, *The Art*, 151; the second phrase Gleber quotes from film theorist Siegfried Kracauer.

70 Jonathan Crary, *Techniques of the Observer: On Vision and Modernity in the Nineteenth Century* (Cambridge, MA: MIT Press, 1990), 11.

71 Walkowitz observes that cosmopolitan practices require "an analysis of self and location": "being a cosmopolitan *flâneur*, to take one example, is a rather different experience for those who have full access to the city than it is for those – women, migrants, colonial subjects – who do not, not only because some observers can move and observe more easily than others but also because some are themselves the objects of intense or hostile scrutiny" (16).

72 Charles Dickens, *American Notes for General Circulation*, ed. John S. Whitley and Arnold Goldman ([1841]; New York: Penguin, 1972), 111.

73 Burton, *Personal Narrative*, I:141.

74 Dickens, *American Notes*, 199.

75 Burton, *Personal Narrative*, I:149.

76 Edith Wharton, *A Motor-Flight through France*, intro. Julian Barnes (London: Picador, 1995), 17.

77 Sidonie Smith, *Moving Lives: Twentieth-Century Women's Travel Writing* (Minneapolis: University of Minnesota Press), 182.

78 Rory Stewart, *The Places in Between* (New York: Harcourt, 2006), 118–119.

79 Jean-François Lyotard, "Answering the Question: What is Postmodernism?" trans. Régis Durand, in *The Postmodern Condition: A Report on Knowledge*, trans. G. Bennington and R. Massumi (Manchester: Manchester University Press, 1984), 74.

80 Peter Osborne, *Traveling Light: Photography, Travel and Visual Culture* (Manchester: Manchester University Press), 5, 9.

81 Isabella Bird, *The Yangtze Valley and Beyond* ([1899] Boston: Beacon, 1987), 302.

82 No substantial studies exist. On Auden specifically, see Marsha Bryant, *Auden and Documentary in the 1930s* (Charlottesville: University Press of Virginia, 1997).

83 See Nancy Armstrong, *Fiction in the Age of Photography: The Legacy of British Realism* (Cambridge, MA: Harvard University Press, 1999).

84 David Spurr, *The Rhetoric of Empire: Colonial Discourse in Journalism, Travel Writing, and Imperial Administration* (Durham, NC: Duke University Press, 1993), 13, 21.

85 Robyn Davidson, *Tracks* (New York: Pantheon, 1980), 102, 237.

86 Pico Iyer, *Video Night in Kathmandu: And Other Reports from the Not-So-Far-East* (New York: Vintage, 1989), 3–5.

87 Chandra Talpade Mohanty, "Under Western Eyes: Feminist Scholarship and Colonial Discourses," *Boundary 2* **12/13** (1984), 333.

Chapter 3   Modernist and Postmodernist Travels

1 W. H. Auden and Louis MacNeice, *Letters from Iceland*, in Auden, *Prose and Travel Books in Prose and Verse*, 2 vols., *The Complete Works of W. H. Auden*, ed. Edward Mendelson (Princeton, NJ: Princeton University Press, 1996), I:183–184. Subsequent references cited in text by page number. Paper editions of *Letters* include silent textual alterations and omit photographs and diagrams.

2 Holland and Huggan and Russell explicitly discard a distinction between "travel narrative" and "novel" when discussing postmodern texts.

3 Paul Fussell, *Abroad: British Literary Traveling between the Wars* (New York: Oxford University Press, 1980), 108. Cf. Helen Carr, "Modernism and Travel (1880–1940)," *The Cambridge Companion to Travel Writing*, ed. Peter Hulme and Tim Youngs (Cambridge: Cambridge University Press, 2002), 85.

4 David Farley, *Modernist Travel Writing: Intellectuals Abroad* (Columbia: University of Missouri Press, 2010), 16.

5 Patrick Holland and Graham Huggan, *Tourists with Typewriters: Critical Reflections on Contemporary Travel Writing* (Ann Arbor: University of Michigan Press, 1998), 4; Debbie Lisle, *The Global Politics of Contemporary Travel Writing* (Cambridge: Cambridge University Press, 2006), 4. The former deals primarily with texts published after 1960, the latter, after 1975.

6 Lisle, *Global Politics*, 3, 4, 5.

7 Holland and Huggan, *Tourists with Typewriters*, xiii, 216, 217.

8 Lisle, *Global Politics*, 21, 261.

9 Rebecca Walkowitz, *Cosmopolitan Style: Modernism beyond the Nation* (New York: Columbia University Press, 2006), 173n.18.

10 Tim Youngs, "Travelling Modernists," *The Oxford Handbook of Modernisms*, ed. Peter Brooker, Andrzej Gąsiorek, Deborah Longworth, and Andrew Thacker (Oxford: Oxford University Press, 2010), 276.

11 W. H. Auden and Christopher Isherwood, *Journey to a War* (New York: Octagon Books, 1972), 291. Subsequent references cited in text by page number.

12 Pico Iyer, *Video Night in Kathmandu: And Other Reports from the Not-So-Far-East* (New York: Vintage, 1989), 15. Subsequent references cited in text by page number.

13 Holland and Huggan, *Tourists with Typewriters*, 115.

14 Beryl Smeeton, *Winter Shoes in Springtime* (London: Rupert Hart-Davis, 1961), 165, 173, 179.

15 Janet Wolff, *Resident Alien: Feminist Cultural Criticism* (New Haven: Yale University Press, 1995), 128.

16 Holland and Huggan, *Tourists with Typewriters*, 100, 109.

17 Peter Fleming, *Brazilian Adventure* (New York: Charles Scribner's, 1933), 49. Subsequent references cited in text by page number.

18 The *Oxford English Dictionary* dates this lightly derogatory term to 1813.

19 "Rover Boys, New Style," *Time* (January 8, 1934)

20 Linda Hutcheon, *A Theory of Parody: The Teachings of Twentieth-Century Art Forms* (New York: Methuen, 1985), 6, 95.

21 Peter Fleming, *One's Company* (London: Jonathan Cape, 1934), 121. Subsequent references cited in text by page number. Fussell identifies Halliburton as among Fleming's targets; Fussell, *Abroad*, 167.

22 Evelyn Waugh, "Mr. Fleming in Brazil," *The Spectator* (August 11, 1933), 195.

23 Fleming – an editor and reviewer for the *Spectator* – also received an advance inquiry regarding a book contract; see Chris Hopkins, "Peter Fleming," *British Travel Writers, 1910–1939*, ed. Barbara Brothers and Julia M. Gergits, *Dictionary of Literary Biography* 195 (Detroit: Gale, 1998), 72–73.

24 On expeditions to find Fawcett, see David Grann, "The Lost City of Oz," *New Yorker* (September 19, 2005), 556–581.

25 Fussell, *Abroad*, 13–14. Hopkins provides details: fifteen impressions within three years of publication, twenty-seven printings by 1946; Hopkins, "Peter Fleming," 75.

26 Waugh, writing of Sakkara, makes the point:

> One is supposed, I know … to conjure up the ruined streets of Memphis and to see in one's mind's eye the sacred procession as it wound up the avenue of sphinxes, mourning the dead bull; perhaps even to give licence to one's fancy and invent some personal romance about the lives of these garlanded hymn-singers, and to generalize sagely about the mutability of all human achievement. But I think we can leave all that to Hollywood.
>
> *Labels: A Mediterranean Journal* (London: Duckworth, 1930), 105.

27 The "warning" occupies a full page immediately after the dedication; the later Penguin paperback inexplicably subordinates it to the foreword.

28 Modernist travel narratives often begin in malaise attributed to political foreboding; see Fussell, *Abroad*, 15–23; and, e. g., H. M. Tomlinson's *Tide Marks* (New York: Blue Ribbon Books, 1924) and Rebecca West's *Black Lamb and Grey Falcon: A Journey through Yugoslavia*, 2 vols. (New York: Viking, 1941). Fleming's narrator, however, attributes his malaise to boredom.

29 V. Sackville-West, "A Modern Elizabethan," *The Spectator* (August 3, 1934), 167.

30 Fleming, *Brazilian Adventure*, 150.

31 Fussell, *Abroad*, 167.

32 Fleming, *One's Company*, 15. His self-consciousness does not, however, extend to the biases of his class and time, which are evident in clichéd comments about women, Jews, and Chinese that he assumes require no qualification.

33 Hutcheon, *A Theory*, 93.

34 "Rover Boys."

35 Hutcheon, *A Theory*, 75.

36 The former ends with Fleming in Dover, picking up a newspaper, the latter with him watching the English coast draw near. *Brazilian Adventure*'s epilogue is archly titled "Home Sweet Home" (401).

37 "Poets in Iceland: Politics and Verse," *Times* (August 6, 1937), 7.

38 For explanatory annotations, see Auden, *Prose and Travel Books* I:781–800.

39 Marsha Bryant, *Auden and Documentary in the 1930s* (Charlottesville: University Press of Virginia, 1997), 65.

40 Bryant, *Auden and Documentary*, 93.

41 Bryant, *Auden and Documentary*, 98.

42 "Cooling Waters: A Byronic Interlude in Iceland," *Times Literary Supplement* (August 7, 1937), 572.

43 "Poets in Iceland."

44 Tim Youngs, "Auden's Travel Writings," *The Cambridge Companion to W. H. Auden*, ed. Stan Smith (Cambridge: Cambridge University Press, 2004), 72–73.

45 Byron was, famously, a swimmer; he crossed the Hellespont in 1810.

46 For a differing view see Tom Paulin, "*Letters from Iceland*: Going North," *Culture, Theory and Critique* **20** (1976), 65–80.

47 For date of composition, see Auden, *Prose and Travel Books* I:769.

48 Maureen Moynagh, "Revolutionary Drag in Auden and Isherwood's *Journey to a War*," *Studies in Travel Writing* **8** (2004), 127.

49 Criticism generally uses "Auden" for the speaker in the poems, "Isherwood" the speaker in the prose. However, the text does not specify authorship, and its composition was collaborative: see Auden, *Prose and Travel Books*, I:822–826; and Douglas Kerr, "Journey to a War: 'a test for men from Europe,'" *W. H. Auden: A Legacy*, ed. David Garrett Izzo (West Cornwall: Locust Hill Press, 2002), 292–293. Bryant credits Auden with the photo captions; *Auden and Documentary*, 131.

50 Marian Osmond's sensational 1923 novel had been adapted for stage and screen.

51 See Nicholas Clifford, *"A Truthful Impression of the Country": British and American Travel Writing in China, 1880–1949* (Ann Arbor: University of Michigan Press, 2001).

52 Bryant, *Auden and Documentary*, 150.

53 Isherwood uses a similarly racial notion of aesthetics in describing the Nationalist war film *Fight to the Last* (167).

54 On Halliburton's performative masculinity, see Charles E. Morris III, "Richard Halliburton's Bearded Tales," *Quarterly Journal of Speech* **95** (2009), 123–147. Isherwood writes of Fleming's renown and exaggerated persona in letters to his mother. From Hong Kong, February 25, 1938: "The Colony is still full of rumours of the approach of Peter Fleming: some even say that he is here, incog." From Shanghai, May 26, 1938: "We both like Fleming extremely. He isn't anything at all resembling the author of his books – that infuriatingly modest well-bred Lucky Strike." Christopher Isherwood, *Kathleen and Christopher: Christopher Isherwood's Letters to His Mother*, ed. Lisa Colletta (Minneapolis: University of Minnesota Press, 2005), 108, 114.

55 Bryant, *Auden and Documentary*, 146; see also Moynagh, "Revolutionary Drag." While staying with Western missionaries, for example, they observe a bathhouse where "little boys" soap men, and a resort they visit features houseboys in shorts (93). One review knowingly declares: "the word that best describes their book – however incongruous it may seem – is 'gay'"; Louis Kronenberger, "Two Travellers and Thirty-eight Philosophers," *New Yorker* (August 12, 1939), 53.

56 "China at War: Travel Diary and Commentary," *Times* March 17, 1939, 10.

57 "Auden and Isherwood in China: Diary and Poetic Commentary," *Times Literary Supplement* (March 18, 1939), 158.

58 Kerr, "'Journey to a War,'" 282, 283.

59 Fleming and his readers debated the rifle's merits in a spirited exchange of letters published in the *Times* in 1935.

60 As Kerr notes, "[t]he formula of the title is that of many historical adventure stories by G. A. Henty, often about boys whose path crosses that of some hero of imperial destiny"; "'Journey to a War,'" 289.

61 Fleming, who read the page proofs because Auden and Isherwood were at sea, made minor revisions to the text; see Auden, *Prose and Travel Books* I:826–828.

62 Kerr, "'Journey to a War,'" 289.

63 Kerr, "'Journey to a War,'" 290.

64 Bryant, *Auden and Documentary*, 133.

65 Speaking on the BBC in 1939, Auden observed, "There is little trench fighting in this war, and the actual front is often impossible to find"; *Prose and Travel Books* I:490. Posing in trenches thus simulates war as imagined more than it represents.

66 Bryant, *Auden and Documentary,* 137, 139, and, on Auden's allusion to Malraux, 165–167.

67 "Auden and Isherwood"; Evelyn Waugh, "Mr. Isherwood and Friend," *The Spectator* (March 24, 1939), 497.

68 Auden published several of the poems in advance of the book and later revised many; see John Fuller, *W. H. Auden: A Commentary* (Princeton, NJ: Princeton University Press, 1998), 230–244.

69 Fuller, *W. H. Auden*, 235.

70 Moynagh, "Revolutionary Drag," 134.

71 Moynagh, "Revolutionary Drag," 126; Bryant, *Auden and Documentary*, 142.

72 Pericles Lewis, *Modernism, Nationalism, and the Novel* (Cambridge: Cambridge University Press, 2000), 5.

73 Scholarship on relations between modernism and postmodernism often blurs historical and aesthetic claims. Some, such as Hutcheon and Walkowitz, foreground continuities in aesthetic and epistemological concerns across the century. Others, such as Russell, focus on differences. The late-century travel narratives examined here retain a commitment to the real – however complicated – that precludes characterizing them as solely postmodern, unlike texts such as Jean Baudrillard's *America*, which declares its subject to be "neither dream or reality" but "hyperreality"; trans. Chris Turner (London: Verso, 1988), 28. As Walkowitz argues of late-century novels, they may be understood as having both modernist and postmodernist elements.

74 On Chatwin, see, e.g., Holland and Huggan, *Tourists with Typewriters*; Russell, *Crossing Boundaries*, and Lisle, *Global Politics*; on Butor and Barthes, see Frances Bartkowski, *Travelers, Immigrants, Inmates: Essays in Estrangement* (Minneapolis: University of Minnesota Press, 1995) and Charles Forsdick, *Travel in Twentieth-Century French and Francophone Cultures: The Persistence of Diversity* (Oxford: Oxford University Press, 2005).

75 Paul Smethurst, "Travels in Globality: Pico Iyer and Jan Morris in Hong Kong," *Studies in Travel Writing* **8**.2 (2004), 186, 191.

76 Euan Cameron, "How the East is Being Won," *The Spectator* (July 30, 1988), 28.

77 *Video Night* includes no photos or other visual images. Auden and Isherwood also watch movie audiences; see *Journey to a War*, 184.

78 Holland and Huggan, *Tourists with Typewriters*, 61.

79 Trinh T. Minh-ha, "Other than myself/my other self," *Travellers' Tales*, ed. Robertson et al., 22, 22–23.

80 Malini Johar Schueller, "Traveling 'Back' to India: Globalization as Imperialism in Pico Iyer's *Video Night in Kathmandu*," *Journeys* **10** (2009), 43. Schueller argues that Iyer's "idea of a supremely unlocated self" forestalls his being identified as "Indian" or "Etonian"; 31.

81 In this scheme of things, Burma is "the queer maiden aunt who lives alone and whom the maid has forgotten to visit," India "as grotesque and fascinating as a hermaphrodite," and Japan "the world's great Significant Other" (199, 215, 361). Cf. Schueller, "Traveling 'Back.'"

82 Holland and Huggan, *Tourists with Typewriters*, 166.

83 Pico Iyer, *The Lady and the Monk: Four Seasons in Kyoto* (New York: Vintage, 1992), 7.

84 Lisle, citing Timothy Brennan, argues that "the 'colonial erotics' of cosmopolitan travel writers like Iyer are not as crude as their predecessors, but the *function* of these narratives remains the same"; *Global Politics*, 120. Cf. Holland and Huggan, *Tourists with Typewriters*, 227n.29.

85 Here his inspiration becomes Emerson; Smethurst, "Travels in Globality," 193.

86 Lisle, *Global Politics*, 120.

87 Kwame Anthony Appiah, *My Father's House: Africa in the Philosophy of Culture* (New York: Oxford University Press, 1992), 155.

Chapter 4   Nostalgia and the Spectacle of Modernity

1 Ella Maillart, *Forbidden Journey*, trans. Thomas McGreevy (London: Heinemann, 1937), 49. Subsequent references cited in text by page number.

2 On nostalgia's modernity, see Svetlana Boym, *The Future of Nostalgia* (New York: Basic Books, 2001).

3 Barry Curtis and Claire Pajaczkowska, "'Getting There': Travel, Time and Narrative," *Travellers' Tales: Narratives of Home and Displacement*, ed. George Robertson et al. (London: Routledge, 1994), 199.

4 Ella Maillart, *Turkestan Solo*, trans. John Rodker (London: Century, 1985), 14. Subsequent references cited in text by page number.

5 Mary Morris, *Nothing to Declare: Memoirs of a Woman Traveling Alone* (New York: Penguin, 1989), 4.

6 Patrick Holland and Graham Huggan, *Tourists with Typewriters: Critical Reflections on Contemporary Travel Writing* (Ann Arbor: University of Michigan Press, 1998), xi, 6–7, 29–30.

7 On nostalgia in fictional narratives, see, e.g., John J. Su, *Ethics and Nostalgia in the Contemporary Novel* (Cambridge, MA: Cambridge University Press, 2005); and Adam Muller, "Notes Toward a Theory of Nostalgia: Childhood and the Evocation of the Past in Two European 'Heritage' Films," *New Literary History* **37** (2007), 739–760.

8 Boym, *The Future of Nostalgia*, 13, 17.

9 Cf. Caren Kaplan, *Questions of Travel: Postmodern Discourses of Displacement* (Durham, NC: Duke University Press), 35.

10 John Frow, "Tourism and the Semiotics of Nostalgia," *October* **57** (1991), 136–137. On the opposition between authentic and inauthentic experience, see Chapter 6.

11 William Cunningham Bissell, "Engaging Colonial Nostalgia," *Cultural Anthropology* **20** (2005), 239. See also Jennifer Wenzel, "Remembering the

Past's Future: Anti-Imperialist Nostalgia and Some Versions of the Third World," *Cultural Critique* **62** (2006), 1–32.

12 Marianne Hirsch and Leo Spitzer, "'We Would Not Have Come Without You': Generations of Nostalgia," *American Imago* **59** (2002), 258. On the late-century variant they call "postmemory," see Chapter 6.

13 E.g., Edward W. Said, *Orientalism* (New York: Random House, 1978), 96–97, 237–240.

14 Maillart, *Turkestan Solo*, 12.

15 Colin Thubron, "Both Seer and Seen: The Travel Writer as Leftover Amateur," *Times Literary Supplement* (July 30, 1999), 13.

16 Holland and Huggan, *Tourists with Typewriters*, 67.

17 Paul Smethurst, "Introduction," *Travel Writing, Form, and Empire: The Poetics and Politics of Mobility*, ed. Julia Kuehn and Paul Smethurst (New York: Routledge, 2009), 7.

18 Custine, a French diplomat, traveled in hopes of seeing a society "uncontaminated by the revolutionary virus gnawing at Europe" but found Russian society innately suspicious and incapable of European rationality: "La Russie est policée non civilisée"; Martin Malia, *Russia Under Western Eyes: From the Bronze Horseman to the Lenin Mausoleum* (Cambridge, MA: Belknap/Harvard University Press, 1999), 98, 98–99. Custine remains a reference point. See, e.g., Colin Thubron, *Among the Russians* (London: Heinemann, 1983), 1. On fiction's influence on English perceptions of Russia, see, e.g., Virginia Woolf, "The Russian Point of View," *The Common Reader* (New York: Harcourt, Brace & World, 1925), 177–187.

19 The USSR was formally recognized by France in 1926, Britain in 1929, and the United States in 1933; Malia, *Russia*, 296.

20 See, e.g., Sylvia R. Margulies, *The Pilgrimage to Russia: The Soviet Union and the Treatment of Foreigners, 1924–1937* (Madison: University of Wisconsin Press, 1968); and Michael David-Fox, "The Fellow Travelers Revisited: The 'Cultured West' through Soviet Eyes," *Journal of Modern History* **75** (2003), 300–335.

21 Peter Fleming, *One's Company* (London: Jonathan Cape, 1934), 33.

22 Robert Byron, *First Russia, Then Tibet* (Harmondsworth: Penguin, 1985), 15, 15–16.

23 Ada Chesterton, *My Russian Venture* (Philadelphia: J. B. Lippincott, 1931), 9, 257.

24 Walter Benjamin, "Moscow," *Reflections: Essays, Aphorisms, Autobiographical Writings*, ed. Peter Demetz, trans. Edmund Jephcott (New York: Schocken, 1986), xxviii, 111.

25 Benjamin, "Moscow," 106.

26 Byron, *First Russia*, 15, 62.

27 Although Guy Debord's critique of the "society of the spectacle" remains provocative, scholarship treats it as a limited analysis. See, e.g., Dean MacCannell, "Spectacles," *Empty Meeting Grounds: The Tourist Papers* (London: Routledge, 1992), 234; and Thomas Richards, *The Commodity Culture of Victorian*

England: Advertising and Spectacle, 1851–1914 (Stanford: Stanford University Press, 1990), 256–257. Richards examines spectacle's role in the Victorian "semiotic consolidation of capitalism" (vii); MacCannell examines its relation to festival, tourism, and postmodern iconic representation. The present discussion deals with spectacle as a way of describing and thus managing what one observes, only indirectly its evolving function in modern societies.

28 Richards, *The Commodity Culture*, 251.

29 Said, *Orientalism*, 158, 188.

30 Said, *Orientalism*, 189, 239.

31 Claude Lévi-Strauss characterizes the premodern traveler's perception of an unfamiliar society as "a stupendous spectacle"; *Tristes Tropiques*, trans. John and Doreen Weightman ([1955] New York: Penguin, 1992), 43.

32 Jonathan Crary, "Spectacle, Attention, Counter-Memory," *October* **50** (1989), 100. Crary takes a historical cue from Debord.

33 Crary, "Spectacle, Attention," 103, 104, 102.

34 Crary, "Spectacle, Attention," 103, 106. On Situationist nostalgia, see Alastair Bonnett, *Left in the Past: Radicalism and the Politics of Nostalgia* (New York: Continuum, 2010), 139–154.

35 Susan Sontag, *Regarding the Pain of Others* (New York: Farrar, Straus, Giroux, 2003), 18.

36 Film appears as analogue precisely for its capability to be mobile and diffuse in ways whose critical potential Crary scrutinizes. Sontag credits narrative with greater capacity to produce comprehension than still images: "Harrowing photographs ... are not much help if the task is to understand. Narratives can make us understand. Photographs do something else: they haunt us" (*Regarding*, 89). Judith Butler reflects on Sontag's argument in *Frames of War: When Is Life Grievable?* (London: Verso, 2010), 63–100. On anthropology's shift, see Mary Louise Pratt, "Fieldwork in Common Places," *Writing Culture: The Poetics and Politics of Ethnography*, ed. James Clifford and George E. Marcus (Berkeley: University of California Press, 1986) and Andres Barry, "Reporting and Visualising," *Visual Culture*, ed. Chris Jenks (London: Routledge, 1995), 52–54.

37 Colin Thubron, *The Lost Heart of Asia* (New York: Harper Collins, 1994), 78. Subsequent references cited in text by page number.

38 Graham Dawson, *Soldier Heroes: British Adventure, Empire and the Imagining of Masculinities* (London: Routledge, 1994), 196. *Seven Pillars* was printed privately for preliminary reading in 1922 (the "Oxford text"), revised extensively before publication in London by subscription in 1926, and finally published for a general readership in 1935. All quotations are from T. E. Lawrence, *Seven Pillars of Wisdom: A Triumph* (New York: Anchor, 1991).

39 Charles Grosvenor, "The Subscribers' *Seven Pillars of Wisdom*: The Visual Aspect," *The T. E. Lawrence Puzzle*, ed. Stephen Tabachnick (Athens: University of Georgia Press, 1984), 177, 165. V. M. Thompson provides bibliographic and visual details in *"Not a Suitable Hobby for an Airman": T. E. Lawrence as Publisher* (Oxford: Orchard Books, 1986); on Kennington's role,

see Jonathan Black, "'King of the Pictures': Eric Kennington, Portraiture and the Illustration of *Seven Pillars of Wisdom*, 1920–26," *The Journal of the T. E. Lawrence Society* **16**.2 (2007), 7–28. Later editions omit, rearrange, and add images. The 1991 Anchor edition includes approximately fifty monochrome images.

40 Grosvenor, "The Subscribers' *Seven Pillars*," 163–164.

41 Dennis Porter, *Haunted Journeys: Desire and Transgression in European Travel Writing* (Princeton, NJ: Princeton University Press, 1991), 226.

42 Dawson, *Soldier Heroes*, 158; Lowell Thomas, *With Lawrence in Arabia*, 2d ed. (Garden City: Doubleday, 1967), 1.

43 D. G. Hogarth, "Lawrence of Arabia: Story of His Book, A Lavish Edition," *Times* (December 13, 1926), 15.

44 Dawson, *Soldier Heroes*, 196.

45 Herbert Read, "The Seven Pillars of Wisdom," *The Bibliophile's Almanack* (1928), 35.

46 "Lawrence of Arabia," *Times Literary Supplement* (August 1, 1935), 487.

47 E. M. Forster, "T. E. Lawrence," *Abinger Harvest* (New York: Harcourt, Brace & World, 1964), 141, 147.

48 See, e.g, Robert Graves's sympathetic *Lawrence and the Arabs* ([1927] New York: Paragon, 1991); Richard Aldington's debunking *Lawrence of Arabia: A Biographical Enquiry* ([1955] London: Collins, 1969); Jeffrey Meyers's *The Wounded Spirit: A Study of* Seven Pillars of Wisdom (London: Martin Brian & O'Keeffe, 1973); Dawson, *Soldier Heroes*; and Marjorie Garber, *Vested Interests: Cross-Dressing and Cultural Anxiety* (New York: Routledge, 1992). Thomas responded to Aldington in his second edition, Graves in "Lawrence Vindicated," *The New Republic* (March 21, 1955), 16–20.

49 On Lawrence and Doughty's *Travels in Arabia Deserta*, see William David Halloran, "Titan, Tome and Triumph: T. E. Lawrence's *Seven Pillars of Wisdom* as a Modernist Spectacle," Ph.D. dissertation, University of California, Los Angeles, 2001, 13–28.

50 Said, *Orientalism*, 240. For Porter, *Seven Pillars* demonstrates Said's fault lines: "because he overlooks the potential contradiction between [Foucauldian] discourse theory and Gramscian hegemony," he finds "always the same triumphant discourse where several are frequently in conflict"; "Orientalism and Its Problems," *The Politics of Theory*, ed. Francis Barker, Peter Hulme, Margaret Iversen, and Diane Loxley (Colchester: University of Essex, 1983), 192.

51 For textual history, see Jeffrey Meyers, "The Revisions of *Seven Pillars of Wisdom*," *PMLA* **88** (1973), 1066–1082; and Jeremy Wilson, "Preface: The Two Texts of *Seven Pillars*," *Seven Pillars of Wisdom: A Triumph. The Complete 1922 Text*, by T. E. Lawrence, ed. Wilson, 2d ed. (n.p.: Castle Hill Press, 2003), xxi–xxvi.

52 E.g., Meyers, *Wounded Spirits* 11, 86; Keith N. Hull, "*Seven Pillars of Wisdom*: The Secret, Contestable Documentary," *The T. E. Lawrence Puzzle*, ed. Tabachnick, 13. Patrick Deer, *Culture in Camouflage: War, Empire, and Modern British Literature* (New York: Oxford University Press, 2009), reads

Seven Pillars as depicting "a futuristic mobile guerilla war, which contrasted appealingly with the horrifying stasis of trench warfare," and asserts that Lawrence "imagined the Arab revolt as a kind of modernist vortex" (67).

53 Read, "The Seven Pillars," 36, 35–36, 41, 39.

54 A. Clare Brandabur and Nasser al-Hassan Athamneh, "Problems of Genre in *The Seven Pillars of Wisdom: A Triumph*," *Comparative Literature* **52** (2000), 324, 336. They propose a diagnosis of "schizophrenic psychosis" but do not explain the causal claim regarding Lawrence's death following a motorcycle accident; 323.

55 Forster, "T. E. Lawrence," 144.

56 Forster, "T. E. Lawrence," 145, 143.

57 Forster, "T. E. Lawrence," 146, 147.

58 Gilles Deleuze, *Essays Critical and Clinical*, trans. Daniel W. Smith and Michael A. Greco (Minneapolis: University of Minnesota Press, 1997), 117.

59 Porter, *Haunted Journeys*, 226, 228.

60 "Some Notes on the Writing of the Seven Pillars of Wisdom by T. E. Shaw," a leaflet for subscribers later incorporated into a preface to *Seven Pillars*, tells the story of Lawrence losing the first draft; Graves thought it fiction. See *Seven Pillars*, 17–22; Graves, "Lawrence Vindicated," 18. On modernist narratives of origin, see Stacy Burton, "Paradoxical Relations: Bakhtin and Modernism," *Modern Language Quarterly* **61** (2000): 519–543. Readers of the Oxford text included Forster and Bell; see Meyers, "The Revisions," 1070.

61 On "literary heightenings," see Stephen E. Tabachnick, "A Fragmentation Artist," *The T. E. Lawrence Puzzle*, 31–32.

62 Andrew Long reads these competing "tendencies" as evidence of internal fissures in imperialist discourse between "elite bourgeois Orientalism" and "Orientalism as mass culture"; "The Hidden and the Visible in British Orientalism: The Case of Lawrence of Arabia," *Middle East Critique* **18** (2009), 23.

63 Edward W. Said, *Culture and Imperialism* (New York: Knopf, 1993), 188, 189.

64 Forster, "T. E. Lawrence," 146.

65 Pericles Lewis, *Modernism, Nationalism and the Novel* (Cambridge: Cambridge University Press, 2000), 5.

66 Porter, *Haunted Journeys*, 234.

67 Carola M. Kaplan, "Conquest as Literature, Literature as Conquest T. E. Lawrence's Artistic Campaign in *Seven Pillars of Wisdom*," *Texas Studies in Language and Literature* **37** (1995), 93.

68 Dennis M. Read, "Ella Maillart," *British Travel Writers, 1910–1939*, ed. Barbara Brothers and Julia Gergits, *Dictionary of Literary Biography* 195 (Detroit: Gale, 1998), 206.

69 Maillart's once-affluent Swiss/Danish family experienced a post-1929 decline in their fortunes; see her memoir, *Cruises and Caravans* (London: Travel Book Club, 1942). *Parmi la jeunesse russe* never appeared in English.

70 *Turkestan Solo* and *Forbidden Journey*, written in French, were published in English within months and reviewed in both languages; Maillart subsequently wrote in English. Scholars discuss her work in both British and Francophone literary contexts.

71 George Orwell, "More News from Tartary," *Time and Tide* (September 4, 1937), 175.

72 Maillart, *Cruises and Caravans*, 29.

73 Ella Maillart, *Parmi la jeunesse russe: de Moscou au Caucase* (Paris: Fasquelle Éditeurs, 1932), 14, 24.

74 Margaret Bourke-White, *Eyes on Russia* (New York: Simon and Schuster, 1931), 22–23. Even Byron acknowledges "the romance of 'construction' at Dnieperstori – as I felt it before at Sukkur"; *First Russia*, 5.

75 "Maillart," *Parmi la jeunesse Russe*, 179. Sara Steinert Borella reads Maillart's depiction of Soviet rulers and peasants in terms of colonizers and "the Other" in *The Travel Narratives of Ella Maillart: (En)Gendering the Quest* (New York: Peter Lang, 2006), 42–45.

76 Maillart's preferred term "Turkestan" designates the region north of the Indian subcontinent and south of Siberia, from the Caspian Sea to the Gobi Desert. It includes areas governed by the Soviet Union and Sinkiang, China's northwestern province.

77 Curtis and Pajaczkowska, "'Getting There,'" 199.

78 Fleming, *Forbidden Journey* 88, 148.

79 Maillart, *Turkestan Solo*, 14, 33.

80 Fleming sneaks exposed film out of the USSR in *One's Company*; Bourke-White must develop her film in a hotel bathtub in order to leave.

81 Charles Forsdick makes a similar point in "Peter Fleming and Ella Maillart in China: Travel Writing as Stereoscopic and Polygraphic Form," *Studies in Travel Writing* **13** (2009), 297. *Des Monts Célestes aux Sables Rouges* originally included fifty-seven photos, three maps; *Turkestan Solo* thirty-two photos, two maps. *Oasis interdites* originally had sixty-two photos, one map; *Forbidden Journey* sixty-four photos, three maps. Photo selection and placement varies between French and English editions; endnotes differ entirely. Later editions have few if any photos or maps.

82 Forsdick, "Peter Fleming," 300.

83 Maillart's foreword silently vanishes in the 1994 edition of *Oasis interdites*. Forsdick cites this as an instance of the kind of textual alteration that constitutes a "re-badging" to which scholars should attend; "Peter Fleming," 300.

84 Peter Fleming, *News from Tartary* (New York: Charles Scribner's, 1936), 32. Maillart remarks the irony of the alliance: "Somebody observed that Peter's last book had been called *One's Company*, and the English edition of my last book, *Turkestan Solo*. Now here we were, contrary to all our principles, going off together!" (15).

85 British reviewers found the narratives complementary; e.g., Orwell, "More News"; Evelyn Waugh, "Companion to Fleming," *Night and Day* (September 2, 1937), 26–27. Forsdick, analyzing them as "an exemplary diptych of parallel narratives," cautions against reductively reading Maillart's text as "feminine," Fleming's "masculine"; "Peter Fleming," 293.

86 Waugh describes a "radical difference of temperament": "Miss Maillart travelled because she liked being abroad, Mr. Fleming because he liked covering

ground. He wanted to be in Scotland for the grouse; she was quite prepared to spend the rest of her life in the desert" ("Companion to Fleming," 26).

87 Fleming, *News from Tartary*, 13, 380, 381.

88 Maureen Mulligan suggests that Maillart prefers "a rhetorical rather than analytical approach" because of political disinterest; "Forbidden Journeys to China and Beyond with the Odd Couple: Ella Maillart and Peter Fleming," *Asian Crossings: Travel Writing on China, Japan and Southeast Asia*, ed. Steve Clark and Paul Smethurst (Hong Kong: Hong Kong University Press, 2008), 145. However, the narrative's use of open-ended questions and exclamations signals a reluctant recognition that politics cannot be avoided.

89 Colin Thubron, "Travel Writing Today: Its Rise and Its Dilemma," *Essays by Divers Hands: Being the Transactions of the Royal Society of Literature, New Series, Volume XLIV*, ed. A. N. Wilson (Woodbridge: Boydell Press, 1986), 173, 175.

90 Thubron, *Behind the Wall*, 67.

91 Colin Thubron, *Journey into Cyprus* (London: Heinemann, 1975), xi. Peter Hulme describes Thubron as "probably the most distinguished of the generation of travel writers whose work confronts the political upheavals of the last thirty years" in "Travelling to Write (1940–2000)," *The Cambridge Companion to Travel Writing*, ed. Peter Hulme and Tim Youngs (Cambridge: Cambridge University Press, 2002), 95.

92 In interviews, Thubron describes the genre's evolution and his own shift from a documentary style to more subjective narration. (His early books about the Levant included photos; beginning with *Among the Russians*, none do.) He attributes some of the genre's conventional presumption of authority to the public school experience (like Fleming, he was schooled at Eton). See, e.g., Susan Bassnett, "Interview with Colin Thubron." *Studies in Travel Writing* **3** (1999), 149, 152, 157.

93 Hulme, "Travelling to Write," 95.

94 Thubron, *Among the Russians*, 1–2, 5.

95 Thubron, *Behind the Wall*, 242. Weary after months traveling alone, Thubron becomes "dourly irritable": "'the people is a sea,' say the Chinese ruefully, and I felt suddenly drowned by them.... Their remorseless, laboratory staring – the stripping of all privacy – had reversed our roles: I had become their subject"; *Behind the Wall*, 226.

96 Colin Thubron, *In Siberia* (London: Chatto & Windus, 1999), 84. Subsequent references cited in text by page number.

97 Thubron, *Behind the Wall*, 179.

98 This theme appears early on in *The Hills of Adonis: A Quest in Lebanon*, when the Six Day War breaks out as Thubron hikes across Lebanon: "The long walk among mountains, and the peasant quietness, seemed irrecoverable. It was decadent to find significance in anything but the tragic present. History was all around us now. There was no meaning left in cities ruined by more ancient wars, or in the intimations of what men had once believed"; (London: Heinemann, 1968), 154–155.

99 Julia M. Gergits and James J. Schramer, "Colin Thubron," *British Travel Writers, 1940–1997*, ed. Barbara Brothers and Julia M. Gergits, *Dictionary of Literary Biography* 204 (Detroit: Gale, 1999), 286.

100 Thubron describes his method in interviews: e.g., "You are attempting to evoke again the journey that you remember, that you have in notes, as accurately as you can, in physical detail, in how people spoke, in what they said, and of course it's exclusion that makes so much of what one writes, particularly when you compress people's conversations"; Bassnett, "Interview," 152.

101 Guy Mannes-Abbott, "Return to the Wild East," *The Independent* (October 2, 1999), 9.

102 William Dalrymple, "Cracked Domes on the Silk Route," *The Independent Weekend Book Review* (October 1, 1994), 26.

103 Dalrymple, "Cracked Domes," 26.

Chapter 5 Perpetual Wartime

1 Stephen Spender, *European Witness* (New York: Reynal & Hitchcock, 1946), 14, 15. Subsequent references cited in text by page number.

2 Margot Norris, *Writing War in the Twentieth Century* (Charlottesville: University Press of Virginia, 2000), 1.

3 Aldous Huxley, *Jesting Pilate* (London: Paladin, 1985), 206.

4 Helen Carr, "Modernism and Travel (1880–1940)," *The Cambridge Companion to Travel Writing*, ed. Peter Hulme and Tim Youngs (Cambridge: Cambridge University Press, 2002), 81.

5 Iain Chambers, "Leaky Habitats and Broken Grammar," *Travellers' Tales: Narratives of Home and Displacement*, ed. George Robertson et al. (London: Routledge, 1994), 245.

6 Scholarship has examined the genre's rhetorical imperialism but largely ignored the violent events it often reports, and the caesura common in literary histories means that narratives from the late 1930s well into the 1960s have received little scrutiny.

7 Bernard Schweizer, *Radicals on the Road: The Politics of English Travel Writing in the 1930s* (Charlottesville: University Press of Virginia, 2001), 2.

8 Here this book differs with Schweizer, who writes that politically engaged travel writing reappears only occasionally until late in the century (*Radicals*, 180–185). For another differing view see Maureen Moynagh, "The Political Tourist's Archive: Susan Meiselas's Images of Nicaragua," *Travel Writing, Form, and Empire*, ed. Julia Kuehn and Paul Smethurst (New York: Routledge, 2009), 199–212.

9 *In Dark Tourism: The Attraction of Death and Disaster* (London: Continuum, 2000), John Lennon and Malcolm Foley see this as chiefly a late twentieth-century phenomenon, though battle-site tourism has a longer history. By 1920, travel guidebooks memorialized sites from "the tragic years 1914–18," offering practical advice regarding "new conditions"; see *Belgium and the Western Front: British and American*, ed. Findlay Muirhead, The Blue Guides

(London: Macmillan, 1920), v. On war tourism, see Elizabeth Diller and Ricardo Scofido (eds), *Visite aux armées: Tourismes de guerre/Back to the Front: Tourisms of War* (Caen: Fonds Régional d'Art Contemporain de Basse-Normandie, 1994).

10 Graham Huggan, *Extreme Pursuits: Travel/Writing in an Age of Globalization* (Ann Arbor: University of Michigan Press, 2009), 5.

11 Norris, *Writing War*, 1.

12 Mary A. Favret, *War at a Distance: Romanticism and the Making of Modern Wartime* (Princeton, NJ: Princeton University Press, 2009), 11, 38.

13 Favret, *War*, 43, 11.

14 Favret, who characterizes the "desire to mark a conflict as unprecedented, new, and therefore 'special'" as "a reflex of modernity," challenges the view that twentieth-century home-front experience had no precedent; *War*, 44.

15 James Joyce, *Ulysses* (New York: Random House, 1961), 34.

16 Brian W. Shaffer, *The Blinding Torch: Modern British Fiction and the Discourse of Civilization* (Amherst: University of Massachusetts Press, 1993), 22; Oswald Spengler, *The Decline of the West*, 2 vols., trans. Charles Francis Atkinson (New York: Alfred A. Knopf, 1926, 1928), I.17.

17 Thomas Mann, "On the Theory of Spengler," *Past Masters and Other Papers*, trans. H. T. Lowe-Porter (London: Martin Secker, 1933), 217, 218, 218–219. While crediting Spengler with "literary brilliance," Mann criticized his pessimism and rejected his politics; 219.

18 Edward Mendelson, *Late Auden* (New York: Farrar, Straus and Giroux, 1999), 292–295; Ella Maillart, *Cruises and Caravans* (London: Travel Book Club, 1942), 29; Motley F. Deakin, *Rebecca West* (Boston: Twayne, 1980), 80–81; John Barry, "*The Waste Land*: A Possible German Source," *Comparative Literature Studies* 9 (1972), 429–442; Kevin McNeilly, "Cultural Morphologies: Yeats, Spengler and Adorno," *Irish University Review* 27 (1997), 245–261.

19 Evelyn Waugh, *Labels: A Mediterranean Journal* (London: Duckworth, 1930), 11.

20 Northrup Frye, "*The Decline of the West*, by Oswald Spengler," *Daedalus* 103 (1973), 6.

21 See Edward W. Said, *Orientalism* (New York: Random House, 1978), 208. Frye celebrates Spengler's ability "to exhilarate the mind" while finding his "specific judgments all too often wrong headed" (10, 11). Roger A. Nicholls explains: "Spengler often writes with dazzling brilliance. He captures an unexpected association or connecting link ... and formulates his insight in succinct and decisive phrases. ... His style is epigrammatic; he aims at effects, and it is often difficult to realize that he intends to build on these insights fixed laws of human development"; "Thomas Mann and Spengler," *The German Quarterly* 58 (1985), 370.

22 Frye, "*The Decline*," 6–7.

23 Quoted in John S. Whitley, "'A Touch of Disaster': Fitzgerald, Spengler and the Decline of the West," *Scott Fitzgerald: The Promises of Life*, ed. A. Robert Lee (London: Vision Press, 1989), 157.

24 John Farrenkopf, *Prophet of Decline: Spengler on World History and Politics* (Baton Rouge: Louisiana State University Press, 2001), 51. Farrenkopf reads Spengler as invoking Goethe and Nietzsche and seeking to counter Hegel.

25 Later grand theorists echo Spenglerian themes; see Alex Callinicos, *Theories and Narratives: Reflections on the Philosophy of History* (Durham, NC: Duke University Press, 1995).

26 Rebecca West, *Black Lamb and Grey Falcon: A Journey through Yugoslavia*, 2 vols. (New York: Viking, 1941), 1089. Subsequent references cited in text by page number.

27 Norris, *Writing War*, 17, citing Barbara Ehrenreich. Martha Gellhorn describes war as modernity's unending state: "War is a malignant disease, an idiocy, a prison, and the pain it causes is beyond telling or imagining; but war was our condition and our history, the place we had to live in"; *The Face of War*, rev. ed. (New York: Atlantic Monthly Press, 1988), 2.

28 Norris, *Writing War*, 18–19.

29 Richard E. Zeikowitz (ed.), *Letters between Forster and Isherwood on Homosexuality and Literature* (New York: Palgrave Macmillan, 2008), 73. On the metropolis as target, see Paul Saint-Amour, "Air War Prophecy and Interwar Modernism," *Comparative Literature Studies* 42 (2005), 130–161. Sven Birkerts, *A History of Bombing*, trans. Linda Haverty Rugg (London: Granta, 2001), and Susan Sontag, *Regarding the Pain of Others* (New York: Farrar, Straus and Giroux, 2003), observe that Franco's bombing of Guernica incurred outrage not because the tactic (previously used in colonies) was new, but because those attacked were European.

30 Gellhorn, *The Face of War*, 53.

31 Norris, *Writing War*, 24.

32 E.g., Kate McLoughlin (ed.), *The Cambridge Companion to War Writing* (Cambridge: Cambridge University Press, 2009); Marina MacKay (ed.), *The Cambridge Companion to the Literature of World War II* (Cambridge: Cambridge University Press, 2009); and Kate McLoughlin, *Authoring War: The Literary Representation of War from the* Iliad *to* Iraq (Cambridge: Cambridge University Press, 2011).

33 E.g., Phillip Knightley, *The First Casualty: The War Correspondent as Hero and Myth-maker from the Crimea to Kosovo*, rev. ed. (London: Prion, 2000); and Fred Inglis, *People's Witness: The Journalist in Modern Politics* (New Haven: Yale University Press, 2002).

34 For an exception, see Leo Mellor, "War Journalism in English," *Cambridge Companion to the Literature of World War II*, ed. MacKay, 68. Schweizer's critical recognition of politically oriented travel narrative implicitly undermines Paul Fussell's view that the genre's turn to war constitutes devolution; see *Abroad: British Literary Traveling between the Wars* (New York: Oxford University Press, 1980), 55.

35 Spender, *European Witness*, ix.

36 E.g., Jonathan Skinner, "Introduction: Writings on the Dark Side of Travel," *Journeys* 11 (2010), 1–28.

37 Maurice Blanchot, *The Writing of the Disaster*, new ed., trans. Ann Smock (Lincoln: University of Nebraska Press, 1995). On the difficulty of reading

and writing "catastrophe on this scale so deliberately inflicted," see, e.g., Inga Clendinnen, *Reading the Holocaust* (Cambridge: Cambridge University Press, 1999), 5; and Edith Wyschogrod, *Spirit in Ashes: Hegel, Heidegger, and Man-Made Mass Death* (New Haven: Yale University Press, 1985). On relations between war writing and Holocaust writing, see, e.g., Mark Rawlinson, "The Second World War: British Writing," *Cambridge Companion to the Literature of World War II*, ed. MacKay, 198; and Susan Rubin Suleiman, *Crises of Memory and the Second World War* (Cambridge, MA: Harvard University Press, 2006), 3.

38 Gellhorn, *The Face of War*, 86.

39 Blanchot, *Writing the Disaster*, 82.

40 Blanchot, *Writing the Disaster,* 11.

41 Gellhorn recalls a poignant exchange with a young soldier who lost his family to wartime horror: "Remembering this boy, and all the others I knew, with their appalling stories of hardship and homelessness, it seemed to me that no American had the right to talk to the Poles, since we had never even brushed such suffering ourselves"; *The Face of War*, 125.

42 Evelyn Waugh, *When the Going Was Good* (Boston: Little, Brown, 1984), 9.

43 Quoted in Gary Saul Morson, *Hidden in Plain View: Narrative and Creative Potentials in* War and Peace (Stanford: Stanford University Press, 1987), 107.

44 Morson, *Hidden in Plain View*, 110–111. Cf. Sidonie Smith, *A Poetics of Women's Autobiography: Marginality and the Fictions of Self-Representations* (Bloomington: Indiana University Press, 1987), 45.

45 Norris, *Writing War*, 22. McLoughlin writes that war "resists depiction, and does so in multifarious ways"; *Authoring War*, 6–7.

46 M. M. Bakhtin, "Author and Hero in Aesthetic Activity," *Art and Answerability: Early Philosophical Essays*, trans. Vadim Liapunov, ed. Michael Holquist and Vadim Liapunov (Austin: University of Texas Press, 1990), 125–126.

47 M. M. Bakhtin, "The Bildungsroman and Its Significance in the History of Realism (Toward a Historical Typology of the Novel)," *Speech Genres and Other Late Essays*, trans. Vern W. McGee, ed. Caryl Emerson and Michael Holquist (Austin: University of Texas Press, 1986), 23.

48 Cf. T. E. Lawrence's narrative rejection of the spectacular media "Lawrence."

49 Ken Hirschkop, *Mikhail Bakhtin: An Aesthetic for Democracy* (Oxford: Oxford University Press, 1999), 234, 239.

50 Leigh Gilmore, *The Limits of Autobiography: Trauma and Testimony* (Ithaca, NY: Cornell University Press, 2001), 14, 143.

51 Psychiatrist Stevan Weine draws on Bakhtin in rethinking the clinical practice of testimony as narrative, a "form of human communication to address a metalinguistic condition." To narrate extreme "cultural trauma" (torture, Bosnia) thus requires both "an open entrée of survivors' stories into culture" and "active-dialogic understanding"; *Testimony after Catastrophe: Narrating the Traumas of Political Violence* (Evanston: Northwestern University Press, 2006), 117, 130.

52 Katherine Woods, "Rebecca West's Brilliant Mosaic of Yugoslavian Travel," *New York Times* October 26, 1941. The original two-volume boxed edition

had a polychrome cover illustration and photographs distributed through the text. The one-volume "reduced wartime format" edition of 1944 grouped the photos in a section; later paperback editions exclude them.

53 On West's journeys, see Carl Rollyson, *Rebecca West: A Life* (New York: Scribner, 1996), 177–216. Although West explains she cannot name Yugoslavian friends because of wartime conditions, at least one reviewer identified "Constantine" as Stanislav Vinaver; Clare Colquitt, "A Call to Arms: Rebecca West's Assault on the Limits of 'Gerda's Empire' in *Black Lamb and Grey Falcon*," *South Atlantic Review* **51**.2 (1986), 89.

54 "Land of Sacrifice: Beauty and Terror in Serbia: An English Writer's Explorations," *Times Literary Supplement* (February 28, 1942), 102.

55 Clifton Fadiman, "Magnum Opus," *New Yorker* (October 25, 1941), 88, 89.

56 Exceptions are Schweizer, *Radicals*; David Farley, *Modernist Travel Writing: Intellectuals Abroad* (Columbia: University of Missouri Press, 2010); and Marina MacKay, *Modernism and World War II* (Cambridge: Cambridge University Press, 2007).

57 Janet Montefiore, *Men and Women Writers of the 1930s* (London: Routledge, 1996), 202. "My husband" – Henry Andrews – remains unnamed until a bibliographical note (1158); on this strategy, see Loretta Stec, "Female Sacrifice: Gender and Nostalgic Nationalism in Rebecca West's *Black Lamb and Grey Falcon*," *Narratives of Nostalgia, Gender and Nationalism.*, ed. Jean Pickering and Suzanne Kehde (London: Macmillan, 1997), 152.

58 Stec, "Female Sacrifice," 139.

59 On gender in *Black Lamb*, see also Vesna Goldsworthy, "Travel Writing as Autobiography: Rebecca West's Journey of Self-discovery," *Representing Lives: Women and Auto/biography*, ed. Alison Donnell and Pauline Polkey (London: Macmillan, 2000), 87–95. Studies of travel and gender, which often examine premises ill-suited to her work, seldom mention West.

60 Schweizer, *Radicals*, 131.

61 Victoria Glendinning aptly describes *Black Lamb* as: "a great work of romantic art constructed over a framework of research and scholarship. Judged by the stiff criteria of this framework, it is excessive, unbalanced, sometimes wrong, sometimes silly.... She was in *Black Lamb* uninhibitedly judgemental, sweepingly certain about things about which no one on earth can be certain.... Some passages sound like self-parody.... She took risks with the equilibrium of something that had started out as a travel book, and she achieved her work of art"; *Rebecca West: A Life* (New York: Knopf, 1987), 177.

62 Schweizer, *Radicals*, 141.

63 Farley, *Modernist Travel Writing*, 23, 159.

64 Stec, "Female Sacrifice," 150.

65 Andrew Hammond, *The Debated Lands: British and American Representation of the Balkans* (Cardiff: University of Wales Press, 2007), 149.

66 Marina MacKay argues that West finds in resurrection a way to reject the myths of her title; see "Immortal Goodness: Ideas of Resurrection in Rebecca West's *Black Lamb and Grey Falcon*," *Renascence* **54**.3 (2002), 177–178.

67 Farley notes the radio's figurative importance; *Modernist Travel Writing*, 170.

68 Saint-Amour, "Air War Prophecy," 130–161.

69 The first newsreel of a political assassination was deemed sufficiently sensational that several countries edited or withdrew it, deeming photos of the dead Alexander "too graphic." See Keith Brown, "The King is dead, Long live the Balkans! Watching the Marseilles Murders of 1934," Watson Institute for International Studies, Brown University, 2001. http://www.watsoninstitute.org/pub_detail.cfm?id=132.

70 Saint-Amour, "Air War Prophecy," 156.

71 Farley links West's work to "modernist epics" such as *Ulysses* and Ezra Pound's *Cantos*; *Modernist Travel Writing*, 155.

72 Adam Piette, "War Zones," *The Cambridge Companion to War Writing*, ed. McLoughlin, 44; MacKay, "Immortal Goodness," 17.

73 On using photographs of the dead, John Taylor writes: "Photographers, editors and readers are all caught in the act of looking, and every act carries various weights of complicity, obligation and shame"; *Body Horror: Photojournalism, Catastrophe and War* (New York: New York University Press, 1998), 54.

74 Michael André Bernstein, "Making Modernist Masterpieces," *Modernism/Modernity* 5.3 (1998), 5, 5–6.

75 Bernstein, "Making Modernist Masterpieces," 13.

76 Saint-Amour, "Air War Prophecy," 148.

77 Mackay, *Modernism*, 69, 70.

78 On Spender's assignment, see John Sutherland, *Stephen Spender: A Literary Life* (Oxford: Oxford University Press, 2005), 302–313.

79 Waugh, *When the Going*, 8, 9, 7.

80 Waugh, *When the Going*, 9.

81 Spender, who had lived in Weimar Germany, published early portions of *European Witness* in *Horizon*, a literary magazine edited by Cyril Connolly. Connolly had used the pseudonym Palinurus for *The Unquiet Grave: A Word Cycle* (1944), a collection of aphorisms and ruminations. Waugh remarks that, had he and others known that "all that seeming-solid, patiently built, gorgeously ornamented structure of Western life was to melt overnight like an ice-castle, leaving only a puddle of mud," "we might have lingered with 'Palinurus'"; *When the Going*, 8.

82 Rose Macaulay, *Pleasure of Ruins* (New York: Thames and Hudson, 1984), 453, 454. On ruins as provocation for "a peculiar kind of scopic desire," see Julia Hell, "Ruins Travel: Orphic Journeys through 1940s Germany," *Writing Travel: The Poetics and Politics of the Modern Journey*, ed. John Zilcosky (Toronto: University of Toronto Press, 2008), 133.

83 Norris, *Writing War*, 25, 26.

84 Spender's use of vignettes is restrained by contemporary mores and, in at least one instance, personal relations. *European Witness* offers no firsthand accounts of German civilians' experience of Allied bombing, a topic still controversial decades later, and it excises much of a previously published vignette

that had offended its subject, a professor who had been Spender's men-
tor; see Stephen Spender, "Rhineland Journal," *Horizon* **12** (December
1945), 394–413; Sutherland, *Stephen Spender*, 311–312; and W. G. Sebald,
On the Natural History of Destruction, trans. Anthea Bell (London: Hamish
Hamilton, 2003).

85 The Allies coined "Displaced Person" to refer to civilians living outside their
countries of origin because of wartime events who were unable or unwilling
to return. In July 1945, approximately 1,270,000 DPs were in the British
zone; by winter, there were approximately 639,000, 510,000 of whom were
Poles; Arieh J. Kochavi, *Post-Holocaust Politics: Britain, the United States, and
Jewish Refugees, 1945–1948* (Chapel Hill: University of North Carolina Press,
2001), 15. Caren Kaplan notes that, by reference, "displacement" includes "a
concept of placement, dwelling, location, or position"; *Questions of Travel:
Postmodern Discourses of Displacement* (Durham, NC: Duke University
Press, 1996), 143. The redrawing of national boundaries at war's end pushes
the concept to the limit: many cannot return because their places of origin
are now different places, in different nations.

86 Norris, *Writing War*, 28, 26.

87 John Xiros Cooper, "'The crow on the crematorium chimney': Germany,
Summer 1945," *English Studies in Canada* **30**.3 (2004), 132.

88 The chapter title he owes to Sartre, as Cooper also notes; "'The
crow,'" 135.

89 Goronwy Rees, "A Poet Abroad," *The Spectator* (November 1, 1946), 456.

90 At a dinner party Spender talks with an American officer who speculates
that the next war "may well be something quite different" (82).

91 On Berlin's future, see Karen E. Till, *The New Berlin: Politics, Memory, Place*
(Minneapolis: University of Minnesota Press, 2005).

92 Spender's turn anticipates a larger cultural shift that Cooper describes, from
the immediate postwar "moment of candor" about the war's ethical consequences to the rhetoric of Cold War politics; "'The crow,'" 142.

93 Campbell, "Travel Writing," 261.

94 See William A. Schabas, *Genocide in International Law: The Crime of Crimes*,
2d ed (Cambridge: Cambridge University Press, 2009), 14; for an overview of Holocaust literature, see, e.g., Phyllis Lassner, "Life Writing and
the Holocaust," *Cambridge Companion to the Literature of World War II*, ed.
MacKay, 179–193.

95 Gellhorn, *The Face of War*, 185, 184, 185.

96 Gellhorn, *The Face of War*, 201.

97 Favret, *War*, 154: "Written, for the most part, in that extended period known
as the Cold War, postwar and subsequently poststructuralist theories tend
rather to celebrate the coincidence of the everyday and war."

98 Inglis, *People's Witness*, 343, 346.

99 Svend Erik Larsen, "Landscape, Identity, and War," *New Literary History* **35**
(2004), 470.

100 Peter Hulme, "Traveling to Write (1940–2000)," *The Cambridge Companion
to Travel Writing*, ed. Hulme and Youngs, 99.

101 Scholars have discussed the nature of witness extensively. Norris, writing of Michael Herr's *Dispatches*, articulates one view: "Herr transformed the temptations of detached journalism into the solitary and painful act of testimony not just to what he saw but to his own experience of seeing. Even when we witness events at some remove, the act of reading can make us vulnerable to penetration by experience, including traumatic experience"; *Writing War*, 31. Clendinnen describes Primo Levi's view, starkly opposite: "after all his years of dedicated reading, writing and witnessing, Levi decided that the saved could not speak for the drowned, that they could not be 'true witnesses' precisely because they had survived"; *Reading the Holocaust*, 47. Cf. Giorgio Agamben, *Remnants of Auschwitz: The Witness and the Archive*, trans Daniel Heller-Roazen (New York: Zone, 2002).

102 Sarah Cole, "People in War," *Cambridge Companion to War Writing*, ed. McLoughlin, 29, 30. Cf. Sontag, *Regarding the Pain*, 3–12.

103 Norris writes that Holocaust and atomic bomb literature "must negotiate the status of their event as a rhetorical figure for unimaginable manmade human suffering and relate this trope to the event's facticity.... The most difficult consequence of that negotiation is the recognition that these events are not detours or aberrations in the advancement of Western civilization but logical products of technological achievement disoriented by incommensurate, unrefunctioned, and broke moral compasses"; *Writing War*, 101.

104 All three have parents who immigrated to the U.S.; Sacco retains Maltese citizenship.

105 Peter Maass, *Love Thy Neighbor: A Story of War* (New York: Knopf, 1996), 1. Subsequent references cited in text by page number.

106 Philip Gourevitch, *We Wish to Inform You That Tomorrow We Will Be Killed with Our Families: Stories from Rwanda.* (New York: Farrar, Straus and Giroux, 1998), 6. Subsequent references cited in text by page number.

107 Joe Sacco, *Palestine* (Seattle: Fantagraphics, 2001), 1, 2. Subsequent references cited in text by page number.

108 Most travel narratives about the former Yugoslavia in the 1990s – e.g., *Love thy Neighbor* and Sacco's *Safe Area Goražde* – mention but refuse the notion that the Balkans are anti-modern. However, Robert Kaplan's *Balkan Ghosts* (1993), whose "discourse of nostalgia" Debbie Lisle takes to be typical, ebraces it; *The Global Politics of Contemporary Travel Writing* (Cambridge: Cambridge University Press, 2006), 209. *Love Thy Neighbor*'s dust jacket features an outline map of Yugoslavia; the Vintage paperback, foregrounding the theme of civilization destroyed, shows a string quartet posed in a ruin.

109 Rachel Moffatt argues that the scene reflects poorly on Gourevitch but serves for "shock value"; "Visiting Rwanda: Accounts of Genocide in Travel Writing," *Journeys* **11**.1 (2010), 100. Gourevitch explains the scene's placement: "You're implicated. You want to get close enough to be able to see it? You're in it"; Dave Welch, "We Wish to Inform You that Philip Gourevitch has Edited a Spectacular Collection of Interviews," Powells.com (December 11, 2006) http://www.powells.com/blog/we-wish-to-inform-you-that-philip-gourevitch-has-edited-a-spectacular-collection-of-interviews/

110 On dark tourism as "collective witnessing," see John Urry, "Death in Venice," *Tourism Mobilities: Places to Play, Places in Play*, ed. Mimi Sheller and Urry (London: Routledge, 2004), 209–211; on memorializing atrocities, Paul Williams, *Memorial Museums: The Global Rush to Commemorate Atrocities* (Oxford: Berg, 2007).

111 Hulme, "Traveling to Write," 98. Cole observes that writing of war's human consequences "almost inevitably follows a deconstructive pattern: war creates distinct types only to miscegenate them; it posits insurmountable differences only to surmount them (at least partially); it organizes the world by animosity only to forge imaginative unities"; "People in War," 26.

112 Aryn Bartley, "The Hateful Self: Substitution and the Ethics of Representing War," *Modern Fiction Studies* **54** (2008), 65.

113 Mary Layoun reads *Palestine* as "a kind of *bildungsroman*, a story of the education of narrator/artist in finding a way to verbally retell and visually represent what he has seen and heard and his own relation to both"; "The Trans-, the Multi-, the Pluri-, and the Global: A Few Thoughts on Comparative and Relational Literacy," *Passages: A Journal of Transnational & Transcultural Studies* **1**.2 (1999), 194.

114 Tristram Walker, "Graphic Wounds: The Comics Journalism of Joe Sacco" *Journeys* **11**.1 (2010), 82.

115 Edward W. Said, "Homage to Joe Sacco," *Palestine*, by Sacco, iv.

116 McLoughlin, *Authoring War*, 107.

Chapter 6   The Allure of Authenticity

1 Andrew X. Pham, *Catfish and Mandala: A Two-Wheeled Voyage through the Landscape and Memory of Vietnam* (New York: Farrar, Straus and Giroux, 1999), 98. Subsequent references cited in text by page number.

2 The *Oxford English Dictionary* gives the first usage of "authentic" as 1340, that of "authenticity," 1657; "inauthentic" does not appear until 1860, "inauthenticity," 1885.

3 Theodor W. Adorno, *The Jargon of Authenticity*, trans. Knut Tranowski and Frederic Will (Evanston: Northwestern University Press, 1973), 59–60.

4 Jean Baudrillard, *Simulacra and Simulation*, trans. Sheila Faria Glaser (Ann Arbor: University of Michigan Press, 1994), 6–7.

5 See, e.g., Fredric Jameson, "Postmodernism, or The Cultural Logic of Late Capitalism," *New Left Review* **146** (1984), 53–92; and Geoffrey Hartman, *Scars of the Spirit: The Struggle Against Inauthenticity* (New York: Palgrave Macmillan, 2002).

6 See, e.g., Marc Manganaro, *Culture, 1922: The Emergence of a Concept* (Princeton, NJ: Princeton University Press, 2002); Carey J. Snyder, *British Fiction and Cross-Cultural Encounters: Ethnographic Modernism from Wells to Woolf* (New York: Palgrave Macmillan, 2008); and Ivan Karp and Steven D. Lavine (eds.), *Exhibiting Cultures: The Poetics and Politics of Museum Display* (Washington: Smithsonian Institution Press, 1991).

7   Dean MacCannell, *The Tourist: A New Theory of the Leisure Class.*, rev. ed. (New York: Schocken, 1989), 94.

8   Erik Cohen, "Phenomenology of Tourist Experiences," *Sociology* **13** (1979), 179–201.

9   MacCannell, *The Tourist*, 94. Cohen views MacCannell's analysis as suited to the third mode but not universally applicable. See also Edward M. Bruner, *Culture on Tour: Ethnographies of Travel* (Chicago: University of Chicago Press, 2005); and Claudio Minca and Tim Oakes (eds.), *Travels in Paradox: Remapping Tourism* (London: Rowman & Littlefield, 2006).

10 Cohen, "Phenomenology," 189, 191.

11 Joan W. Scott, "The Evidence of Experience," *Critical Inquiry* **17** (1991), 781.

12 Matthew Wickman, *The Ruins of Experience: Scotland's "Romantick" Highlands and the Birth of the Modern Witness* (Philadelphia: University of Pennsylvania Press, 2007), 5.

13 Cf. Adorno, *Jargon*, 18.

14 H. V. Morton, *In Search of Scotland* (London: Methuen, 2000), 292; H. V. Morton, *In Search of Wales* (London: Methuen, 2000), 55. Subsequent references cited by title or in text by page number.

15 Caren Kaplan, *Questions of Travel: Postmodern Discourses of Displacement* (Durham, NC: Duke University Press, 1996), 46.

16 Susan Stewart, *On Longing: Narratives of the Miniature, the Gigantic, the Souvenir, the Collection* (Durham, NC: Duke University Press, 1993), 22.

17 Stewart, *On Longing*, 22–23.

18 Scott, "The Evidence," 797.

19 Trinh T. Minh-ha, *Woman, Native, Other: Writing Postcoloniality and Feminism* (Bloomington: Indiana University Press, 1989), 94. Ken Hirschkop, reading Bakhtin, argues that the mediation that autobiography requires can serve ethical purpose: "Constituting one's life as a coherent narrative ... depends upon the existence of a context where you are forced to adopt the *other's* perspective"; *Mikhail Bakhtin: An Aesthetic for Democracy* (Oxford: Oxford University Press, 1999), 130.

20 Hilton Obenzinger, *American Palestine: Melville, Twain, and the Holy Land Mania* (Princeton, NJ: Princeton University Press, 1999), xvii. Military actions, political debate over Ottoman territories, and archaeological discoveries all renewed interest in the region.

21 Mary Baine Campbell, *The Witness and the Other World: Exotic European Travel Writing, 400–1600* (Ithaca, NY: Cornell University Press, 1988), 19–20.

22 Obenzinger, *American Palestine*, 40–41.

23 Twain anticipates the "post-tourist," who matches disinterest in "authentic experience" with delight in "the obviously inauthentic"; Patrick Holland and Graham Huggan, *Tourists with Typewriters: Critical Reflections on Contemporary Travel Writing* (Ann Arbor: University of Michigan Press, 1998), 24.

24 Frank S. DeHass, *Buried Cities Recovered; Or, Explorations in Bible Lands, Giving the Results of Recent Researches in the Orient, and Recovery of Many Places of Sacred and Profane History Long Considered Lost*, 5th ed.

(Philadelphia: Bradley, Garretson, 1884), 253, 254. On nineteenth-century Holy Land travel, see Guy Galazka, *A la découverte de la Palestine* (Paris: Les presses universitaires de Paris-Sorbonne, 2011).

25 John Finley, *A Pilgrim in Palestine: Being an Account of Journeys on Foot by the First American Pilgrim after General Allenby's Recovery of the Holy Land* (New York: Scribner's, 1919), vii, 7–8, 12. Finley contrasts Allenby's decorum with the "august and farcical entry" of Kaiser Wilhelm II in 1898 (85).

26 Finley, *A Pilgrim*, 16.

27 Finley, *A Pilgrim*, 240, 218, 234.

28 Pericles Lewis, *Religious Experience and the Modernist Novel* (Cambridge: Cambridge University Press, 2010), 25; Lewis cites "age of authenticity" from Charles Taylor's *A Secular Age* (2007).

29 Stewart, *On Longing*, 139. Colin Thubron and Mary Morris each use tense scenes with Soviet border officials to suggest that losing the narrative could constitute losing the experience; see Colin Thubron, *Among the Russians* (London: Heinemann, 1983), 212; Mary Morris, *Wall to Wall: From Beijing to Berlin by Rail* (New York: Penguin, 1992), 233–234.

30 Jed Esty, *A Shrinking Island: Modernism and National Culture in England* (Princeton, NJ: Princeton University Press, 2003), 34, 39, 40.

31 Esty, *A Shrinking Island*, 42; cf. John Taylor, *A Dream of England: Landscape, Photography and the Tourist's Imagination* (Manchester: Manchester University Press, 1994), 129. On nostalgia and Englishness, see, e.g., Robert Hemmings, *Modern Nostalgia: Siegfried Sassoon, Trauma and the Second World War* (Edinburgh: Edinburgh University Press, 2008).

32 Morton often traveled with others: *In Search of England* is dedicated to a mistress who sometimes joined him, and *In the Steps of the Master* gives photo credits to his second wife Mary, who accompanied him; see Michael Bartholomew, *In Search of H. V. Morton* (London: Methuen, 2006), 100.

33 Bartholomew, *In Search*, 224, 225.

34 Bartholomew, *In Search* 109; Paul Fussell, *Abroad: British Literary Traveling between the Wars* (New York: Oxford University Press, 1980), 55.

35 H. V. Morton, *In Search of England* (New York: Dodd, Mead, 1984), 1. Subsequent references cited by title or in text by page number.

36 This opening mimes "the officer in the trenches dreaming of the English shires"; the narrator does not claim to be a soldier but imagines he might die and never return home; Michael Bartholomew, "H. V. Morton's English Utopia," *Regenerating England: Science, Medicine and Culture in Inter-War Britain*, ed. Christopher Lawrence and Anna-K. Mayer (Amsterdam: Rodopi, 2000), 32.

37 Bartholomew, *In Search*, 108.

38 Morton, *In Search of Wales*, 149.

39 Morton, *In Search of Scotland*, 294.

40 H. V. Morton, *In Search of Ireland* (London: Methuen, 1930), 273. Subsequent references cited by title or in text by page number.

41 Morton, *In Search of Wales*, 55.

42 The original introduction to *In Search of England* attests to the vital nature of villages while celebrating the motor car, which allows new "explorers" to see them; New York: Robert M. McBride & Co., 1930, viii.

43 Morton, *In Search of Ireland*, 129; Morton, *In Search of Wales*, 115.

44 Bartholomew, *In Search*, xviii.

45 Carol Huebscher Rhoades, "H. V. Morton," *British Travel Writers, 1910–1939*, ed. Barbara Brothers and Julia Gergits, *Dictionary of Literary Biography* 195 (Detroit: Gale, 1998), 254. Morton defends himself in *In Search of Ireland*, declaring that two columns whose veracity readers had doubted (including the one about Connemara) were "literal reporting" of events that "happened just as I describe them" (viii).

46 Bartholomew, *In Search*, 94.

47 Morton's revisions in adapting newspaper columns into a book intensify the effect: he minimizes the role of the motor car, adds an earnest introduction, and uses visual images that depict preindustrial village life; Bartholomew, *In Search*, 99–101.

48 Bartholomew, *In Search*, 137.

49 Morton, *In Search of Scotland*, 89; Morton, *In Search of Wales*, 278.

50 C. R. Perry, "In Search of H. V. Morton: Travel Writing and Cultural Values in the First Age of British Democracy," *Twentieth Century British History* 10 (1999, 437.

51 Similarly, though he tries to subordinate the "Troubles" to Ireland's earlier history, they seep into view when he describes the ruins of an estate whose owner narrowly escaped execution by Irregulars in 1922; Morton, *In Search of Ireland*, 115–118.

52 Morton, *In Search of England*, 185; Morton, *In Search of Ireland*, 143; Morton, *In Search of Wales*, 164.

53 The scene echoes moments in James Joyce's "The Dead" and Virginia Woolf's *To the Lighthouse* in which a narrator reveals a man's thoughts as he gazes on a woman, thinking of her beauty and supposing he knows her mind, then uses the woman's thoughts or speech to show the man to be wrong.

54 Wren Sidhe argues that Morton's books about England locate "Englishness" in a heterosexual bond between a masculine national subject and a feminine nature or landscape" and place women outside the bond as too urban and international, their Englishness questionable; "H. V. Morton's Pilgrimages to Englishness," *Literature & History*, 3d ser. **12**.1 (2003), 57.

55 Esty, *A Shrinking Island*, 40.

56 Morton, *In Search of England*, 266.

57 H. V. Morton, *In the Steps of the Master* (London: Rich & Cowan, 1934), v. Subsequent references cited in text by page number. The 1984 paper edition excludes the twenty-four photographs used in the original. Morton uses both "Palestine" and "Holy Land" throughout, preferring the former.

58 Campbell, *The Witness*, 20.

59 Morton excuses the hawkers by blaming mass tourists less sincere than his presumed readers: "If they behave badly it is the fault of tourists who swarm

into Nazareth as people swarm into Stratford-on-Avon; and in exactly the same attitude of mind" (166).

60 Cohen, "Phenomenology," 49.

61 "I Walked Today Where Jesus Walked," a popular religious song with lyrics by Daniel S. Twohig published in 1937, shares Morton's theme.

62 In this pilgrim the narrator sees "a symbol not only of the questioning ache at the heart of Humanity, but also of the answer" (14). Here Morton fore-shadows Rebecca West, who also finds something admirable though alien in Balkan piety.

63 Bartholomew, *In Search*, 152.

64 Fussell's reading of Morton's book as "gravely naïve" misses its ambiguity; his description – "an important bourgeois devotional classic" – accurately identi-fies the audience that made it a success; *Abroad*, 55. Morton adapted mate-rial from *In the Steps of the Master* and two sequels in *Middle East: A Record of Travel in the Countries of Egypt, Palestine, Iraq, Turkey and Greece* (1941), designed for military personnel assigned to the region.

65 Similar themes figure in later texts as varied as Bettina Selby's *Riding to Jerusalem: A Journey through Turkey and the Middle East* (1985), in which political realities frustrate an attempt to replicate a medieval pilgrimage by bicycle; Sacco's *Palestine*; and Bruce Feiler's *Walking the Bible: A Journey by Land through the Five Books of Moses* (2001), a best seller in the United States.

66 Morton's narrator notices the history of Judaism only as the context for Christianity. Traveling through villages, he even pronounces which identi-ties are authentic: "one of the fantastic things about Palestine is that people so obviously ancient Canaanites should be called Arabs and should worship Allah!" (148).

67 Morton's devout readers "wrote to him saying how their faith had been enriched by his books. They also tried to coax him into being more explicit about his own beliefs. Morton always declined"; Bartholomew, *In Search*, 162.

68 Morton notes primly that the "national home for the Jews" pledged in the Balfour Declaration is "an uninterpreted phrase" (99). In the 1962 introduc-tion, he regrets contemporary national borders, remembering "with nostalgia the ease of travel, and the air of friendly co-operation which existed when this part of the world was administered by Britain and France. That was the perfect moment to have visited the Holy Land" (1984 ed., ix).

69 Bartholomew comments that Morton "certainly wanted to enlarge his Christian readers' understanding of their faith, and he seems to have wanted to imply, though never directly state, that he shared that faith.... He also wanted – let it never be forgotten – to enlarge his income. The books the [Middle Eastern] project produced are sometimes a bit tangled and indigest-ible"; *In Search*, 170.

70 Michael Ignatieff, *The Russian Album* (London: Penguin, 1988), 1.

71 Baudrillard, *Simulacra*, 10.

72 Morton, *In Search of England*, 1930 ed., viii. The original introduction using this phrase was replaced in 1959. On Morton's depiction of "Englishness" as racial, see Sidhe, "H. V. Morton's Pilgrimages."

73 Morton, *In Search of Scotland*, 30.

74 Morton comments:

> As soon as I saw him I knew that he was embarked on one of those sentimental journeys which happen to all successful Americans.... [E]very American with English, Scottish, or Irish blood in him comes back at some time to find his roots. They drift about unlikely towns and villages like prosperous ghouls. (*In Search of Scotland*, 30)

75 In largely ignoring contemporary politics even in Ireland and Palestine, Morton's narratives reflect the fact that "events of the 1920s neither utterly destroyed the imperial 'illusion of permanence' nor fully roused England to alarm about its shrinking domain"; Esty, *A Shrinking Island*, 37. This stance suits his themes and an intended audience less politically engaged than those of West or T. E. Lawrence.

76 Jean Baudrillard, *America*, trans. Chris Turner (London: Verso, 1988), 76.

77 See Vincent Cheng, *Inauthentic: The Anxiety over Culture and Identity* (New Brunswick: Rutgers University Press, 2004).

78 Marianne Hirsch, *Family Frames: Photography, Narrative, and Postmemory* (Cambridge, MA: Harvard University Press, 1997), 21–23; Marianne Hirsch and Leo Spitzer, "'We Would Not Have Come Without You': Generations of Nostalgia," *American Imago* **59** (2002), 261–263.

79 Rebecca Solnit, *A Book of Migrations: Some Passages in Ireland* (London: Verso, 1997), 6. Alan Cheuse cites Alex Haley's *Roots* (1976) as inspiration, but such narratives tend to refute *Roots*' premises by demonstrating that genealogy does not guarantee identity and traveling to places of origin does not resolve the search for home; *Fall Out of Heaven: An Autobiographical Journey across Russia* (New York: Atlantic Monthly Press, 1989), 5.

80 Hirsch, *Family Frames*, 22.

81 On the fragility of the autobiographical "I" see, e.g., Leigh Gilmore, *Autobiographics: A Feminist Theory of Women's Self-Representation* (Ithaca, NY: Cornell University Press, 1994), 65, 105.

82 The chapters of *Catfish and Mandala* bear bifurcated titles; the italicized intercalary sections, which tell family stories or fragments of memories, are all titled "Fallen-Leaves."

83 Early on Pham remembers a man who "once revealed something which disturbed me too much to be discounted. He said, 'Your sister died because she became too American'" (7). Much later, however, he himself describes Minh as dying "the most Vietnamese of deaths, a brokenhearted suicide" (299). Minh's journey to his "true self" is also physically rigorous: years of breast-binding, then sex-change surgery.

84 Peter Bishop reads Pham's work – and Gourevitch's – as instances of "reconciliation travel" in "To Witness and Remember: Mapping Reconciliation Travel," *Travel Writing, Form, and Empire*, ed. Julia Kuehn and Paul Smethurst (New York: Routledge, 2009), 180–198.

85 Though Pham's memories include the violent with the idyllic, Eva Hoffman's description of the "overdetermined" nature of such "undertakings" pertains: "Because I had loved and lost [Poland], because I had been cut off from it summarily and, it seemed, irrevocably, it stayed arrested in my imagination as a land of childhood sensuality, lyricism, vividness, and human warmth"; *Exit into History: A Journey through the New Eastern Europe* (New York: Penguin, 1994), ix.

86 Solnit, *A Book*, 117–118.

87 Solnit, *A Book*, 14–15.

88 See Delores B. Phillips, "Quieting Noisy Bellies: Moving, Eating, and Being in the Vietnamese Diaspora," *Cultural Critique* **73** (2009), 47–87.

89 Anita J. Duneer argues that Pham's journey is "not only a way of reconnecting with the Vietnamese part of his own identity but also an effort to put Chi's spirit to rest"; "Postpositivist Realism and Mandala: Toward Reconciliation and Reunification of Vietnamese and American identities in Andrew X. Pham's *Catfish and Mandala*," *a/b: Auto/Biography Studies* **17** (2002), 209.

90 Phillips writes: "Instead of vacillating, Pham learns to oscillate, how to find the rhythm that characterizes the spaces around him and move with them"; "Quieting Noisy Bellies," 76.

91 Solnit, speaking for Americans generally, describes the challenge Pham faces:

> Many of us are children of refugees from countries that no longer exist, from atrocities no one spoke of, from traditions that had been trampled over earlier by the same forces; and in living on a new continent, most of us have begun to be something else, transplanted and hybridized. This evolving something else has never been resolved adequately, and perhaps it is irresolvable – unless *resolution* itself returns to its linguistic roots, which meant to unloose or dissolve, to clarify by liquefying, not solidifying. (*A Book*, 6)

92 Peter Kivy, *Authenticities: Philosophical Reflections on Musical Performance* (Ithaca, NY: Cornell University Press, 1995), 108, 7.

93 Kivy, *Authenticities*, 286.

94 Rosemary Mahoney, *The Singular Pilgrim: Travels on Sacred Ground* (Boston: Houghton Mifflin, 2003), 5. Subsequent references cited in text by page number.

95 Rosemary Mahoney, *Whoredom in Kimmage: Irish Women Coming of Age* (New York: Anchor, 1994), 222.

96 Mahoney explains in the introduction that she spent two years traveling, but the narrative is not obviously chronological and refers to episodes it omits, such as a 150-mile walk on a medieval pilgrimage route (96).

97 Tourism and pilgrimage come intertwined in Mahoney's narrative: she values the "pilgrim's record" that certifies her progress toward Santiago yet notes with amusement advertisements seeking to attract participants to "The Lough Derg Challenge" (76, 398).

98 Mahoney characterizes acts of pilgrimage that heed tradition:

> We were going not for the arrival but for the experience of getting there. Our journey would be arduous because we wanted it to be. It seemed to me that walking to Santiago by choice in the twentieth century was – among many other things – a reenactment of sorts, not unlike the efforts of American Civil War buffs who dress in period uniforms and stage mock battles at Antietam. (88)

Chapter 7   Conclusion

1 W. G. Sebald, *The Rings of Saturn: An English Pilgrimage*, trans. Michael Hulse (New York: New Directions, 1999), 235–237. Subsequent references cited in text by page number.

2 Daphna Erdinast-Vulcan, "The *I* That Tells Itself: A Bakhtinian Perspective on Narrative Identity," *Narrative* **16** (2008), 12.

3 See Simon Ward, "Ruins and Poetics in the Works of W. G. Sebald," *W. G. Sebald – A Critical Companion*, ed. J. J. Long and Anne Whitehead (Seattle: University of Washington Press, 2004), 58–71.

4 W. H. Auden and Christopher Isherwood, *Journey to a War* (New York: Octagon Books, 1972), 274.

5 The image comes from Penelope Lively, *Moon Tiger* (New York: Harper & Row, 1989), 1.

6 M. M. Bakhtin, *The Dialogic Imagination: Four Essays*, trans. Caryl Emerson and Michael Holquist, ed. Holquist (Austin: University of Texas Press), 39.

7 Jed Esty, *Unseasonable Youth: Modernism, Colonialism, and the Fiction of Development* (Oxford: Oxford University Press, 2012), 18.

8 Rory Stewart, *The Places in Between* (New York: Harcourt, 2006), xi.

9 Mary Louise Pratt, *Imperial Eyes: Travel Writing and Transculturation*, 2d ed. (New York: Routledge, 2008), 238, 243.

10 Iain Chambers, "Leaky Habitats and Broken Grammar," *Travellers' Tales: Narratives of Home and Displacement*, ed. George Robertson et al. (London: Routledge, 1994), 246.

Selected Bibliography

Adams, David. *Colonial Odysseys: Empire and Epic in the Modernist Novel.* Ithaca, NY: Cornell University Press, 2003.

Adams, Percy G. *Travel Literature and the Evolution of the Novel.* Lexington: University Press of Kentucky, 1983.

Adorno, Theodor W. *The Jargon of Authenticity.* 1964. Trans. Knut Tranowski and Frederic Will. Evanston, IL: Northwestern University Press, 1973.

Agamben, Giorgio. *Remnants of Auschwitz: The Witness and the Archive.* Trans Daniel Heller-Roazen. New York: Zone, 2002.

Auden, W. H. *Prose and Travel Books in Prose and Verse.* 2 vols. *The Complete Works of W. H. Auden.* Ed. Edward Mendelson. Princeton, NJ: Princeton University Press, 1996.

Auden, W. H., and Christopher Isherwood. *Journey to a War.* 1939. Rpt. New York: Octagon Books, 1972. Rev. ed. London: Faber & Faber, 1973.

Auden, W. H., and Louis MacNeice. *Letters from Iceland.* 1937. London: Faber & Faber, 1967.

Bakhtin, M. M. *Art and Answerability: Early Philosophical Essays.* Trans. Vadim Liapunov. Ed. Michael Holquist and Liapunov. Austin: University of Texas Press, 1990.

   The Dialogic Imagination: Four Essays. Trans. Caryl Emerson and Michael Holquist. Ed. Holquist. Austin: University of Texas Press, 1984.

   Problems of Dostoevsky's Poetics. Trans. and ed. Caryl Emerson. Minneapolis: University of Minnesota Press, 1984.

   Speech Genres and Other Late Essays. Trans. Vern W. McGee. Ed. Caryl Emerson and Michael Holquist. Austin: University of Texas Press, 1986.

Bartholomew, Michael. "H. V. Morton's English Utopia." *Regenerating England: Science, Medicine and Culture in Inter-War Britain.* Ed. Christopher Lawrence and Anna-K. Mayer. Amsterdam: Rodopi, 2000, 25–44.

   In Search of H. V. Morton. London: Methuen, 2006.

Bartkowski, Frances. *Travelers, Immigrants, Inmates: Essays in Estrangement.* Minneapolis: University of Minnesota Press, 1995.

Bartley, Aryn. "The Hateful Self: Substitution and the Ethics of Representing War." *Modern Fiction Studies* **54** (2008): 50–71.

Bassnett, Susan. "Interview with Colin Thubron." *Studies in Travel Writing* **3** (1999): 148–171.

Baudrillard, Jean. *America*. 1986. Trans. Chris Turner. London: Verso, 1988.
    Simulacra and Simulation. 1981. Trans. Sheila Faria Glaser. Ann Arbor: University of Michigan Press, 1994.
Beasley-Murray, Tim. *Mikhail Bakhtin and Walter Benjamin: Experience and Form*. New York: Palgrave Macmillan, 2007.
Begam, Richard, and Michael Valdez Moses, eds. *Modernism and Colonialism: British and Irish Literature, 1899–1939*. Durham, NC: Duke University Press, 2007.
Behdad, Ali. *Belated Travelers: Orientalism in the Age of Colonial Dissolution*. Durham, NC: Duke University Press, 1994.
Bell, Gertrude. *The Desert and the Sown*. 1907. London: Virago, 1985.
Benjamin, Walter. *The Arcades Project*. Trans. Howard Eiland and Kevin McLaughlin. Cambridge, MA: Belknap/Harvard University Press, 1999.
    Charles Baudelaire: A Lyric Poet in the Era of High Capitalism. Trans. Harry Zohn. London: NLB, 1973.
    "Moscow." 1927. *Reflections: Essays, Aphorisms, Autobiographical Writings*. Ed. Peter Demetz. Trans. Edmund Jephcott. New York: Schocken, 1986, 97–130.
Bernstein, Michael André. "Making Modernist Masterpieces." *Modernism/Modernity* **5**.3 (1998): 1–17.
Bissell, William Cunningham. "Engaging Colonial Nostalgia." *Cultural Anthropology* **20** (2005): 215–248.
Black, Jonathan. "'King of the Pictures': Eric Kennington, Portraiture and the Illustration of *Seven Pillars of Wisdom*, 1920–26." *The Journal of the T. E. Lawrence Society* **16**.2 (2007): 7–28.
Blanchot, Maurice. *The Writing of the Disaster*. 1980. New ed. Trans. Ann Smock. Lincoln: University of Nebraska Press, 1995.
Bourke-White, Margaret. *Eyes on Russia*. New York: Simon and Schuster, 1931.
Boym, Svetlana. *The Future of Nostalgia*. New York: Basic Books, 2001.
Brandabur, A. Clare, and Nasser al-Hassan Athamneh. "Problems of Genre in *The Seven Pillars of Wisdom: A Triumph*." *Comparative Literature* **52** (2000): 321–338.
Brothers, Barbara, and Julia M. Gergits, eds. *British Travel Writers, 1910–1939*. Dictionary of Literary Biography 195. Detroit: Gale, 1998.
    British Travel Writers, 1940–1997. Dictionary of Literary Biography 204. Detroit: Gale, 1999.
Bruner, Edward M. *Culture on Tour: Ethnographies of Travel*. Chicago: University of Chicago Press, 2005.
Bryant, Marsha. *Auden and Documentary in the 1930s*. Charlottesville: University Press of Virginia, 1997.
Burton, Stacy. "Paradoxical Relations: Bakhtin and Modernism." *Modern Language Quarterly* **61** (2000): 519–543.
Butor, Michel. *Mobile: étude pour une représentation des États-unis*. Paris: Gallimard, 1962.
Buzard, James. *The Beaten Track: European Tourism, Literature, and the Ways to 'Culture,' 1800–1918*. Oxford: Clarendon, 1993.
Byron, Robert. *First Russia, Then Tibet*. 1933. Harmondsworth: Penguin, 1985.

Campbell, Mary Baine. *The Witness and the Other World: Exotic European Travel Writing, 400–1600.* Ithaca, NY: Cornell University Press, 1988.

"Travel Writing and Its Theory." *The Cambridge Companion to Travel Writing.* Ed. Peter Hulme and Tim Youngs. Cambridge: Cambridge University Press, 2002, 261–278.

Carr, Helen. "Modernism and Travel (1880–1940)." *The Cambridge Companion to Travel Writing.* Ed. Peter Hulme and Tim Youngs. Cambridge: Cambridge University Press, 2002, 70–86.

Chambers, Iain. "Leaky Habitats and Broken Grammar." *Travellers' Tales: Narratives of Home and Displacement.* Ed. George Robertson, Melinda Mash, Lisa Tickner, Jon Bird, Barry Curtis, and Tim Putnam. London: Routledge, 1994, 245–249.

Chatwin, Bruce. *The Songlines.* New York: Penguin, 1988.

Cheng, Vincent. *Inauthentic: The Anxiety over Culture and Identity.* New Brunswick, NJ: Rutgers University Press, 2004.

Chesterton, Ada [Mrs. Cecil]. *My Russian Venture.* Philadelphia: J. B. Lippincott, 1931.

Clendinnen, Inga. *Reading the Holocaust.* Cambridge: Cambridge University Press, 1999.

Clifford, James. *The Predicament of Culture: Twentieth-Century Ethnography, Literature, and Art.* Cambridge, MA: Harvard University Press, 1988.

Routes: Travel and Translation in the Late Twentieth Century. Cambridge, MA: Harvard University Press, 1997.

Cohen, Erik. "Phenomenology of Tourist Experiences." *Sociology* **13** (1979): 179–201.

Cohen, Ralph. "Do Postmodern Genres Exist?" *Genre* **20** (1987): 241–258.

Colquitt, Clare. "A Call to Arms: Rebecca West's Assault on the Limits of 'Gerda's Empire' in *Black Lamb and Grey Falcon.*" *South Atlantic Review* **51**.2 (1986): 77–91.

Cooper, John Xiros. "'The crow on the crematorium chimney': Germany, Summer 1945." *English Studies in Canada* **30**.3 (2004): 129–144.

Crary, Jonathan. "Spectacle, Attention, Counter-Memory." *October* **50** (1989): 96–107.

Techniques of the Observer: On Vision and Modernity in the Nineteenth Century. Cambridge, MA: MIT Press, 1990.

Davidson, Robyn. *Tracks.* New York: Pantheon, 1980.

Dawson, Graham. *Soldier Heroes: British Adventure, Empire and the Imagining of Masculinities.* London: Routledge, 1994.

Deer, Patrick. *Culture in Camouflage: War, Empire, and Modern British Literature.* New York: Oxford University Press, 2009.

Diller, Elizabeth, and Ricardo Scofido, eds. *Visite aux armées: Tourismes de guerre/Back to the Front: Tourisms of War.* Caen: Fonds Régional d'Art Contemporain de Basse-Normandie, 1994.

Duneer, Anita J. "Postpositivist Realism and Mandala: Toward Reconciliation and Reunification of Vietnamese and American identities in Andrew X. Pham's *Catfish and Mandala.*" *a/b: Auto/Biography Studies* **17**.2 (2002): 204–220.

Erdinast-Vulcan, Daphna. "The *I* That Tells Itself: A Bakhtinian Perspective on Narrative Identity." *Narrative* **16** (2008): 1–15.

Esty, Jed. "The British Empire and the English Modernist Novel." *The Cambridge Companion to the Twentieth-Century English Novel*. Ed. Robert Caserio. Cambridge: Cambridge University Press, 2009, 23–39.

A Shrinking Island: Modernism and National Culture in England. Princeton, NJ: Princeton University Press, 2003.

Unseasonable Youth: Modernism, Colonialism, and the Fiction of Development. Oxford: Oxford University Press, 2012.

Farley, David G. *Modernist Travel Writing: Intellectuals Abroad*. Columbia: University of Missouri Press, 2010.

Favret, Mary A. *War at a Distance: Romanticism and the Making of Modern Wartime*. Princeton, NJ: Princeton University Press, 2009.

Finley, John. *A Pilgrim in Palestine: Being an Account of Journeys on Foot by the First American Pilgrim after General Allenby's Recovery of the Holy Land*. New York: Scribner's, 1919.

Fleming, Peter. *Brazilian Adventure*. New York: Charles Scribner's, 1933.

News from Tartary. New York: Charles Scribner's, 1936.

One's Company. London: Jonathan Cape, 1934. New York: Charles Scribner's, 1934. London: Penguin, 1956.

Forsdick, Charles. "Peter Fleming and Ella Maillart in China: Travel Writing as Stereoscopic and Polygraphic Form." *Studies in Travel Writing* **13** (2009): 293–303.

Travel in Twentieth-Century French and Francophone Cultures: The Persistence of Diversity. Oxford: Oxford University Press, 2005.

Forster, E. M. "T. E. Lawrence." *Abinger Harvest*. 1936. New York: Harcourt, Brace & World, 1964, 141–147.

Frow, John. "Tourism and the Semiotics of Nostalgia." *October* **57** (1991): 123–151.

Frye, Northrup. "*The Decline of the West*, by Oswald Spengler." *Daedalus* **103**.1 (1973): 1–13.

Fuller, John. *W. H. Auden: A Commentary*. Princeton, NJ: Princeton University Press, 1998.

Fussell, Paul. *Abroad: British Literary Traveling between the Wars*. New York: Oxford University Press, 1980.

Gardiner, Michael. *The Dialogics of Critique: M. M. Bakhtin and the Theory of Ideology*. London: Routledge, 1992.

Gellhorn, Martha. *The Face of War*. Rev. ed. New York: Atlantic Monthly Press, 1988.

Gikandi, Simon. *Maps of Englishness: Writing Identity in the Culture of Colonialism*. New York: Columbia University Press, 1996.

Gilmore, Leigh. *Autobiographics: A Feminist Theory of Women's Self-Representation*. Ithaca, NY: Cornell University Press, 1994.

The Limits of Autobiography: Trauma and Testimony. Ithaca, NY: Cornell University Press, 2001.

Gleber, Anke. *The Art of Taking a Walk: Flanerie, Literature, and Film in Weimar Culture*. Princeton, NJ: Princeton University Press, 1999.

Glendinning, Victoria. *Rebecca West: A Life.* New York: Knopf, 1987.

Gluck, Mary. "The *Flâneur* and the Aesthetic Appropriation of Urban Culture in Mid-19th-century Paris," *Theory, Culture & Society* **20**.5 (2003): 53–80.

Godzich, Wlad. "Correcting Kant: Bakhtin and Intercultural Interactions." *Boundary 2* **18**.1 (1991): 5–17.

Gourevitch, Philip. *We Wish to Inform You That Tomorrow We Will Be Killed with Our Families: Stories from Rwanda.* New York: Farrar, Straus and Giroux, 1998.

Greene, Graham. *Journey without Maps.* 1936. 2d ed. London: Heinemann & Bodley Head, 1978.

Hammond, Andrew. *The Debated Lands: British and American Representation of the Balkans.* Cardiff: University of Wales Press, 2007.

"'The Unending Revolt': Travel in an Era of Modernism." *Studies in Travel Writing* **7** (2003): 169–189.

Hartman, Geoffrey. *Scars of the Spirit: The Struggle Against Inauthenticity.* New York: Palgrave Macmillan, 2002.

Hell, Julia. "Ruins Travel: Orphic Journeys through 1940s Germany." *Writing Travel: The Poetics and Politics of the Modern Journey.* Ed. John Zilcosky. Toronto: University of Toronto Press, 2008, 123–160.

Hirsch, Marianne. *Family Frames: Photography, Narrative, and Postmemory.* Cambridge, MA: Harvard University Press, 1997.

Hirsch, Marianne, and Leo Spitzer. "'We Would Not Have Come Without You': Generations of Nostalgia." *American Imago* **59** (2002): 253–276.

Hirschkop, Ken. *Mikhail Bakhtin: An Aesthetic for Democracy.* Oxford: Oxford University Press, 1999.

Hoffman, Eva. *Exit into History: A Journey through the New Eastern Europe.* New York: Penguin, 1994.

Holland, Patrick, and Graham Huggan. *Tourists with Typewriters: Critical Reflections on Contemporary Travel Writing.* Ann Arbor: University of Michigan Press, 1998.

Huggan, Graham. *Extreme Pursuits: Travel/Writing in an Age of Globalization.* Ann Arbor: University of Michigan Press, 2009.

Hulme, Peter. *Colonial Encounters: Europe and the Native Caribbean, 1492–1797.* London: Methuen, 1986.

"Travelling to Write (1940–2000)." *The Cambridge Companion to Travel Writing.* Ed. Peter Hulme and Tim Youngs. Cambridge: Cambridge University Press, 2002, 87–101.

and Tim Youngs, eds. *The Cambridge Companion to Travel Writing.* Cambridge: Cambridge University Press, 2002.

Hutcheon, Linda. *A Theory of Parody: The Teachings of Twentieth-Century Art Forms.* New York: Methuen, 1985.

Huxley, Aldous. *Along the Road: Notes and Essays of a Tourist.* 1925. London: Paladin, 1985.

Jesting Pilate. 1926. London: Paladin, 1985.

Inglis, Fred. *People's Witness: The Journalist in Modern Politics.* New Haven: Yale University Press, 2002.

Isherwood, Christopher. *Kathleen and Christopher: Christopher Isherwood's Letters to His Mother*. Ed. Lisa Colletta. Minneapolis: University of Minnesota Press, 2005.

Iyer, Pico. *The Global Soul: Jet Lag, Shopping Malls, and the Search for Home*. New York: Vintage, 2001.

   The Lady and the Monk: Four Seasons in Kyoto. New York: Vintage, 1992.

   Video Night in Kathmandu: And Other Reports from the Not-So-Far-East. New York: Vintage, 1989.

Jameson, Fredric. "Postmodernism, or The Cultural Logic of Late Capitalism." *New Left Review* **146** (1984): 53–92.

Jenks, Chris, ed. *Visual Culture*. London: Routledge, 1995.

Kaplan, Caren. *Questions of Travel: Postmodern Discourses of Displacement*. Durham, NC: Duke University Press, 1996.

Kaplan, Carola M. "Conquest as Literature, Literature as Conquest: T. E. Lawrence's Artistic Campaign in *Seven Pillars of Wisdom*." *Texas Studies in Literature and Language* **37** (1995): 72–97.

Katz, Tamar. *Impressionist Subjects: Gender, Interiority, and Modernist Fiction in England*. Urbana: University of Illinois Press, 2000.

Kerr, Douglas. "Journey to a War: 'a test for men from Europe.'" *W. H. Auden: A Legacy*. Ed. David Garrett Izzo. West Cornwall: Locust Hill Press, 2002, 275–296.

Kivy, Peter. *Authenticities: Philosophical Reflections on Musical Performance*. Ithaca, NY: Cornell University Press, 1995.

Knightley, Phillip. *The First Casualty: The War Correspondent as Hero and Myth-maker from the Crimea to Kosovo*. Rev. ed. London: Prion, 2000.

Korte, Barbara. *English Travel Writing from Pilgrimages to Postcolonial Explorations*. Trans. Catherine Matthias. London: Macmillan, 2000.

Kuehn, Julia, and Paul Smethurst, eds. *Travel Writing, Form, and Empire: The Poetics and Politics of Mobility*. New York: Routledge, 2009.

Larsen, Svend Erik. "Landscape, Identity, and War." *New Literary History* **35** (2004): 469–490.

Lawrence, Karen R. *Penelope Voyages: Women and Travel in the British Literary Tradition*. Ithaca, NY: Cornell University Press, 1994.

Lawrence, T. E. *Seven Pillars of Wisdom: A Triumph*. London: privately printed, 1926. New York: Doubleday, Doran & Co., 1935. New York: Anchor, 1991.

Layoun, Mary. "The Trans-, the Multi-, the Pluri-, and the Global: A Few Thoughts on Comparative and Relational Literacy." *Passages: A Journal of Transnational & Transcultural Studies* **1** (1999): 173–213.

Lennon, John, and Malcolm Foley. *Dark Tourism: The Attraction of Death and Disaster*. London: Continuum, 2000.

Lewis, Pericles. *Modernism, Nationalism, and the Novel*. Cambridge: Cambridge University Press, 2000.

   Religious Experience and the Modernist Novel. Cambridge: Cambridge University Press, 2010.

Lisle, Debbie. *The Global Politics of Contemporary Travel Writing*. Cambridge: Cambridge University Press, 2006.

Long, Andrew. "The Hidden and the Visible in British Orientalism: The Case of Lawrence of Arabia." *Middle East Critique* **18** (2009): 21–37.

Lowe, Lisa. *Critical Terrains: French and British Orientalisms*. Ithaca, NY: Cornell University Press, 1991.

Lukács, Georg. "Narrate or Describe?" *Writer and Critic and Other Essays*. Trans. and ed. Arthur Kahn. London: Merlin Press, 1970, 110–148.

Lyotard, Jean-François. "Answering the Question: What is Postmodernism?" Trans. Régis Durand. *The Postmodern Condition: A Report on Knowledge*. Trans. George Bennington and Brian Massumi. Minneapolis: University of Minnesota Press, 1984, 71–82.

Maass, Peter. *Love Thy Neighbor: A Story of War*. New York: Knopf, 1996. New York: Vintage, 1997.

Macaulay, Rose. *Pleasure of Ruins*. 1953. New York: Thames and Hudson, 1984.

MacCannell, Dean. "Spectacles." *Empty Meeting Grounds: The Tourist Papers*. London: Routledge, 1992, 230–254.

   The Tourist: A New Theory of the Leisure Class. Rev. ed. New York: Schocken, 1989.

MacKay, Marina. "Immortal Goodness: Ideas of Resurrection in Rebecca West's *Black Lamb and Grey Falcon*." *Renascence* **54** (2002): 177–196.

   Modernism and World War II. Cambridge: Cambridge University Press, 2007.

   ed. *The Cambridge Companion to the Literature of World War II*. Cambridge: Cambridge University Press, 2009.

Mahoney, Rosemary. *The Singular Pilgrim: Travels on Sacred Ground*. Boston: Houghton Mifflin, 2003.

   Whoredom in Kimmage: Irish Women Coming of Age. New York: Anchor, 1994.

Maillart, Ella. *Cruises and Caravans*. London: Travel Book Club, 1942.

   Des Monts Célestes aux Sables Rouges. Paris: Éditions Bernard Grasset, 1934. Paris: Éditions Payot, 1991.

   Forbidden Journey. Trans. Thomas McGreevy. London: Heinemann, 1937.

   Oasis interdites: de Pékin au Cachemire. Paris: Éditions Bernard Grasset, 1937. Paris: Éditions Payot, 1994.

   Parmi la jeunesse russe: de Moscou au Caucase. Paris: Fasquelle Éditeurs, 1932.

   Turkestan Solo. Trans. John Rodker. 1934. London: Century, 1985.

Malia, Martin. *Russia Under Western Eyes: From the Bronze Horseman to the Lenin Mausoleum*. Cambridge, MA: Belknap/Harvard University Press, 1999.

Manganaro, Marc. *Culture, 1922: The Emergence of a Concept*. Princeton, NJ: Princeton University Press, 2002.

Mann, Thomas. "On the Theory of Spengler." 1924. *Past Masters and Other Papers*. Trans. H. T. Lowe-Porter. London: Martin Secker, 1933, 215–227.

Mao, Douglas, and Rebecca L. Walkowitz. "The New Modernist Studies." *PMLA* **123** (2008): 737–748.

Maugham, W. Somerset. *On a Chinese Screen*. 1922. London: Heinemann, 1935.

McLoughlin, Kate. *Authoring War: The Literary Representation of War from the Iliad to Iraq*. Cambridge: Cambridge University Press, 2011.

 ed. *The Cambridge Companion to War Writing*. Cambridge: Cambridge University Press, 2009.

Meyers, Jeffrey. "The Revisions of *Seven Pillars of Wisdom*." *PMLA* **88** (1973): 1066–1082.

 The Wounded Spirit: A Study of Seven Pillars of Wisdom. London: Martin Brian & O'Keeffe, 1973.

Miller, Tyrus. *Late Modernism: Politics, Fiction, and the Arts Between the World Wars*. Berkeley: University of California Press, 1999.

Mills, Sara. *Discourses of Difference: An Analysis of Women's Travel Writing and Colonialism*. London: Routledge, 1991.

Minca, Claudio, and Tim Oakes, eds. *Travels in Paradox: Remapping Tourism*. London: Rowman & Littlefield, 2006.

Moffatt, Rachel. "Visiting Rwanda: Accounts of Genocide in Travel Writing." *Journeys* **11**.1 (2010): 89–106.

Montefiore, Janet. *Men and Women Writers of the 1930s*. London: Routledge, 1996.

Morris, Mary. *Nothing to Declare: Memoirs of a Woman Traveling Alone*. New York: Penguin, 1989.

 Wall to Wall: From Beijing to Berlin by Rail. New York: Penguin, 1992.

Morris, Meaghan. "At Henry Parkes Motel." *Cultural Studies* **2** (1988): 1–47.

Morson, Gary Saul. *Hidden in Plain View: Narrative and Creative Potentials in* War and Peace. Stanford: Stanford University Press, 1987.

Morson, Gary Saul, and Caryl Emerson. *Mikhail Bakhtin: Creation of a Prosaics*. Stanford: Stanford University Press, 1990.

Morton, H.V. *In Search of England*. 1927. New York: Robert M. McBride & Co., 1930. New York: Dodd, Mead, 1984.

 In Search of Ireland. London: Methuen, 1930.

 In Search of Scotland. 1929. London: Methuen, 2000.

 In Search of Wales. 1932. London: Methuen, 2000.

 In the Steps of the Master. London: Rich & Cowan, 1934. London: Methuen, 1984.

Moynagh, Maureen. "Revolutionary Drag in Auden and Isherwood's *Journey to a War*." *Studies in Travel Writing* **8** (2004): 125–148.

Muirhead, Findlay, ed. *Belgium and the Western Front: British and American*. The Blue Guides. London: Macmillan, 1920.

Muller, Adam. "Notes Toward a Theory of Nostalgia: Childhood and the Evocation of the Past in Two European 'Heritage' Films." *New Literary History* **37** (2007): 739–760.

Mulligan, Maureen. "Forbidden Journeys to China and Beyond with the Odd Couple: Ella Maillart and Peter Fleming." *Asian Crossings: Travel Writing on China, Japan and Southeast Asia*. Ed. Steve Clark and Paul Smethurst. Hong Kong: Hong Kong University Press, 2008, 141–148.

New Literary History. Special issues: "Theorizing Genres I" and "Theorizing Genres II." *34*.2–3 (2003).

Nixon, Rob. *London Calling: V. S. Naipaul, Postcolonial Mandarin*. Oxford: Oxford University Press, 1992.

Norris, Margot. *Writing War in the Twentieth Century*. Charlottesville: University Press of Virginia, 2000.

North, Michael. *Reading 1922: A Return to the Scene of the Modern*. New York: Oxford University Press, 1999.

Osborne, Peter D. *Traveling Light: Photography, Travel and Visual Culture*. Manchester: Manchester University Press, 2000.

Parsons, Deborah L. *Streetwalking the Metropolis: Women, the City and Modernity*. Oxford: Oxford University Press, 2000.

Paulin, Tom. "*Letters from Iceland*: Going North." *Culture, Theory and Critique* **20** (1976): 65–80.

Pechey, Graham. "On the Borders of Bakhtin: Dialogization, Decolonization." *Bakhtin and Cultural Theory*. Ed. Ken Hirschkop and David Shepherd. Manchester: Manchester University Press, 1989, 39–67.

Perry, C. R. "In Search of H. V. Morton: Travel Writing and Cultural Values in the First Age of British Democracy." *Twentieth Century British History* **10** (1999): 431–456.

Pham, Andrew. *Catfish and Mandala: A Two-Wheeled Voyage through the Landscape and Memory of Vietnam*. New York: Farrar, Straus and Giroux, 1999.

Phillips, Delores B. "Quieting Noisy Bellies: Moving, Eating, and Being in the Vietnamese Diaspora." *Cultural Critique* **73** (2009): 47–87.

Porter, Dennis. *Haunted Journeys: Desire and Transgression in European Travel Writing*. Princeton, NJ: Princeton University Press, 1991.

"Orientalism and Its Problems." *The Politics of Theory*. Ed. Francis Barker, Peter Hulme, Margaret Iversen, and Diane Loxley. Colchester: University of Essex, 1983, 179–193.

Pratt, Mary Louise. "Fieldwork in Common Places." *Writing Culture: The Poetics and Politics of Ethnography*. Ed. James Clifford and George E. Marcus. Berkeley: University of California Press, 1986, 27–50.

Imperial Eyes: Travel Writing and Transculturation. New York: Routledge, 1992; 2d ed., 2008.

Read, Herbert. "The Seven Pillars of Wisdom." *The Bibliophile's Almanack*, 1928, 35–41.

Richards, Thomas. *The Commodity Culture of Victorian England: Advertising and Spectacle, 1851–1914*. Stanford: Stanford University Press, 1990.

Riemer, Andrew. *Inside Outside: Life Between Two Worlds*. Sydney: Angus & Robertson, 1992.

Robertson, George, Melinda Mash, Lisa Tickner, Jon Bird, Barry Curtis, and Tim Putnam, eds. *Travellers' Tales: Narratives of Home and Displacement*. London: Routledge, 1994.

Rojek, Chris, and John Urry, eds. *Touring Cultures: Transformations of Travel and Theory*. London: Routledge, 1997.

Rollyson, Carl. *Rebecca West: A Life*. New York: Scribner, 1996.

Rosmarin, Adena. *The Power of Genre*. Minneapolis: University of Minnesota Press, 1985.

Roth, Michael S. "Foucault's 'History of the Present.'" *History and Theory* **20** (1981): 32–46.

Rushdie, Salman. *Imaginary Homelands: Essays and Criticism 1981–1991*. New York: Viking Penguin, 1991.

Russell, Alison. *Crossing Boundaries: Postmodern Travel Literature*. New York: Palgrave, 2000.

Sacco, Joe. *Palestine*. 1993–1996. Seattle: Fantagraphics, 2001.

Safe Area Goražde. Seattle: Fantagraphics, 2000.

Said, Edward W. *Culture and Imperialism*. New York: Knopf, 1993.

"Homage to Joe Sacco." *Palestine*. By Joe Sacco. Seattle: Fantagraphics, 2001, i–v.

Orientalism. New York: Random House, 1978.

Saint-Amour, Paul. "Air War Prophecy and Interwar Modernism." *Comparative Literature Studies* **42** (2005): 130–161.

Schueller, Malini Johar. "Traveling 'Back' to India: Globalization as Imperialism in Pico Iyer's *Video Night in Kathmandu*." *Journeys* **10**.1 (2009): 29–50.

Schweizer, Bernard. *Radicals on the Road: The Politics of English Travel Writing in the 1930s*. Charlottesville: University Press of Virginia, 2001.

Scott, Joan W. "The Evidence of Experience." *Critical Inquiry* **17** (1991): 773–797.

Sebald, W. G. *On The Natural History of Destruction*. Trans. Anthea Bell. 1999. London: Penguin, 2004.

The Rings of Saturn: An English Pilgrimage. 1995. Trans. Michael Hulse. New York: New Directions, 1999.

Shaffer, Brian W. *The Blinding Torch: Modern British Fiction and the Discourse of Civilization*. Amherst: University of Massachusetts Press, 1993.

Sidhe, Wren. "H. V. Morton's Pilgrimages to Englishness." *Literature & History* 3d ser. **12**.1 (2003): 57–71.

Skinner, Jonathan. "Introduction: Writings on the Dark Side of Travel." *Journeys* **11**.1 (2010): 1–28.

Smeeton, Beryl. *Winter Shoes in Springtime*. London: Rupert Hart-Davis, 1961.

Smethurst, Paul. "Travels in Globality: Pico Iyer and Jan Morris in Hong Kong." *Studies in Travel Writing* **8** (2004): 179–197.

Smith, Sidonie. *Moving Lives: Twentieth-Century Women's Travel Writing*. Minneapolis: University of Minnesota Press, 2001.

A Poetics of Women's Autobiography: Marginality and the Fictions of Self-Representations. Bloomington: Indiana University Press, 1987.

Snyder, Carey J. *British Fiction and Cross-Cultural Encounters: Ethnographic Modernism from Wells to Woolf*. New York: Palgrave Macmillan, 2008.

Solnit, Rebecca. *A Book of Migrations: Some Passages in Ireland*. London: Verso, 1997.

Sontag, Susan. *Regarding the Pain of Others*. New York: Farrar, Straus and Giroux, 2003.

Spender, Stephen. *European Witness*. London: Hamish Hamilton, 1946. New York: Reynal & Hitchcock, 1946.

"Rhineland Journal." *Horizon* **12** (December 1945): 394–413.

Spengler, Oswald. *The Decline of the West.* 2 vols. Trans. Charles Francis Atkinson. New York: Alfred A. Knopf, 1926, 1928.

Spurr, David. *The Rhetoric of Empire: Colonial Discourse in Journalism, Travel Writing, and Imperial Administration.* Durham, NC: Duke University Press, 1993.

Stark, Freya. *The Zodiac Arch.* New York: Harcourt, Brace & World, 1968.

Stec, Loretta. "Female Sacrifice: Gender and Nostalgic Nationalism in Rebecca West's *Black Lamb and Grey Falcon.*" *Narratives of Nostalgia, Gender and Nationalism.* Ed. Jean Pickering and Suzanne Kehde. London: Macmillan, 1997, 138–158.

Stewart, Rory. *The Places in Between.* New York: Harcourt, 2006.

Stewart, Susan. *On Longing: Narratives of the Miniature, the Gigantic, the Souvenir, the Collection.* Durham, NC: Duke University Press, 1993.

Su, John J. *Ethics and Nostalgia in the Contemporary Novel.* Cambridge: Cambridge University Press, 2005.

Sutherland, John. *Stephen Spender: A Literary Life.* Oxford: Oxford University Press, 2005.

Tabachnick, Stephen E., ed. *The T. E. Lawrence Puzzle.* Athens: University of Georgia Press, 1984.

Taylor, John. *Body Horror: Photojournalism, Catastrophe and War.* New York: New York University Press, 1998.

   A Dream of England: Landscape, Photography and the Tourist's Imagination. Manchester: Manchester University Press, 1994.

Thomas, Lowell. *With Lawrence in Arabia.* 1924. 2d. ed. Garden City, NY: Doubleday, 1967.

Thompson, V. M. *"Not a Suitable Hobby for an Airman": T. E. Lawrence as Publisher.* Oxford: Orchard Books, 1986.

Thubron, Colin. *Among the Russians.* London: Heinemann, 1983. Published as *Where Nights Are Longest: Travels by Car through Western Russia.* New York: Random House, 1984.

   Behind the Wall: A Journey through China. New York: Atlantic Monthly Press, 1988.

   "Both Seer and Seen: The Travel Writer as Leftover Amateur." *Times Literary Supplement* July 30, 1999: 12–13.

   The Hills of Adonis: A Quest in Lebanon. London: Heinemann, 1968.

   In Siberia. London: Chatto & Windus, 1999.

   Journey into Cyprus. London: Heinemann, 1975.

   The Lost Heart of Asia. New York: Harper Collins, 1994.

   "Travel Writing Today: Its Rise and Its Dilemma." *Essays by Divers Hands: Being the Transactions of the Royal Society of Literature, New Series, Volume XLIV.* Ed. A. N. Wilson. Woodbridge: Boydell Press, 1986, 167–181.

Till, Karen E. *The New Berlin: Politics, Memory, Place.* Minneapolis: University of Minnesota Press, 2005.

Todorov, Tzvetan. "The Journey and Its Narratives." *The Morals of History.* 1991. Trans. Alyson Waters. Minneapolis: University of Minnesota Press, 1995, 60–70.

Trinh T. Minh-ha. *Woman, Native, Other: Writing Postcoloniality and Feminism.* Bloomington: Indiana University Press, 1989.

Urry, John. *Consuming Places.* London: Routledge, 1995.

"Death in Venice." *Tourism Mobilities: Places to Play, Places in Play.* Ed. Mimi Sheller and John Urry. London: Routledge, 2004, 205–215.

The Tourist Gaze: Leisure and Travel in Contemporary Societies. London: Sage, 1990.

Walker, Tristram. "Graphic Wounds: The Comics Journalism of Joe Sacco." *Journeys* **11**.1 (2010): 69–88.

Walkowitz, Rebecca L. *Cosmopolitan Style: Modernism beyond the Nation.* New York: Columbia University Press, 2006.

Ward, Simon. "Ruins and Poetics in the Works of W. G. Sebald." *W. G. Sebald – A Critical Companion.* Ed. J. J. Long and Anne Whitehead. Seattle: University of Washington Press, 2004, 58–71.

Waugh, Evelyn. *Labels: A Mediterranean Journal.* London: Duckworth, 1930.

When the Going Was Good. 1946. Boston: Little, Brown, 1984.

Weine, Stevan. *Testimony after Catastrophe: Narrating the Traumas of Political Violence.* Evanston, IL: Northwestern University Press, 2006.

West, Rebecca. *Black Lamb and Grey Falcon: A Journey through Yugoslavia.* 2 vols. New York: Viking, 1941. Rpt. 1 vol. New York: Viking, 1944.

Wharton, Edith. *A Motor-Flight through France.* 1908. Intro. Julian Barnes. London: Picador, 1995.

White, Hayden. "Anomalies of Genre: The Utility of Theory and History for the Study of Literary Genres." *New Literary History* **34** (2003): 597–615.

Williams, Paul. *Memorial Museums: The Global Rush to Commemorate Atrocities.* Oxford: Berg, 2007.

Wilson, Elizabeth. "The Invisible Flâneur." *New Left Review* **191** (1992): 90–110.

Wilson, Jeremy. "Preface: The Two Texts of *Seven Pillars*." *Seven Pillars of Wisdom: A Triumph. The Complete 1922 Text.* By T. E. Lawrence. Ed. Wilson. 2d ed. n.p.: Castle Hill Press, 2003, xxi–xxvi.

Wolff, Janet. *Resident Alien: Feminist Cultural Criticism.* New Haven: Yale University Press, 1995.

Woods, Katherine. "Rebecca West's Brilliant Mosaic of Yugoslavian Travel." *New York Times* October 26, 1941.

Woolf, Virginia. "Mr. Bennett and Mrs. Brown." *Collected Essays.* Ed. Leonard Woolf. London: Hogarth, 1966–1967. I: 319–337.

Three Guineas. 1938. New York: Harcourt Brace Jovanovich, 1966.

Wyschogrod, Edith. *Spirit in Ashes: Hegel, Heidegger, and Man-Made Mass Death.* New Haven: Yale University Press, 1985.

Youngs, Tim. "Auden's Travel Writings." *The Cambridge Companion to W. H. Auden.* Ed. Stan Smith. Cambridge: Cambridge University Press, 2004, 68–81.

"Travelling Modernists." *The Oxford Handbook of Modernisms.* Ed. Peter Brooker, Andrzej Gąsiorek, Deborah Longworth, and Andrew Thacker. Oxford: Oxford University Press, 2010, 267–280.

Index